A DISTURBANCE
IN THE FORCE

A DISTURBANCE IN THE FORCE

HOW AND WHY THE STAR WARS HOLIDAY SPECIAL HAPPENED

STEVE KOZAK

APPLAUSE
THEATRE & CINEMA BOOKS

APPLAUSE
THEATRE & CINEMA BOOKS

An imprint of Globe Pequot, the trade division of
The Rowman & Littlefield Publishing Group, Inc.
4501 Forbes Blvd., Ste. 200
Lanham, MD 20706
www.rowman.com

Distributed by NATIONAL BOOK NETWORK

Book design by Tom Seabrook

Library of Congress Cataloging-in-Publication Data available upon request

ISBN 978-1-4930-7527-0 (paperback)
ISBN 978-1-4930-7528-7 (ebook)

♾™ The paper used in this publication meets the minimum requirements
of American National Standard for Information Sciences—Permanence
of Paper for Printed Library Materials, ANSI/NISO Z39.48-1992

FOR ELLIOTT

Yes, a powerful agent and a successful producer, but off the charts as the best father a kid could have.

"The greatest teacher, failure is."
YODA, *The Last Jedi*

"The *Star Wars Holiday Special*
sucked so bad, I was amazed
that I wasn't in it."
GILBERT GOTTFRIED

CONTENTS

PREFACE

IN THE LATE 1970S, my father, Elliott, left Bob Hope after several years of producing and running his production company to oversee the TV variety department at one of the top talent agencies of the time, International Creative Management (ICM). Unlike my high-school friends who were working in fast food, I soon had the coolest job of all: working after school in the ICM mailroom, where nearly all of their agents' careers had begun. We sorted the mail, washed the bosses' cars, and read and synopsized scripts. It sure beat flipping burgers.

While delivering the mail, I would pass through the sixth-floor offices of music agents like Hal Lazareff, blasting the music of his clients, Aerosmith. But even cooler was one floor up: the seventh-floor film department. Rounding the first corner office, I dropped off mail for the slick Jack Gilardi, a sweetheart of a man who was then married to Annette Funicello. Gilardi practically created the "Hollywood agent" stereotype with his expensive Italian suits and gold chains, rocking his jet-black, rock-hard pompadour right up until he died in 2019. The next corner office belonged to Sue Mengers, who had not one but two assistants, represented a slew of Hollywood heavyweights (Cher, Michael Caine, Steve McQueen, Gene Hackman, Barbra Streisand), and had even been *portrayed* in several films and TV shows.

There was always a bit of a slowdown midway down the next walkway. The hubbub was usually coming from the office of thirty-year-old Jeff Berg, who at the time was the agency's Man of the Hour. While he represented several of the top writers and directors of "The New Hollywood," by far his most important client was George Lucas. Not only had Berg set up Lucas's deal at Universal to write and direct *American Graffiti*, he had also negotiated with 20th Century Fox for Lucas to write and direct *Star Wars*. More importantly, after the success of *American Graffiti*, Berg had *re*-negotiated with the studio for Lucas to retain half of *Star Wars'* merchandising rights, as well as its sequel rights, which would be vital to Lucas if he ever planned on turning this single film into a multibillion-dollar franchise.

Unlike flashy social butterflies like Gilardi and Mengers, Berg was part of a new generation of agents who were quite the opposite: mild-mannered, bookish, and armed with college degrees (Berg himself had an MA from Lucas's alma mater, the University of Southern California). In the midst of this golden age of scriptwriting, there were just too many amazing scripts waiting to be read for them to waste their time socializing.

I would regularly stop about ten feet before reaching Berg's office and talk to Dan Ostroff, who had just been promoted from the mailroom to become an assistant for literary agent Jane Sindall. Like two *Star Wars*–crossed fans, we would gaze at Berg, this fairly ordinary-looking man, like he was Han Solo himself. Agents and assistants scurried in and out of his office, leaving the uninvited to wonder what new project Berg was hammering out for Lucas. What we would give to be a fly on the wall in that office, we thought; they probably knew all about *The Empire Strikes Back*, the second installment in the brand new *Star Wars* franchise.

But it turns out that even with all of this unparalleled access to Berg and company, I would learn hardly anything about Lucas and next to nothing about *Star Wars*. If we had only known at the time that just two floors down, back in the TV variety department, just two offices over from my father's corner office, sat one of his top agents, Dan Stevens, who represented comedy writers Pat Proft, Lenny Ripps, and Bruce Vilanch. Strangely, that was where all the real *Star Wars* action was happening.

Stevens had just gotten offers for all of them to write for some sort of *Star Wars*–themed CBS television special for Lucas. Stevens had recommended they take the offers, telling Vilanch, "This will be a clusterfuck, but it's got George Lucas, so it might be something really unusual and different."

Dan Stevens represented some of the biggest actors and writers in television at the time. He was smart and usually had great instincts. But in hindsight . . . he should have had a bad feeling about this.

INTRODUCTION

FOR MANY YEARS, at Thanksgiving time, comedy writer Bruce Vilanch would throw a big dinner at his house up in Laurel Canyon for forty to fifty of his friends who weren't welcome home for the holidays. He called it "The Lost Boys' Thanksgiving." Vilanch explains, "There were a lot of guys back then who had come from towns in the Midwest and Catholic upbringings and whatnot, and their families had rejected them. So they had no real contact with their families, and the holidays would come around and it would be really tough."

Although the *Star Wars Holiday Special* aired the week *before* Thanksgiving 1978, Vilanch celebrated the same way: he and his friends spent the Thursday together, "cooking, eating, [and] partying," and the next night they all returned for leftovers. Consequently, on that Friday night, November 17th, Vilanch had quite an audience for the one and only broadcast of the Special.

Vilanch had worked for several months on the Special, and he was looking forward to seeing the final result of so many different voices and opinions—as well as how the audience he had invited to his home was going to react.

While the basic script had been hammered out from a plot by George Lucas, Vilanch's job had been to come up with the comedy elements. The segments ranged from Harvey Korman's four-armed alien version of Julia Child giving cooking lessons; to a circus of imp-sized jugglers, gymnasts, and tumblers; to a cantina bar full of extraterrestrials led by barkeep Bea Arthur singing songs at closing time.

The show was a success, as far as Vilanch and his friends were concerned. "We just rolled a doob and sat back and watched it, and we thought it was fabulous!" he recalls. "They loved Bea, and they loved Harvey. They loved all the crap, of course—all the camp stuff. But what wasn't camp in that show?"

But many weren't laughing at what was supposed to be a galactic sweeps-period extravaganza. Up in Northern California, Lucas was likely still stewing over what had happened to his Special.

"He was not happy about it, not proud of it," biographer Dale Pollock says. *Star Wars* producer Gary Kurtz said that after he and Lucas watched the final cut, "It was a bit too late then to do much about it. We couldn't pull the show. And I guess . . . well, it wasn't really that bad compared to other Christmas specials, so what the hell."

However, there are countless fans who disagreed with Kurtz. For them, the Special is not just the worst *Star Wars*–related production ever. No, their hatred goes even further: it qualifies for Outer Rim status, ranking among the worst television specials *ever produced*. Thus, it is something Lucas *loathes* talking about. "Weird Al" Yankovic, one of the biggest *Star Wars* fans on the planet, advises that it's best to watch it in short increments: "Your brain melts if you have to watch all two hours."

Nearly all who have seen the Special can attest to its truly bizarre elements: Harvey Korman drinks his cocktails through a hole in the top of his head. Bea Arthur flirts with a giant rat. Mark Hamill, as Luke, appears to be wearing way too much makeup. Chewbacca's father watches a sexy dancer talk intimately with him through a "mind evaporator" in the Special's most bizarre scene, which has been referred to over the years as "Wookiee porn."

And Princess Leia sings.

* * *

Just down Laurel Canyon into West Hollywood, another writer from the Special was also having a viewing party. Lenny Ripps had hired a caterer and had waiters with trays serving the two dozen or so friends he had invited over for the broadcast.

For nearly twelve minutes, Ripps and his guests took in the opening scene of the Special. Chewbacca's family takes center stage, with his wife, Malla, his son, Lumpy, and his father, Itchy, all grunting back and forth with no overdubs and no subtitles, all situated in a modern-day, sitcom-styled living room in their carpeted treehouse on the planet Kashyyyk.

It frustrated Ripps tremendously because he, Vilanch, and nearly every producer on the staff had warned Lucas about centering the story around a family of grunting Wookiees.

Ripps got up and turned off the television set.

"Let's eat."

As his guests headed toward the food, Ripps sat back, contemplating his fate. CBS would never rerun that horrific show, he thought. In the morning, he would tell his agent to get him a gig—any gig—and fast, before word got out that he was a part of this galactic embarrassment.

Luckily for him, most home viewers were not able to record programs off air, not able to print and distribute bootleg versions of such recordings, and certainly not able to share that content with one another digitally.

No, he was safe. For now, at least.

* * *

The two-hour Special was CBS's attempt at cashing in on the popularity of *Star Wars* by inviting Lucasfilm to produce a TV version of the film that had recently surpassed *Jaws* as the highest-grossing movie of all time. ABC had experimented with *Star Wars* on the television show *Donny and Marie*, and NBC had booked the infamous cantina-scene aliens for *The Richard Pryor Show*. Both had earned massive ratings for their respective networks. Now, CBS wanted its turn.

However, that would mean Lucas would have to co-mingle with a genre that, today, no longer exists. Variety was one of the dominant forms of TV programming from the 1950s through the mid-1980s, filling prime-time network schedules with shows hosted by such popular entertainers as Andy Williams, Sonny and Cher, the Smothers Brothers, and Carol Burnett. Now extinct, these variety shows contained an hour or more of various entertainments, including singing, dancing, comedy, and off-the-wall novelty. But the genre eventually became an embarrassment when too many mediocre talents started hosting their own shows in the 1980s; variety went the way of disco, stripped from prime-time programming schedules and leaving very little trace of its existence.

The Special would never be broadcast again. Lucas shelved it, and he has spent most of his adult life trying to keep it buried deep in his closet—deeper even than the remnants of *Howard the Duck, More American Graffiti,* and Jar-Jar Binks. For the next two decades, the Special would remain perfectly hidden and largely undiscoverable in the lost world of analog technology.

Ironically, it would be the same sort of digital technology that Lucas embraced, and eventually invested in, that would be instrumental in bringing the Special to a brand-new generation of *Star Wars* fans. Back in the late 1970s, when the Special was initially broadcast, Betamax consumer video recorders had just hit the market, and although there was uncertainty about the legality of recording copyrighted content off air, buyers had already begun doing so.

Unfortunately for Lucas, part of that copyrighted content included a few off-air recordings of the Special that were made available on videotape and traded by *Star Wars* fans and collectors. By the mid-'90s—thanks to the advent of DVD recording technology—higher-quality versions of the Special were now being sold at comic-book conventions and through mail-order ads in the back of science-fiction magazines. Its sudden reappearance was a major cause of concern for Lucas, who had omitted it from the newly released *Star Wars* collector's editions. He has famously been quoted as saying, "If I had the time and a hammer, I would personally smash every one of these bootlegged copies of the Special."

However, by the turn of the century and the emergence of the internet, Lucas's hammer was too little, too late. With the launch of YouTube in 2005, digital versions of the entire Special could now be accessed online and available to all who had been waiting decades to see it. Despite Lucas's best efforts, he was unable to keep his darkest secret away from curious fans to watch, share, and mock.

And mock they did.

Some who were involved with the Special remain reluctant to talk about it, even today. Gene Crowe, the Special's technical director, is willing only to say that it was "a difficult experience. There were a lot of people there that expected it to be something else, and it fell short of those marks. I think that's about as much as I'd like to say about it."

Vilanch is not particularly ashamed of the end result, explaining that it was just one of dozens of projects the Special's production company, Smith–Hemion Productions, was juggling at the time: "The thing of it is, if we would have known forty years ago that we'd be doing this now, we would've paid closer attention. But it was just another show at the time."

From the 1960s through the early 1990s, Smith–Hemion was arguably the top TV variety production company in the industry—the go-to team the networks brought in to produce specials for such A-list acts as Barbra Streisand, Julie Andrews, and Neil Diamond. That this bizarre product was among its hundreds of critically acclaimed shows baffles many to this day.

"Smith and Hemion were two of the most talented people in the business," recalls Bob Newhart, who worked with Hemion as a director as far back as 1964 on *Perry Como's Kraft Music Hall.* "So, the fact that this *didn't* turn out well is surprising."

Even the late Dwight Hemion—who, along with partner Gary Smith, led the production company—described the Special afterward as "the worst piece of crap [he'd] ever done." So how did such a highly creative and technically sophisticated outfit—the gold standard in variety television—produce a show that, in the words of David Hofstede, is "the worst two hours of television ever"?

Many place the blame on Lucas, but the fault is not his alone. *Many* people had their hands in the Special's creative pie, but it was Lucas who was left with egg on his face after convincing Mark Hamill, Carrie Fisher, and Harrison Ford to appear in it, against their own initial reservations. "To be honest, it's almost like a very bad parody of *Star Wars* made with the blessing of the people who made *Star Wars,*" says Dan Madsen, founder and former publisher of *Star Wars Insider* magazine.

One of the most often-asked questions is how the same Lucas who fought so hard for creative control over his first three films (*THX 1138, American Graffiti,* and *Star Wars*) could hand over the reins to his new franchise to the writers and producers of *Donny and Marie* and *The Carol Burnett Show.* What would prompt him to take this newly enriched brand of science fiction and submerge it into a fluffy concoction—part soap opera, part Bob Hope special—while dragging his fresh new strain of digital mastery into bed with vaudevillian schtick from such TV veterans as Harvey Korman and Art Carney?

And why did Lucas fight so hard to push a plot focused almost exclusively on a family of Wookiees who do not speak any known language—against the resistance and advice of his own team of experienced variety-show writers and producers—for a project he would wind up skipping out on altogether, once things got messy at Burbank Studios?

There are *several* reasons for the Special's strange outcome, but among the most notable was a rift that pitted a creative team of TV variety producers and film auteurs against each other, with both sides unable to respect—or even *recognize*—the talents of the other, resulting in a shoddy, welded-together fusion of the worst of both worlds.

The idea that Kurtz and Lucas actually compared this Special to *any* of the era's other prime-time entertainment means somebody slipped on the fun sticks. Anyone who thinks that this was just another 1970s TV special is terribly mistaken. The bizarre amalgamation of people, places, and things that are part of the story of this two-hour show reads like a pop culture puzzle of sorts: Elvis Presley, Sonny and Cher, Led Zeppelin, *The Exorcist*, Raquel Welch, Altamont, *Deep Throat*, Bob Hope, the Great Gazoo, Perry Como, *Mork and Mindy*, Mick Jagger, *Maude*, *Donny and Marie*, the Manson Family, *Easy Rider*, David Bowie, *Chariots of the Gods*, Sid and Marty Krofft, *Gilligan's Island*, Richard Pryor, Olivia Newton-John, *The Honeymooners*, and Motown. (For some reason, Lyle Waggoner never came up.)

Among the questions that will be answered in this book:

Was this Special a possible precursor for the Wookiees starring in their own sitcom?

How did Bing Crosby and David Bowie's remarkable "Little Drummer Boy" duet help persuade Lucas to test the television waters?

Why does a Special that was targeted at kids feature a scene with an older Wookiee watching virtual-reality porn?

What is Life Day, and why are all the Wookiees wearing *Eyes Wide Shut* robes and walking toward a ball of light?

Most importantly, what made Lucas so obsessed with prime-time television as to pressure Hamill, Ford, Fisher, Anthony Daniels, and Peter Mayhew into dipping their feet in the genre?

Many say that Lucas's driving preoccupation with TV stemmed from his paranoia that, despite *Star Wars* being the monstrous hit that it was, he still needed to keep the soon-to-be franchise alive in the public's minds for the next three years, until the release of his much-anticipated sequel, *The Empire Strikes Back.*

Although he denies much involvement in the *Star Wars Holiday Special,* George Lucas came up with the original plot, spent significant hours with the show's writers, moved to have his friend David Acomba direct it, and begged the film's leading actors to appear in it—against their better judgment. *Photofest © Lucasfilm Ltd./Twentieth Century Fox Film Corp*

Others contend that the TV appearances were intended to sustain interest until the following holiday season, when a tidal wave of delayed *Star Wars* toys and other merchandise would finally be available in stores.

While these are both valid reasons, the true impetus for the Special that I'll put forth here is *spite*. Although no actual blood would be shed in its making, Lucas's relentless desire to keep *Star Wars* prospering in theaters for as long as possible was a way to strike back at one of the non-believers from his not-so-distant past.

For the first time, it is revealed here that a major rival studio chief was a tremendous adversary of Lucas's. Their longtime feud began in 1971 and lasted through and beyond the release of *Star Wars* six years later. It would be pure ego that made Lucas double down on extending the theatrical life of *Star Wars* by pushing Lucasfilm's marketing maven, Charles Lippincott, to go on a revenge-fueled PR blitz, booking the film's stars and characters on a dozen different talk and TV variety shows. That holiday season, Mark Hamill would even appear on a campy Bob Hope Christmas special. (Perhaps Hope's producers made producing a holiday special look easier than it was.)

To appreciate the most unique and misunderstood endeavor in the *Star Wars* universe, one must understand the true origins of the Special—why it was conceived, how it was produced, and, more importantly, why, after its initial broadcast, Lucas tried so hard to keep it hidden from current and future generations.

True, the Holiday Special is in a class of its own. Nonetheless, is it fair to compare anything from that time period, and shot on inexpensive, recyclable videotape, with the digitally fortified content streaming in high definition today? Further, how much worse is the Special than other TV specials of the era, like NBC's *KISS Meets the Phantom of the Park* or ABC's *Paul Lynde Halloween Special*? Where does the Carpenters' *Space Encounters* musical special rank? Or how about *Ringo*, featuring the former Beatle playing his alter ego, "Ognir Rrats"? And why does Carrie Fisher get minced alive for singing in the Special when, several months before, she sang an equally mediocre version of "You're Sixteen" with Starr?

To understand Lucas's decision to do this special, one must also look at the brilliant but naive Lucasfilm team who were doing their best to navigate through the thousands of opportunities offered to them in the three years between *A New Hope* and *The Empire Strikes Back*.

Filmmaker Kyle Newman sympathizes with Lucas over the brand-new position he was in, with countless offers pouring through his front door. "It's probably hard to say no to the volume of things he was offered," Newman says. "It's never happened before, that type of explosion. How do you know the dangers of saying yes to too many things? You don't. It's not like there were Burger King cups for *Gone with the Wind*. This is something that never happened before, and we can't fault him for being a visionary, a purveyor. . . . To have other brands come at you, and opportunities on television, you're going to seize them."

And, at that point in history, seize them he did.

"It was a period of civil wars," as Lucas once wrote, via Brian De Palma, in *A New Hope*'s opening crawl. To understand the making of this unique TV special, as well as Lucas's conflicts with those who had power and wielded it unfairly, and how they subsequently influenced his filmmaking and business acumen, one must go way back to before *Star Wars* was even conceived, *a long time ago in a galaxy far, far away . . .*

CHAPTER 1

NOT A PLAN
IN SIGHT

AUGUST 1973. Alan Ladd Jr., a production executive at 20th Century Fox, had been an admirer of George Lucas since his 1971 film debut with Warner Bros, the critically acclaimed but commercially unsuccessful *THX 1138*. It looked to Ladd that the Boy Wonder had finally struck gold. "Laddie," as he was known by his friends and colleagues, was excited by the glowing reviews and hefty box-office earnings Universal Pictures' *American Graffiti* had just gotten in its opening weekend.

He was glowing; a signature away from completing a deal memo between Lucas and 20th Century Fox to produce and distribute Lucas's next film, which at the time was titled *The Star Wars*. Lucas and Ladd had a mutual respect for each other: Ladd saw an amazing filmmaker in Lucas, who in turn appreciated Ladd as one of the few out-of-the-box studio executives in town willing to take a chance on his new space project.

But now, Lucas's stock had just shot up considerably, and there was even early talk of an Oscar nomination for him as director, as well as for the overall film, lead actor Richard Dreyfuss, and supporting actors Cindy Williams, Candy Clark, and Paul Le Mat.

Jeff Berg, Lucas's agent, told him that, with the reviews and box-office numbers for *American Graffiti*, they could ask 20th Century Fox for an additional $500,000 in salary, as well as additional percentage points from the film's profits, as a condition of Fox getting the new film. But Lucas wasn't interested in leveraging Ladd for more cash. He was far more interested in control. He wanted his own company, Lucasfilm, to produce *The Star Wars*, and he didn't want the studio adding unnecessary expenses that would subsequently eat into his profits. He also wanted final-cut approval, as well as control over any potential sequels. Lastly, he wanted to retain all of the film's merchandising rights.

The 20th Century Fox executives had already been expecting to pay a huge additional sum to Lucas as a result of the success of *American Graffiti*, so, when they heard Lucas's non-cash option, they thought they had won the battle. They probably couldn't believe a filmmaker would sacrifice so much cash to retain something like a portion of a film's merchandising rights.

The deal went through with minor compromises: notably, Lucas did not receive final-cut approval, but he *was* allowed to retain sequel rights, with the caveat that he had to offer 20th Century Fox the option of distributing. Most importantly, the studio allowed Lucas to share the merchandising rights, with Fox deducting a fifteen percent administrative fee off the top. In a highly unusual agreement, not only would Fox and Lucasfilm split the rights, but both would be allowed to shop them around.

"It was unprecedented," says Dale Pollock, who in 1983 wrote the first biography of Lucas. "No filmmaker had ever retained merchandising rights to his own films. I don't think it ever would've occurred to another filmmaker to do that. But it occurred to Lucas, because he imagined it from the outset."

From the first incarnation of *Star Wars*, Pollock explains, "When he first started writing his pencil drafts, Lucas envisioned a *Star Wars* toy universe." The director foresaw the potential rewards from "giving kids toys to play with that would both foster their imagination and, critically, keep their interest in . . . *Star Wars*. So, from the beginning, you had this dual message of education but also allegiance to a product."

Meanwhile, the executives at 20th Century Fox were celebrating what they considered to be their savvy negotiating tactics, saving potentially hundreds of thousands of dollars in additional salary. *What a chump that Lucas was*, they must have thought.

Even as late as 1976, the concept of film or television merchandising was virtually nonexistent. By that time, toymakers had only started to achieve limited success selling action figures based on TV shows like *The Six Million Dollar Man*, and toys based upon films had achieved even lesser success once the theatrical run ended. In the days before home video and the widespread adoption of cable, films would disappear until they debuted on television. At least television shows went into syndication and gave retailers the potential for *some* staying power.

Beginning in early 1976, 20th Century Fox offered the *Star Wars* merchandising rights to several different toy companies, notably Mego Corporation, at that time the leading producer of action figures. However, Mego—like most of the other toy companies, including Mattel—had passed (Lucasfilm VP of merchandising Charles Lippincott was rejected so brutally at the 1977 Toy Fair that he was asked to leave the Mego booth). By the time they had gotten to Kenner, it was even later in the development process, says the company's then senior product designer, Jim Swearingen. "Everybody else had turned it down because it was a movie that could be in and out of theaters in a month or two, or even less."

Located in Cincinnati, Kenner was a subsidiary of General Mills that had made its mark with toys like the Spirograph and the Easy-Bake Oven but wanted to dive into the action-figure market. However, the problem with licensing these types of products is that a manufacturer needs a two-to-three-year lead to make the toys, according to Marc Pevers, former vice president of licensing for 20th Century Fox. "Lucas had a fetish for secrecy and didn't want people to see the images of the characters," thus delaying the approval process, which subsequently tightened the manufacturing time frame. "George was concerned about his unique characters getting out and was worried about knockoffs. So, by the time we received the go-ahead from Lucas for licensing, it was in August of 1976. Now, bear in mind, [*Star Wars*] was released in May of 1977."

Another factor in the delay was perfectionism. It's no secret that Lucas has a history of being dissatisfied with projects even after their completion, and of going back and trying to improve upon them, like the "Special Editions" of the first three *Star Wars* movies he released in the late 1990s. (He has also sometimes tried to bury past projects altogether, as with the *Star Wars Holiday Special*.)

"George was very strong on quality. I mean *super* quality," says Charles Weber, who was hired as CEO of Lucasfilm shortly after the release of *Star Wars*. "He made the toy companies jump through hoops. I don't mean it badly; he was just qualitatively interested in making it right."

Two months before the release of *Star Wars*, Kenner president Bernie Loomis sent his creative team to a screening of a rough cut of the film that had just been made available to them. The team came back invigorated by what they had seen and got to work immediately, coming up with several different ideas for toys. Kenner had extraordinarily little time to design and produce a product, and, on top of everything, the movie was a long shot: science fiction was still an unproven film genre. But the gamble was tempting. Loomis knew that the better the film did, the better they would do. If *Star Wars* was even a moderate success, Kenner Toys would have successfully made the jump to action figures.

Would it be worth the risk? Kenner thought so. Loomis's endgame was to rise from the world of Easy Bake Ovens and make it with the big boys in the action-figure industry he had yet to enter. To Loomis, it would be completely worth the risk to end up with just one Kenner-produced toy in retailers' action-figure aisles for Christmas. Hopefully, Loomis thought, they would at least break even.

* * *

The early 1970s is often referred to as one of the golden ages of cinema. It was a sort of changing of the guard, where—for various reasons—the old studio system was replaced by a new generation of young independent filmmakers. It was a time when most of the studios had stopped paying big money to the industry's biggest movie stars and instead invested their resources in these younger directors, writers, and actors. Big-budget films were becoming a thing of the past. Several of them—such as *Cleopatra* (1963), *Hello Dolly* (1964), and *Doctor Dolittle* (1967)—had nearly sunk a few of the major studios in the prior decade.

One major reason for the change was the recent success of *Easy Rider*, which had become an overnight sensation on its release in July 1969. From a budget of a little over a half-million dollars, the Dennis Hopper–directed film would eventually gross *$60 million* worldwide, which made the studios begin to re-think their bottom lines.

Another reason was simple mathematics. It had been about sixty years since the studios had started, and that crop of filmmakers who were in their twenties and thirties back then were now reaching retirement age, opening up new opportunities. "The studios were being bought up by corporations," Lucas explained. "The corporations didn't have any idea how to run a studio, so they were hiring film students. All of us, this whole group that I was a part of, got ushered into the film business because the studios didn't know what they were doing."

This new group included a huge crop of young American directors who would hijack the industry over the next few decades and beyond, among them Francis Ford Coppola, Martin Scorsese, Steven Spielberg, William Friedkin, Brian De Palma, Robert Altman, Hal Ashby, Peter Bogdanovich—and Lucas himself.

However, despite the critical acclaim the films from these new directors received, audiences were still not coming to the theaters in droves. There were a few legitimate blockbusters throughout this period—*The Godfather* (1972), *The Exorcist* (1973), and *Jaws* (1975)—but the film studios were still in a major "financial recovery" mode. Even with the shoestring budgets that these films were being produced on, the studios were still healing from the budgetary excesses of the previous decade. The upcoming release of *Star Wars* would help not just 20th Century Fox's recovery but also that of the entire film industry as a whole. Studios *and* theaters would benefit.

By the time *Star Wars*' Memorial Day weekend release came around, critics had already produced a barrage of positive advance reviews, nearly all of them fawning over the space adventure from another dimension. Despite an unusual Wednesday release date (timed to come just before the holiday weekend) and showings in only thirty-two theaters nationwide, *Star Wars* grossed about $11 million in its first weekend, selling out nearly every screening.

It was not a hit. It was a certified freak sensation.

Fox would keep *Star Wars* under its initial limited release through the end of July, when it would expand to more theaters. By that time, excitement about the film had grown even more via word of mouth, and it was on a collision course to becoming not just the biggest hit of the year but ultimately one of the most successful films of all time.

"It's hard to overstate how much of an impact *Star Wars* had when it came out," recalls "Weird Al" Yankovic, who would later produce several parodies involving the franchise. "We'd all seen science-fiction movies before, but not like this. This was different. It was kind of like a nuclear explosion had gone off in pop culture. It blew people's minds."

The recent appearance of high-capacity multiplex theaters also helped *Star Wars*. There was a huge demand for screenings throughout the country, and photos of people waiting in line around city blocks helped fuel the excitement. The new multi-theater venues helped exhibitors shoehorn millions of moviegoers through their doors and would soon help *Star Wars* dethrone *Jaws* as the highest-grossing film in history.

Peter Frampton had recently shown the then-waning music industry that serious money could still be made when, in 1976, he sold several million copies of the live double album *Frampton Comes Alive*. Similarly, *Star Wars* proved to the flailing film studios that there were still thirsty movie audiences—and that, if they liked what they saw, they would not only return but also bring along their friends. Additional box-office revenue was now coming from a source that the film studios and exhibitors had never before considered: the repeat customer. Although *Jaws* was a huge summer hit as well, it could not compare to the numbers of moviegoers who were coming back to wait in line all over again just to see *Star Wars* for a second, third, or fourth time.

"I remember people waiting in line all day to see this movie," recalls Yankovic. "I think it was the first movie that I paid to see in the theaters twice, because you just couldn't get it all in one viewing. You had to see it multiple times."

However, toy stores were not as lucky as the multiplexes. Their shelves were still void of any *Star Wars* merchandise, and Kenner was completely unprepared for the film's unprecedented success. Parents were scrambling to find *Star Wars* toys as Kenner went into overdrive trying to expedite the arrival of *any* merchandise ahead of the upcoming holiday season.

"As a store owner, you're always protecting yourself from being in that situation," says Larry Ross, owner of Blast from the Past, one of the world's largest film and TV collectible stores. "Not being able to meet the demand is a store owner's worst nightmare."

Most stores began their holiday merchandising in the fall, so Kenner was seemingly out of luck for the 1977 season. "That Christmas, every kid in

America want[ed] a *Star Wars* toy, but they had nothing to sell," says Ross. However, one of Kenner's marketing executives came up with what Ross calls "a pretty darn brilliant idea" to meet the demand. It was called the "Early Bird Certificate Special"; Ross and many *Star Wars* fans refer to it as "the empty box."

"It was just that . . . an empty box. But it worked," Ross says. Parents could pay $14 for a certificate that could be redeemed for four *Star Wars* action figures of their choice, which would arrive the following spring. This preorder solution would still give Kenner only six months to deliver the product, so the company went into hyperdrive to meet that deadline. But at least parents had something they could put under the tree that year.

The concept worked brilliantly, and by spring 1978, Kenner's *Star Wars* toys were delivered as promised, accounting for a staggering $100 million in sales. But the point of the action figures had not been simply to generate merchandising revenue; they were used to extend the *Star Wars* merchandising appetite through to the following holiday season, when Kenner would be caught up and ready to line toy stores' shelves with an even wider selection of products.

How could *Star Wars* be kept fresh in the minds of its fans through the 1978 holiday season? Lucas and his colleagues would soon come up with a solution. At the time, it must have seemed like an entirely sensible one.

CHAPTER 2
THE SECRET WEAPON

NOVEMBER 1975. When George Lucas was in film school at USC, he was among a throng of students that would become friends and eventually collaborators. They called themselves "The Dirty Dozen," after the 1967 film about a group of Nazi hunters in World War II, although Lucas actually preferred "The USC Mafia." Among the mafioso: screenwriters John Milius (*Dirty Harry*), Willard Huyck (*American Graffiti*), and Matthew Robbins (*Crimson Peak*); director Randall Kleiser (*Grease*); cinematographer Caleb Deschanel (*Being There*); editor Walter Murch (*Apocalypse Now*); and Gary Kurtz, who would eventually become Lucas's producer for *American Graffiti*, *Star Wars*, and *The Empire Strikes Back*.

On the periphery of this group of type-A personalities was Charles Lippincott.

"Charley was a good guy," recalls Craig Miller, who launched and ran the Official *Star Wars* Fan Club for Lucasfilm. "He had kind of an oddball sense of humor."

Marc Pevers says that what he loved about Lippincott was that he was a square peg in a round hole, far different from the narcissistic filmmakers he was used to working with. He was a people person who didn't try to fit into the Hollywood establishment, swapping his dress shoes for sneakers and living out of his secondhand leather briefcase. Most importantly, Pevers says, he wasn't the "Hollywood type."

Unlike the rest of the mafia, this low-key film student was less interested in writing and directing films than he was in marketing, promoting, and celebrating them. "I don't remember Charley ever making any movies," says Matthew Robbins. "He was like a den mother, but when I learned . . . that Charley was becoming a publicist, it made perfect sense to me."

Eventually, this immensely talented and resourceful prodigy would literally *invent* film marketing, yet he would never reach anywhere near the pinnacle of filmmaking notoriety that his colleagues did. Aside from Lucas, Kurtz, composer John Williams, and conceptual artist Ralph McQuarrie, one would be hard-pressed to cite another person more responsible for the off-the-chart success of *Star Wars* than Lippincott, who has gone strangely unmentioned amid the countless histories of, tributes to, and awards received by the film over the years. Any account of the success of *Star Wars* would be incomplete without his story. Further, a full history of marketing and licensing across media—whether books, comics, or television—would be impossible without explaining the role Lippincott played in creating these ancillary opportunities in the film industry.

Specifically, Lippincott was the solitary force who convinced Lucas to use television to further promote and extend the life of the newly established *Star Wars* brand—a kind of experimental crossbreeding that took a cutting-edge science-fiction film story and intermingled it with the world of lower-budget shows filmed on disposable videotape. Lippincott was the one who encouraged a brief testing of the Nielsen waters in which Lucas—with *Star Wars* still enjoying record-breaking box-office success in theaters throughout the summer of 1977—first allowed the film's characters, costumes, and intellectual property to be exploited in campy musical comedy skits on *Donny and Marie*. And it was that appearance that would lay the groundwork for the Holiday Special.

In late 1974, several years after graduating from USC, Lucas and Gary Kurtz bumped into Lippincott on the Universal lot, where he had just started as a unit publicist on Alfred Hitchcock's *Family Plot*. Lucas and Kurtz were fresh off the mega-success of *American Graffiti*, and although Fox had just greenlit *Star Wars*, they were still renting offices at Universal, following a lesson Lucas had learned since producing *THX 1138* at Warner Bros: if you want to keep the studio brass out of your hair, never keep an office at the actual studio where your film is being produced.

Charles Lippincott, who attended film school with George Lucas, created an out-of-the-box pre-release marketing buzz for *Star Wars* nearly two years before its eventual release. More significantly, he steered Lucas toward using television to promote the movie during its theatrical run. *Photo by Bob Seidemann, courtesy Belinda Seidemann*

"We chatted," Lippincott recalled in a 2015 interview, "and they told me about this new picture they were working on called *The Star Wars*." Lucas offered him a script to read over the weekend, and when they spoke on Monday, Lippincott couldn't contain his enthusiasm. He told Lucas he thought they had a great project on their hands, and the two discussed all of the film's marketing possibilities, including toys that would be sold in comic-book stores. "I was very excited because I'm a true fanboy, a die-hard science-fiction fan and comic-book collector," Lippincott recalled. He was such a fanboy, in fact, that he was willing to leave Alfred Hitchcock to work on Lucas's film.

To harness Lippincott's enthusiasm, Lucas urged Fox to hire him. Fox insisted they already had a marketing department, but after some back and forth they finally gave in and hired Lippincott at a minimal rate to market *Star Wars*, as well as several of the studio's other films. Then, with Fox paying Lippincott's salary, Lucas named him vice president of advertising, publicity, promotion, and merchandising for his own newly created subsidiary, the Star Wars Corporation. It was quite a win for Lucas: Lippincott would end up spending little time, if any, on Fox's other films, and thus Fox was, in effect, paying him to work exclusively on marketing *Star Wars*.

After all, Lucas was going to need all the help he could get to encourage audiences to see a film in a relatively unproven genre. Word of mouth only works if there are people in the theater in the first week or two to see the film. Only then can they start talking about it.

Even if a film got great reviews, in 1977 theater owners still relied on movie stars to bring people in, and other than Alec Guinness and Peter Cushing (who had supporting roles as Obi-Wan Kenobi and Grand Moff Tarkin, respectively), there were no stars in *Star Wars*. They were all newcomers, none of them big enough names to get booked on programs like *The Tonight Show* to promote the film. There simply wasn't a good hook for marketing science fiction, so Lippincott came up with the idea of marketing *Star Wars* directly to fans.

To do this, Lippincott went directly to his wheelhouse. An avid fan of both comic books and science-fiction films, he was very familiar with the market, and he planned to promote *Star Wars* almost a year before its release date at conventions all over the country. "My thinking was that we should sell to the science-fiction and comic-book crowd early on," he said in a 2011 interview. "Why not tailor a campaign and build off of that? Do a novelization and comic-book adaption early?"

Although mega-conventions like Comic-Con existed in 1977, they had not nearly begun to attract the tens of thousands they pull in today. However, the smaller conventions Lippincott was targeting were still a great way to get the niche film and comic-book fans committed to seeing *Star Wars* during its first week.

These days, building a brand before a film's release is practically Marketing 101. Propelled by social media, today's film marketers create campaigns that begin several months or even a year before a film's release. Back when *Star Wars* was still being developed at Fox, however, the term "film marketing" didn't even exist. In 1975, Lippincott invented it.

Craig Miller says one of the smartest things that the detail-oriented Lippincott did was methodically file all of the copyrights and trademarks for *Star Wars*. "He made sure everything was covered." Most importantly, Lippincott trademarked the names of the characters, as he was well aware of the countless legal issues that had befallen Paramount after the studio had not secured copyrights on every element of *Star Trek*. This looseness with the *Star Trek* brand's ownership created a void where fans began to use the franchise's characters and ideas in their own works. "To prevent this, I copyrighted everything I could think of," Lippincott later recalled. "If it was possible to copyright a paperclip, I would have. Folks at Fox thought I was crazy."

In November 1975—*eighteen months* before the film's release—Lippincott made plans to sell the novelization of Lucas's original screenplay. The novel would be called *Star Wars*, and although it would actually be written by Alan Dean Foster—who had written a few movie and TV novelizations—the book would be credited to Lucas. Some of the folks at Lucasfilm wanted to create a bidding war for it, but Lippincott wasn't interested in selling the rights for the largest possible amount. He felt it was much more valuable, marketing-wise, to have the novel published by the top science-fiction publisher of the time, Ballantine Books, which had released Ray Bradbury's *Fahrenheit 451* and J. R. R. Tolkien's *Lord of the Rings*. Lippincott eventually negotiated a reasonable financial offer from Ballantine, who—more importantly—agreed to his extraordinary requirement that it publish the novel *nine months* before the film's release.

Soon after, Lippincott began negotiating with Marvel to produce a *Star Wars* comic book. Again, he was looking for promotional opportunities, not necessarily a revenue stream, so he pushed Marvel to release several of the comics before the film came out. "The real problem was, I didn't want one comic book, and I didn't want two comic books," Lippincott said in 2018. "I wanted five-to-six comic books telling the story of the film. And I wanted at least three issues out before the film came out, and nobody had done that up to that time. So that was a bit of a hard sell at first."

According to Lippincott, Stan Lee initially turned down the project, until he learned that Alec Guinness would be appearing in the film. After further negotiations about the number of issues to be released prior to the film's release, Marvel—encouraged by editor Roy Thomas—agreed to produce three comic books before the film's debut. They would be written and drawn by Thomas and Howard Chaykin, respectively. Production began immediately.

Fox criticized the Marvel arrangement, calling the deal "stupid" and saying it didn't care about the added revenue. But neither did Lippincott, who—as with the novelization—was just looking for another avenue to reach the film's intended audience. To him, these ancillary media projects weren't a source of revenue but a source of free advertising, so any actual profit made from these ventures was just gravy.

The Fox folks who criticized these deals either didn't believe in *Star Wars* or thought this potential revenue was a drop in the hat compared to the film's budget, which was increasing with every month it was in production. (Generally speaking, *most* at Fox didn't really believe in *Star Wars*. To be fair, Ladd—who almost solely championed the film at Fox—didn't really understand *Star Wars* either; he was more invested in Lucas, the director, making another great film.)

Now, with the release of the novel slated for November 12, 1976, and three Marvel comic books coming out several months before the film, Lippincott was well on his way to generating the pre-release buzz he had been trying to create.

In the spring of 1976, Lippincott hired Craig Miller, a local comic-book and science-fiction enthusiast who was even more immersed in this unique world. Miller regularly attended conventions and narrowed down the best events for Lippincott to attend and potentially present sneak-peak presentations of *Star Wars* at. By that time, Thomas and Chaykin had already submitted some of the comic books' test designs to Lucasfilm. With these, plus Ralph McQuarrie and Joe Johnston's artwork of the film's costumes and spaceships, Lippincott had enough material to host one of the first ever film-related presentations at San Diego's Comic-Con that July.

Lippincott had been prodding Lucas about the importance of winning over this niche audience, so Lucas paid out of pocket to send him out on the convention circuit. Lippincott passed out press materials, sold posters, and joined Thomas and Chaykin in answering questions about the film. Even though he had no footage to show, his ace in the hole wound up being a preview of the film's stupendous artwork, particularly Johnston's amazing drawings and McQuarrie's extravagant paintings.

"A year before *Star Wars* came out, Charley went and showed slides about this movie and got this amazing groundswell," says Mick Garris, who was the receptionist at the *Star Wars* offices in 1976 and has since become a prominent film director. "Fandom was never really a part of the marketing plan until Charley Lippincott made it so."

Previews in such film magazines as *American Film* and *Sight and Sound* also helped keep cinephiles curious. In September 1976, Lippincott hosted a presentation at MidAmeriCon, a science-fiction convention held in Kansas City, this time accompanied by Kurtz and Hamill. Costumes of Darth Vader and the robots C-3PO and R2-D2 were displayed, along with a stormtrooper's helmet and blaster and a wall of McQuarrie's amazing conceptual artwork.

However, most important was an hour-long presentation made up of 35 mm slides of the film's production artwork and on-set photos. A standing-room-only crowd listened as Lippincott introduced the film's plot, and a lengthy question-and-answer session followed. The die-hard science-fiction fans in the audience were mostly supportive, although a few suspicious ones grilled Kurtz and Hamill over their sincerity about the genre.

Lippincott even went so far as crossing the aisle and boldly going where no publicist had gone before. "He went to the *Star Trek* conventions and got the Trekkies interested," recalls Marc Pevers. "He had stills from the film, and he could explain to people what the film was about. And this is something right up their alley. The idea is, if you get the enthusiasm with them, that will spread. These are the kind of people that will see a movie ten times if they like it."

Miki Herman, who began as a production assistant on *Star Wars* and eventually became Lucas's liaison for the Holiday Special, also credits Lippincott for the tremendous following the film had before it was even released. "He knew how to get people excited and how to stir up interest and word of mouth. And, from these science-fiction conventions, people [were] interested to see what this film was going to be like. And then they would tell their friends about it."

Lucas eventually praised Lippincott for his brilliant pre-release strategy. "It had an effect because there was a whole world of fanatics out there that were crazy to see this movie six months before it came out."

Lippincott's goal of guaranteeing people in the seats for the first week—both through direct promotion and by getting excitement to spread via word of mouth—had been met. Additionally, through Lippincott's merchandising efforts, "Lucasfilm began to make a lot more money from these ancillary revenue streams," explains Dale Pollock. "And those were often invented by Charley Lippincott."

The pre-release strategies that Lippincott used to promote *Star Wars* would soon become the standard for all film marketing departments. With *Star Wars* set on a course to become the highest-grossing film in history, Lippincott would soon venture into other mediums, continuing to find new audiences for his film. He was just getting started.

* * *

Two months into the summer of *Star Wars'* release, the madness surrounding the film was showing no signs of stopping, and people were still waiting hours in lines to see it. After the film's momentous release, Lippincott had found some additional ways to attract attention to the *Star Wars* brand, while also generating extra money for Lucasfilm. The Official *Star Wars* Fan Club was one such idea: for five dollars, a member would be given stills, a poster, and other memorabilia, generating what Pollock describes as "a significant revenue stream." Still, overall, Lucasfilm's post-release marketing strategy was largely the result of the extraordinary word of mouth that was propelling the film.

For the most part, *Star Wars* was pretty much running on autopilot, but managing the onslaught of various inquiries coming into the Lucasfilm offices was a colossal job. Everything from interview requests to advertising opportunities, to invitations for charity event appearances were coming through the main line, and the young staffers were doing their best to handle what could only be described as a promotional explosion.

"I love the world between *Star Wars* and *Empire*," says action-figure designer Jason Lenzi. "To me, it's bizarre. It's not completely thought out. There's no mythology built up. The merchandise is crazy. And it wasn't until *Empire* that everything became more fully formed. So, I have a real affection for that time where it was this wild thing that nobody could figure out— whether it was *Donny and Marie* or the Holiday Special. Everybody was kind of making it up as they went along, and then it became much more refined as it went on. So, I love the strangeness of that period, and the Holiday Special falls smack dab in the heart of that."

In the history of movies, there had never been a phenomenon like *Star Wars*, says *Fanboys* director Kyle Newman, who calls this period "an unprecedented, unrivaled wild time. Everybody's coming at them for a piece of it. Everyone wants to be affiliated with it. Anything that *Star Wars* touches is gold—read-alongs and inflatables and lightsabers. Everybody wants in on this."

Newman, who has directed and produced several projects for Lucas, knows that his years of struggling with Warner Bros over *THX 1138* frustrated him tremendously. For Lucas, in Newman's view, the success of *Star Wars* "must have been extremely rewarding, having been doubted for years, and having all your films be maligned and chopped up and deemed failures by a studio."

To capitalize on the success of *Star Wars*, in late July Warner Bros reached out to Lucas about re-releasing his directorial debut, *THX 1138*. The 1971 science-fiction film starred Robert Duvall and was the first of a seven-picture deal that Warner Bros had made with Francis Ford Coppola's newly created American Zoetrope Studios, a scrappy film company based in downtown San Francisco that Coppola was trying to launch with Lucas.

It was the future of this scrappy little film company that was the focus of a deep-seated grudge held by both Lucas and Coppola against Warner Bros. The resentment had begun six years earlier, while the two were working on *THX 1138*—when *Star Wars* was just a glimmer in young George's eye— which is where the motive for the *Star Wars Holiday Special* strangely begins.

Coppola and Lucas had met under the strangest of coincidences. Coppola was five years older and working as a writer for the Canadian film company Seven Arts when suddenly, Seven Arts bought Warner Bros and Coppola was assigned to the Warner backlot to direct *Finean's Rainbow*, a musical starring Fred Astaire.

Lucas, fresh from USC, had just entered and won a competition sponsored by Warner Bros, enabling a student to observe the studio's operations for six months. However, when he arrived in July 1967, the only production on the entire lot was *Finean's Rainbow*. It was not exactly Lucas's cup of tea, but he headed over anyway and subsequently met Coppola—only to learn that the musical wasn't his cup of tea either.

Being the only people there who were under fifty, the two became immediate friends. Frustrated with the Astaire project, they talked about developing their own ideas. *THX 1138* was originally a student film Lucas had made at USC, and since he already had a completed script in hand, it became the first project Coppola formally pitched to the newly formed Warner Bros–Seven Arts film group. But, to Coppola's surprise, it was rejected.

Two years later, however, two factors would help Coppola sell *THX 1138*. First, he learned that the film group was being acquired by Kinney National Services—a nationwide company largely known for managing parking facilities—and would be bringing in former talent agent Ted Ashley as chairman and film producer John Calley as the studio's new head of production. Coppola immediately went to Warner with a whopper of a pitch, explaining to the new regime that the prior management had *already greenlit THX 1138* and that they had already begun production on it. He also told them about his new company that would produce low-budget films targeted at the youth market. He assured them that Zoetrope would deliver *THX 1138* for under a million dollars—and that he had six additional films he could also bring in at under a million apiece, as well.

The second factor was the recent success of *Easy Rider*, which resulted in what Lucas called "a real eight-month renaissance." In a recently unearthed 1971 interview, he explained the studios' sudden respect for younger filmmakers like him and Coppola. "All of a sudden there was freedom," Lucas recalled, adding that the studios were basically thinking, "These kids are crazy, but we'll let them do it because it seems to make money."

The financial success of *Easy Rider* soon sent a message to the studios that any kid armed with a vague idea for a film and a shoestring budget could make a profit for them. With this new appetite for smaller independent films—coupled with Coppola's promise to keep his budgets in check—Ashley lent him $300,000 in seed money to help develop *THX 1138*, as well as the six other ideas he had included in his pitch. In addition, Ashley agreed to loan Coppola another $300,000 to help establish Zoetrope as a functioning company. With the latter, Coppola would be able to purchase cameras and sound, lighting, and editing equipment, and then he and Lucas could "continue" production on *THX 1138*.

However, the loan came with a huge stipulation: if the scripts Coppola was developing did not meet Warner's expectations, they would have to be reimbursed the entire $600,000. Coppola was aware of the risk but knew of no other way to get the financing to produce *THX 1138*. And he was certain a few of those seven projects would be a success.

Of the six additional films Coppola pitched to Ashley, one was *Apocalypse Now*, the Vietnam War story Lucas had been writing with USC alum John Milius. Also among the stories Coppola pitched were Carroll Ballard's *Vesuvio* and *The Conversation*, a thriller Coppola had been developing on his own.

Although Lucas was infuriated that Coppola had bartered with *THX 1138* and Milius's *Apocalypse Now* script without their approval, he was now behind the eight ball to begin production on the movie. Lucas hired another USC graduate, Walter Murch, to co-write a revised version of *THX 1138*, and production began on September 21, 1969. Filming was completed in mid-November, but Lucas was still editing seven months later. The studio executives were getting increasingly anxious about Coppola's first project under the new deal, and in May of 1970, they demanded a screening of what Lucas had assembled to date.

The night before the screening, Coppola stopped by Lucas's place to view his latest cut. He was not impressed, and he warned Lucas that the studio would probably not like it. Nonetheless, Coppola drove the film down to Burbank to screen it for Ashley, Calley, and a roomful of other executives, including vice president of production Dick Lederer, story editor Barry Beckerman, and head of business affairs Frank Wells.

Wells was not a typical showbiz executive. Standing six foot four, he was a physically fit middle-aged specimen. A Stanford graduate and Rhodes Scholar, Wells became an attorney for both Roy Disney and Clint Eastwood. He was soon hired to run Warner's business-affairs department and is credited with stripping the Man with No Name from Universal and bringing him to Warner to star in the mega-successful *Dirty Harry* franchise.

He fit into the role at business affairs perfectly. He was a no-nonsense numbers guy who could effectively play the "Bad Cop" to Calley's "Good Cop" persona with the prowess of Lawrence Olivier.

He also wanted to be the first man to climb the highest mountain on all seven continents.

When the Warner executives saw the film, their response was as expected. They were horrified. "They freaked out," Lucas recalled.

"This is not the screenplay we said we were going to do," one said. "This isn't a commercial movie."

As the executives started to leave, their conversation became focused on how to recut the film. Wells—who again was head of the business-affairs department—*actually dictated* what needed to be done to fix the film. He assigned the implementation to Fred Weintraub, the studio's informal "connection to the younger generation," who was currently supervising the editing of *Woodstock*.

Lucas dodged Weintraub's calls, trying to delay the inevitable. Finally, the studio got its veteran head editor, Rudy Fehr, to extract four minutes from Lucas's most recent cut. Lucas later recalled, "The studio tried to recut it, tried to shorten it. 'You can't understand it anyway,' I said. 'Why are you trying to shorten it? It's not going to make it make any more sense. I put my heart and soul into this thing and to me it means something. You just come in and whack a few fingers off it and think there's nothing to it.'"

Lucas was less upset at *what* they cut from the film than *why* they cut it. "I'm more upset at the idea," he lamented, just after the release of *THX 1138*. "It's more of a young idealist facing the reality of the fact that these people exist. I guess it's like what most kids face when they see the government—I just faced it with Warner Bros." The experience left him with a bitterness that would later manifest itself in an almost obsessive desire for total creative control of all of his future films—films that he would wind up owning outright.

While Calley and Ashley were disappointed with the film, they assured Coppola that Warner Bros would still distribute *THX 1138*, but they weren't interested in producing any more of his projects, closing the door on any future collaborations with Zoetrope. Wells had been less cordial, telling Coppola—even before the business-affairs executive had seen any of *THX 1138*—they expected him to refund the $600,000 Warner had loaned him. Specifically, beyond the $300,000 Warner loaned Coppola to build Zoetrope, Wells wanted him to reimburse Warners–Seven for the additional $300,000 they had spent developing the scripts for *THX 1138*, as well as the six other projects Coppola pitched them.

Author Gene Phillips succinctly describes Warner's move: "In effect, the studio was making Coppola buy back his own scripts." *THX 1138* co-writer Walter Murch put it more bluntly: "Warner Bros not only pulled the rug out from Francis. They tried to sell it back to him." Upon his departure, Coppola reportedly signed off to Wells and his colleagues, "I'm a fucking artist. You're fucking Philistines."

The incident resonated with both of them for several years. "Warner Bros loaned me $300,000," Coppola recalled, "and they financed about $300,000 against development of our projects."

Ironically, the need to make up for the huge financial losses they had just suffered meant Lucas and Coppola immediately took "money gigs." Lucas started writing a more commercially viable film called *American Graffiti*, and Coppola finally agreed to take on the mafia film that Paramount's Robert Evans had been begging him to direct.

* * *

As soon as Coppola started on *The Godfather*, Wells called up Paramount and told them about Coppola's debt, and that they might as well turn over Coppola's salary to them. After the tremendous success of the film, Coppola paid back the initial $300,000 but asked Warner to reconsider demanding the additional $300,000 back, noting it was standard procedure for studios to invest in scripts "on spec." No-nonsense Wells responded that a deal was a deal.

At the Oscars presentation in March of 1973, Wells was sitting with Dick Lederer at the Warner Bros table when he spotted Coppola. Even though he had lost the "Best Director" award to Bob Fosse (for *Cabaret*), he and the novelist Mario Puzo won "Best Adapted Screenplay," and the film itself won "Best Picture." Wells said they should go congratulate him, to which Lederer warned, "Don't Frank, don't. He's a Sicilian, he will not shake hands with you." Wells ignored Lederer and approached Coppola, who recognized him from about ten feet away: "No. No. I'm not shaking hands with you."

As Coppola began *The Godfather Part II*, Wells again called Paramount about the debt. Paramount, tired of the drama and wanting Coppola to be free of this distraction, paid Warner, subsequently deducting the amount from Coppola's earnings.

Back in 1971, Frank Wells demanded that Lucas and the producer of *THX 1138*, Francis Ford Coppola, return the start-up money Warner Bros had "loaned" them to develop six other American Zoetrope films. Both men went on to take "money gigs": Lucas wrote and directed *American Graffiti* for Universal, and Coppola finally accepted Paramount's offer to direct *The Godfather*. *Photofest © Warner Bros*

Six years after the *THX 1138* melodrama, Lucas was still just as angry at the studio. Common sense also dictated that he had no interest in the studio re-releasing *THX 1138* while *Star Wars* was enjoying such insane box-office numbers. Obviously, Warner wanted to use Lucas's name to reinvigorate a film that the studio had never believed in anyway, just to capitalize on his recent success. Why would Lucas give his blessings to a rival studio releasing another science-fiction film that would lure potential ticket-buyers from seeing *Star Wars* again? Why would he want to do anything for Warner Bros, the studio that had allowed Frank Wells—its head of *business affairs*—to circumvent Lucas and supervise the editing of his final cut?

Although he still harbored resentment toward Warner Bros, Lucas was a tad curious when a meeting request came in not from a lowly film executive but from the vice chairman of the company. Maybe he was hoping for an apology. He asked Kurtz and Lippincott to join him, and the three went to Burbank to meet with the vice chairman, Wells, who had risen up the corporate ranks from the business-affairs department rather quickly.

Shortly after the release of *Star Wars*, the late Warner Bros executive Frank Wells (*right*) tried to cash in on its success by re-releasing Lucas's 1971 directorial debut, *THX 1138*. Wells died fourteen years later in a helicopter crash while serving as president of Walt Disney. He is shown here with Disney CEO Michael Eisner. *Courtesy Scott Wolf*

When they arrived, Wells got up from behind his large desk, his wall-to-wall corner office window revealing an amazing view of the San Fernando Valley behind him. "He sat in a big, leather chair facing us, twiddling his fingers," Lippincott recounted in a journal discovered after his passing. Wells then brought up the idea of re-releasing *THX 1138* in theaters, and Lucas expressed his disapproval, telling him he didn't want *THX 1138* to compete with *Star Wars*.

According to Lippincott's journal, Wells went on to explain that Warner was planning on re-releasing the film in September, because "*Star Wars* is a big deal now, but by Labor Day, it will be a flash in the pan." He told the three of them that he had seen his share of summer blockbusters, and "none of them ever make it past September."

The three other men sat shell-shocked. According to the journal, this meeting occurred in late July. The box-office figures for the week of July 15–21 had been up ten percent from the previous week. The film's total box-office revenue was just under $60 million for just its first eight weeks, most of which had been under limited release.

Ironically, if there was someone in the room that knew a thing or two about summer blockbusters, it was Lucas, whose own *American Graffiti*, released in the summer of 1973, had grossed $55 million.

Lucas, Kurtz, and Lippincott were incensed by Wells's patronizing dismissal of *Star Wars*. *By Labor Day, it'll be history.*

"You should have seen the steam pour out of George's ears," Lippincott recalled. "We left the office pissed," he wrote in his journal. "George was furious. So [were] Gary and I. At that point, we decided we were going to prove the jerk wrong."

Craig Miller adds that Lucas's anger helped to fuel their new directive: "It kind of redoubled George's interest in making sure *Star Wars* succeeded and continued to be in theaters."

That afternoon, Lippincott's mission became clear: by whatever means necessary, Lucasfilm was to be saber-focused on extending the life of *Star Wars*' theatrical run—through Labor Day and beyond, if possible. For nearly two months, *Star Wars* had been on autopilot, using word of mouth to gain its numbers. Now they were going to be actually, proactively *promoting* the film. There was no telling what that would do for the box-office receipts.

Lucas kept Lippincott fixated on discovering more ways to promote *Star Wars* to even *newer* audiences, using talk shows, variety shows ... nothing was exempt. Lippincott started booking the cast members wherever he could, as well as creating live promotional events—anything that might help keep people in theater seats through September. This August promotional surge, they hoped, might help cushion the eventual slowdown of ticket sales, and clearly show Wells how wrong he was about the longevity of *Star Wars*.

At this point, that's all that mattered.

CHAPTER 3
MEDIA ONSLAUGHT

LIPPINCOTT DID NOT have a huge post-release marketing plan for *Star Wars*. The media coverage the film had been receiving was not the result of publicists' efforts. It was getting amazing news coverage because it was clearly newsworthy: it was an insane box-office draw, it was getting outstanding reviews, and it was in the unusual genre of science fiction. This all made the actual film an event unto itself, and one that was now being propelled organically by its own newsworthiness in a way that was impossible to buy or engineer.

Now, with the new directive, Lippincott started working proactively again.

"It's almost as if, at that time in the entertainment world, there were two tracks, and it had been going on since the silent movies," explained former LucasBooks executive editor Jonathan Rinzler, in one of his last interviews before his death in 2021. "You did your kind of high art form, which is the movie. Then you did a lot of stuff to support it, whatever it took. If you had to put on the disguise in front of a shopping mall, you did it."

The track that Lippincott decided to use to promote *Star Wars* was television. These were the days when the preferred medium for most connoisseurs was film, and television was dismissed by self-styled artists as a lesser medium—a destination for those who couldn't make it in the movies. Critics aside, however, the number of eyeballs watching television during the '50s, '60s, and '70s was far above that of any other medium—and it was growing exponentially.

In February 1977, three months before the release of *Star Wars*, Merv Griffin walked into his daily production meeting raving about a trailer he had just seen for an upcoming film. At the time, Griffin was hosting a ninety-minute syndicated talk show that aired during prime time in Los Angeles and New York. The bookers were doing their best to fill up each of the shows with entertaining guests that also attracted viewers. Griffin had the answer.

"Book everyone from that movie you can," he told the room. "It's going to be an insane hit. It'll be bigger than *Jaws*. It's rocket ships and sword fights. It's like a Western in outer space." However, Griffin also emphasized that, in addition to action and adventure, the film had sex appeal. "Girls were screaming for it," he said. "Book it!"

"Booking *it*" likely meant that Griffin wanted the producers to do a special show about the film. *The Merv Griffin Show* had distinguished itself from the rest of the TV talkers by producing themed shows focusing on one specific TV, film, theater, or musical project. One night they might book the entire cast of *Grease*, the following night the entire cast of *The Golden Girls*. These were riskier because, if the audience liked the project, they'd likely watch the entire show; but if they didn't like the project, the entire show would go down the tubes.

Apparently, the producers didn't think *Star Wars* would attract the kind the viewership needed for a themed show, so they booked the actors individually. However, since they were early to the game (thanks to Griffin), they were able to book Ford and Hamill before most of the competition. "On the day Mark Hamill was on, all the girls in the building came down to the studio to watch his interview," recalls writer/producer Peter Barsocchini. "They didn't care about rocket ships, sword fights, or science fiction. They cared about *him*. They *screamed* when he walked onstage."

During the commercial break, Barsocchini walked up to the set and dropped some notes on a table beside him. He says that Merv just looked at me and said, "Told ya."

Lippincott locked in on the rest of the TV talk-show circuit. In the summer of 1977, there was just a handful of other talk shows: besides Merv in prime time, there was *Dinah!* and *The Mike Douglas Show* in the daytime, and after hours there was *The Tonight Show Starring Johnny Carson*. (*The Dick Cavett Show*, which also aired in late night, was far too political for this kind of popcorn movie fodder.)

An important demographic Lucasfilm was trying to attract was women,

Often misidentified as being of *Star Wars'* opening day, this photograph was in fact taken over a month after its amazing debut at Mann's Chinese Theater. Fox had been forced to relocate the record-breaking film to make room for a prior commitment by the theater to William Friedkin's *Sorcerer;* Lippincott turned its return into a huge media event, negotiating for Darth Vader, C-3PO, and R2-D2 to have their "feet" enshrined in cement out front. *Photofest*

so the next call was to *Dinah!*, where Carrie Fisher and Mark Hamill were booked to appear together the following week. Hamill, who had been working in television for several years, had much more experience in front of audiences than the low-key Fisher, who pretty much allowed Hamill to take most of the questions.

The following week, on July 20, *The Mike Douglas Show*—which was taped in Philadelphia—aired a live broadcast of the entire *Star Wars* triumvirate: Hamill, Fisher, and Ford. Later that evening, Hamill's *Merv Griffin Show* appearance aired in prime time.

For the month of August, Lippincott ratcheted things up a bit, having conceived an amazing promotional event by taking what had been a massive blow to the film's first few weeks and creating one of the biggest hooplas ever produced on Hollywood Boulevard.

Prior to *Star Wars'* theatrical release, Lucas had told Fox he really wanted the film to play at Mann's Chinese Theater (formerly known as Grauman's, before Mann's Theaters purchased it in 1973). However, Mann's had only a two-week slot available before Paramount began a six-week theatrical run of *Sorcerer*, William Friedkin's highly anticipated follow-up to his 1973 blockbuster *The Exorcist*. At the time, Fox didn't hold much stock in *Star Wars* anyway and was betting that *The Other Side of Midnight*, the film adaption of Sidney Sheldon's best-selling novel, would be its summer hit. In fact, Mann's president Larry Gleason says that Fox "was not a fan of the movie." He recalls the studio's head of distribution, Peter Myers, saying, "We're fine, we'll take the two weeks. I just hope we get a second week out of it . . . it's a pretty weird movie."

No one at Fox nor Mann's envisioned *Star Wars'* run lasting two weeks, much less while fans were still lining around the block to see it. After the film's massive opening weekend, however, Gleason appealed to Paramount to let them keep *Star Wars* running instead of swapping it out for *Sorcerer*, but the studio wouldn't budge.

Mann's owned another venue down the street called the Hollywood—a five-hundred-seat theater, but not a very nice one. It ran twenty-four hours a day, Gleason explains. "We used to call it 'the Flop House' . . . because some people would go in there to sleep. People would go in there at midnight, buy a ticket, and leave at seven o'clock in the morning."

Mann's gave the theater a quick renovation—repainting it and installing new seats—and then moved *Star Wars* in. However, *Sorcerer* underperformed at Grauman's, resulting in Paramount pulling it from the theater after just two weeks, allowing *Star Wars* to return to the Chinese four weeks early.

For this return, Lippincott negotiated for his three stars—not Hamill, Fisher, and Ford, but C-3PO, R2-D2, and Darth Vader—to have their footprints enshrined in cement in front of the theater. Special feet would need to be created for the robots, which had only flat pieces of metal on their soles. The newly modified feet looked exactly like those of the original costumes, except for the special patterns on the bottom that were created to look like some sort of robotic footwear. Attention to detail was one of the hallmarks of Rick Baker, a future winner of multiple Oscars who had not only overseen this specific modification but had supervised the creation of many alien creatures for the *Star Wars* cantina sequence.

It all went off pretty smoothly, except for Regis Philbin's faux pas: as the droids were ready to be dipped in front of a phalanx of camera crews, the then-KABC entertainment reporter accidentally stepped in the wet cement, requiring the theater crew to repair it before starting again.

Of the three "inductees," only Anthony Daniels was flown in from London for the event; Kenny Baker and David Prowse (the actor who wore Darth Vader's suit in *A New Hope*) were not. Lucasfilm receptionist Mick Garris had since been promoted to be R2-D2's remote-control operator, so he would be the brains of the miniature robot for the day, and for many events and R2-D2 appearances to come.

Wearing the Darth Vader suit was six-foot-five Kermit Eller. Lippincott had been getting daily requests for the *Star Wars* characters to make appearances at children's charity events and at promotional events like the Grauman's ceremony. Now his robotic stars had several prime-time television appearances coming up, too. He couldn't afford—timewise or financially— to fly the actors back and forth from London. He would need to find a solution for these characters, and the hardest of all was recruiting a full-time domestic Lord Vader.

Hiring for such a job was not easy. This was decades before you could use craigslist to find day-hires for gigs like this, and you couldn't just look one up in the "411" book (the industry's directory at the time for all things TV and film). However, a solution presented itself through the studio of costume and mask designer Don Post, nicknamed "The Godfather of Halloween," and for good reason. After the tremendous success of 1930s horror films like *Phantom of the Opera*, *Dracula*, and *Frankenstein*, Post had begun working with studios to create consumer versions of its costumes for the public— specifically, plastic masks of movie monsters. (He would eventually partner with Verne Langdon, who would go on to do makeup for the *Planet of the Apes* franchise, as well as some television projects—including the *Star Wars Holiday Special*.)

By the 1970s, Post's son, Don Jr., had pretty much taken over the family business and had hired Kermit Bryce Eller to assist with the mask-making. Lippincott had reached out to Post's studio to explore licensing masks during the pre-release merchandising blitzkrieg for *Star Wars*. Eller had been one of the first to respond to Lippincott's offer, and the two met in person. A year later, Lippincott remembered Eller's towering physique and offered him a job as the touring Vader, which he accepted. Eller would make all of Vader's personal appearances, including charity events, record and book signings—and, most importantly, the prime-time variety shows Lippincott had begun booking the film's characters on.

According to Eller, Prowse was not well-liked among the Lucasfilm lot. After the Grauman's event, Eller and Daniels had dinner, where Eller asked what sort of an actor Prowse was. "Tony said, 'David Prowse is not an actor,'" Eller recalls. "David Prowse is a shape.'" In fact, he was so disliked that there were reportedly discussions about Eller replacing him on *The Empire Strikes Back*. "But there was no way that Actors Equity in England would allow somebody that's in a costume, whose face you cannot see, to be played by an American actor if there was an Englishman that could do it."

Lippincott had covered the talk-show circuit pretty well, and now, with a local Darth Vader on the payroll, he pushed the brand into other areas of the television sphere. First, he booked Eller on *The Midnight Special*, where he pretended to choke host Wolfman Jack (to whom Lucas had been extremely indebted after he agreed to appear in *American Graffiti* at low cost). He also booked him to make cameos on campy variety shows like *Wacko* and promotional appearances alongside Shaun Cassidy and the Harlem Globetrotters.

"You saw the proliferation of *Star Wars* on television in the late 1970s, and in 1977 specifically on these variety shows, as a way to keep *Star Wars* cemented in the zeitgeist," says Kyle Newman. As Lucas (and Lippincott) had predicted, *Star Wars* was indeed a merchandising dream, so it would be pretty easy to drop these characters into a television variety show. There was lots of talent in *Star Wars* to choose from, whether it was the lead actors or its assortment of aliens and Wookiees. "Prior to that, the big movie was *Jaws*, right?" says comedian and *Star Wars* superfan Kevin Smith. "But we couldn't just throw *Jaws* onto a thing: 'Look, ladies and gentlemen—*Jaws* is here to sing.'"

Lippincott had several decisions to make regarding which television programs he was going to have the *Star Wars* characters appear on. *Saturday Night Live* was preparing for its third season and had already been established as a bona-fide hit. For the upcoming season, the producers were trying to add some youth to the lineup of guest hosts, instead of the older stable of comedians they were pulling from. Thus, they reached out to Lippincott for a *Star Wars* cast member to change things up a bit. Lippincott was selective, however, and a bit worried about overexposure within certain demographics, so he ultimately went with *The Richard Pryor Show* over *SNL*.

In early 1977, NBC had rolled the dice on a Richard Pryor special whose executive producer, Burt Sugarman, had earned his stripes at the network with his successful late-night series *The Midnight Special*. It was a risky move on NBC's part, as Pryor was a lightning rod for controversy at the time. Just three years earlier, he had been hired by Mel Brooks to co-write and co-star in *Blazing Saddles*, but although he definitely had the comedy chops to join Brooks's writing team, Warner Bros was skittish about his alleged drug use and only allowed him to stay on as a writer, putting the kibosh on a co-starring role. (Pryor recommended a then-unknown Cleavon Little to replace him as "Black Bart" in what would be Little's most iconic role ever.)

NBC won the bet hands down after Pryor's special became a huge critical and commercial success, and as a result the network gave him a chance to host his own weekly TV sketch show, which premiered in September 1977.

"It was Richie's idea from the beginning to incorporate *Star Wars* into the show," series producer Rocco Urbisci recalls. "He had seen it and thought we could do a parody of the cantina scene. [Pryor said he] could be the bartender, and he could be going off on all the freaks in the cantina."

Another reason for going with Pryor's show was that it aired at 8 p.m., as compared to *SNL*, which was famously "not ready for prime time." It was also the series-premiere episode, so the audience could potentially be vast. And Lippincott and Lucas already knew the Pryor producers from their involvement with *The Midnight Special*.

However, the most likely reason for choosing the Pryor show might have been that Lucas was starting to get criticism for *Star Wars* having an all-white cast; working with Pryor would certainly work wonders in repairing that rift with the African American community.

So, Urbisci brought in designer Rick Baker to fill Pryor's bar with aliens. Baker had Lucasfilm robot wrangler Miki Herman pull particular cantina creature costumes from storage, specifically Momaw Nadon (also known as "Hammerhead"), to go alongside the new ones he would create.

"Star Bar" was scheduled to be the second comedy bit of the premiere episode. However, Pryor's cold open was deemed so over-the-top by the

NBC executives that they killed the bit, fired Urbisci, and pushed "Star Bar" up to the top of the show. Despite the bloodshed, Pryor's performance in the bit was magnificent; most who have seen it feel that he knocked it out of the galaxy.

The *AV Club*'s Mike Vanderbilt has attributed at least part of the success of the bit to its being centered around one of *Star Wars*' most iconic scenes: "In previous science-fiction films, alien visitors were generally clad in matching silver jumpsuits and were of the same species, and usually pretty stiff. The cantina scene in *Star Wars*, on the other hand, features aliens of all shapes and sizes co-mingling in a very relatable environment, driving home the concept of George Lucas's lived-in universe." (Vanderbilt does point out, however, that on Pryor's show, the scenery looked less like the Mos Eisley cantina and more like *Three's Company*'s Regal Beagle.) As the late Roger Ebert put it in his original review of *Star Wars*, "As that incredible collection of extraterrestrial alcoholics and bug-eyed martini drinkers lined up at the bar, and as Lucas so slyly let them exhibit characteristics that were universally human, I found myself feeling a combination of admiration and delight."

The show premiered on Tuesday, September 13, to a very healthy audience. However, there were no ratings high enough to balance out the stress that both the NBC executives—and the censors—were experiencing in dealing with Pryor's editorial swagger. NBC re-hired Urbisci, but the series only lasted four weeks before it was abruptly canceled.

Technically, *The Richard Pryor Show* was a sketch-comedy program, which is different than a TV variety show. Variety shows were normally one-hour television productions, often built around the specific talents of well-known, likable entertainers who would host a weekly program with singing and dancing, comedy bits, and cheesy novelty acts, all presented to a studio audience. Nowadays, variety shows are virtually extinct—a genre whose proof of actual existence can only be found on YouTube, if at all.

With the advent of television in the '50s, variety dominated most network programming. "The variety show was nothing more than a burlesque kind of show," says Kim LeMasters, who was president of CBS Entertainment in the late 1980s. "It was the theater that was being done in individual cities with traveling troupes and all that. [*The*] *Ed Sullivan* [*Show*] was the quintessential variety show where you just have somebody who is the interlocutor for different acts to come up. Then it became where you would [hire] a star [and have supporting talent] pivoting around [that] one person."

The most successful variety shows of TV's first decade were one-hour shows hosted by Sullivan, Milton Berle, and Jackie Gleason. In the 1960s, the genre grew further with shows hosted by Judy Garland, Carol Burnett, Dean Martin, Glen Campbell, Rowan and Martin, and the Smothers Brothers.

Although the genre got a huge shot in the arm in the 1970s, with variety shows hosted by likable talents like Sonny and Cher and Donny and Marie, by halfway through the decade the luster was starting to fade. Bob Hope was in his mid-seventies, eyes shot but still singing and dancing alongside performers a third or a quarter his age, still churning out a half-dozen specials a year.

A lot of people had variety shows at the time, says Donny Osmond, the co-star and executive producer of *Donny and Marie*, which ran on ABC for five seasons. "Many tried but seemed to fail. About a four-year life span is about all the life that a variety show had back then."

By the end of the decade, the talent pool of TV variety hosts had been watered down considerably. "Suddenly, the idea got into some execs' heads to give anyone who had any small trace of talent their own show," notes TV historian Brian Ward. "Some of these people had no business hosting their own shows." At one point, it seemed as though anyone with a face had been given a weekly TV show. These included the husband-and-wife mime team of Shields and Yarnell, the one-hit wonders barely known as the Starland Vocal Band, the Scottish teen idols the Bay City Rollers, and the "King of Banter," sportscaster Howard Cosell. That's not to dismiss country singer Barbara Mandrell and her sisters, as well as the even lesser-known Hudson Brothers, whose brand of music and comedy was CBS's juvenile answer to ABC's hit series *The Partridge Family*.

The saddest entry on this list is *Pink Lady and Jeff*, the brainchild of TV programming maestro Fred Silverman. The NBC executive had taken one of the top stand-up comics of the time, Jeff Altman, and paired him with a female singing duo from Japan, Pink Lady, who barely spoke English.

The only variety series that critics rank lower than *Pink Lady and Jeff* is *The Brady Bunch Hour*, for which the TV family recorded eight episodes of fairly horrific song-and-dance pandemonium.

"The Brady Bunch, in *The Brady Bunch*, was a family," Gilbert Gottfried recalled. "Not like any family you've ever met, but they were a family. And then somehow they come back and they're a song-and-dance family. And I don't know that any of them ever sang or danced before."

The Brady children had actually already started singing on the last few seasons of the sitcom. Who could forget the kids singing "Keep On" and "It's a Sunshine Day," or Bobby's breakout performance on "Time to Change"? That's not including the musical prowess of Barry Williams, who would soon be known by his alter ego, Johnny Bravo.

After ABC canceled *The Brady Bunch* in 1974, Williams actually began touring with such productions as *Grease* and *Pippin*. While on the road, he got a call from Marty Krofft, who told him to come back to Hollywood to star in his own variety show. According to TV historian Ted Nichelson, "This is how Marty Krofft talked him into coming back. So, Barry had this expectation that he was going to be the lead and they were going to center all the musical numbers around him."

The Brady Bunch Hour wound up being about an hour too long. It combined comedy sketches and musical covers of current hits, most of them brutally sung by Williams. The family massacred songs like "Car Wash" and "Southern Nights," and Williams covered the Jacksons' "Enjoy Yourself" while hopping around the stage with the gracefulness of a jackhammer.

"It was wonderfully '70s," Gottfried said of the ill-fated series. "Horrible '70s music and '70s outfits. When '70s TV was bad, there was no description for it."

The bottom line is there were astronomically worse shows than the *Star Wars Holiday Special* that aired around this time period. They just didn't carry the name *Star Wars*.

Nonetheless, when they first appeared, variety shows were a departure from the many situation comedies, dramas, and news and talk shows that filled the programming schedules of the three networks of the day. They had a "live" feel to them, and they carried a vibe of excitement and spontaneity. It was as if the network's directive was to air anything to break up the monotony.

Growing up in the 1970s, comedy writer Anthony Caleca hated the sameness of most TV shows and appreciated the unpredictability of a special.

"Anything different worked," he recalls. "Not a sitcom, not just some movie of the week, not a drama that you can care less about. For us, anything that was different from what was on ordinary network television was magical."

The most obvious difference between variety shows and other programs came down to production values. Most dramas, and certain sitcoms, were shot on film. It was a worthwhile investment, since after each show's initial network run was over, the producers could re-sell, or syndicate, episodes into other local and international markets. Those shows usually avoided references to specific news events that would put a time stamp on them, instead keeping the show's time frame as generic and "evergreen" as possible.

Variety shows, on the other hand, "did not repeat well," as comedy writer Bruce Vilanch explains. "A lot of the humor on them was topical. As a result, they look arcane today." Since these shows were pretty much destined to air just once, producers didn't bother recording them using the higher-quality format of film. They used videotape instead.

Lance Guest, who starred in *The Last Starfighter* (1980), also worked in television. "I do remember that era in television. A lot of those guys, they just did weekly shows, and it was somewhat disposable comedy. They might have been rerun maybe once, but it's not like people were gonna hold on to these shows for posterity."

Donny Osmond agrees. "It was disposable television," he says. "People are gonna see this once, and that's it."

If anyone should know variety TV, it's Donny. He made his television debut on *The Andy Williams Show* at the ripe old age of five, as the youngest member of the Osmond Brothers. From there, along with his brothers, he spent most of his early life singing, dancing, and performing, whether for Williams or *The Glen Campbell Goodtime Hour*, *The Flip Wilson Show*, or a Bob Hope special or two.

In 1975, ABC Entertainment president Fred Silverman happened to catch Donny and his sister, Marie, co-hosting a week of *The Mike Douglas Show*. Donny had been performing solo, without his brothers, for a while, and Marie had just re-recorded Anita Bryant's 1960 hit "Paper Roses," taking it to number one on the *Billboard* Country Music chart. Silverman thought the chemistry between the two was dynamic; not only were they great musically, but comedically he thought Marie's quick wit and good-natured ability to poke fun at her brother—coupled with Donny's self-deprecating way of taking it—could make them an instant family hit on Friday nights in the eight o'clock hour.

Donny and Marie debuted on January 23, 1976, to massive ratings, launching the duo as a successful television act and, eventually, as a brand. Ruth Buzzi and Paul Lynde joined the four remaining Osmond brothers, who had become the show's executive producers, cementing their decision to leave their careers behind to work on the series. The series' showrunners were Sid and Marty Krofft, the production team behind such successful family fare as *H. R. Pufnstuf, Lidsville,* and *Land of the Lost.*

"The Donny and Marie show was fun Mormon comedy," remarked the late Gilbert Gottfried. "It's like those Mormons were always known for their sense of comedy and timing."

By May 1977, as *Donny and Marie* was finishing its second season, Marty Krofft saw *Star Wars* and instantly thought it would be a great film to lampoon for the huge musical production numbers they would do at the end of their shows. "I went right to the top guy ... I called Laddie," Krofft recalls, referring to Fox president Alan Ladd. "I just said, 'Hey, I want *Star Wars* on our show,' and it eventually happened."

"The *Star Wars* producers wanted to get on television shows and do musicals," recalls Jay Osmond. "And our show was the one that did the musicals." The *Star Wars* stars had appeared on various other talk shows already, but Jay thought they would have fun with the Osmonds. "There's a part in the course of *Star Wars* where they do the silly musical thing with the aliens in the cantina," he recalls. "That's what kind of sparked the idea."

Plans began for a *Star Wars* production number: sets were designed and built, and a script was written, all under the watchful eye of Miki Herman, whom Lippincott assigned to be on set as Lucasfilm's liaison with the show. It was Herman's responsibility to make sure that all of the sets, costumes, and visual and audio effects were in line with the official storyline of *Star Wars*—or "canon," as it would come to be called—which fans would increasingly treat as sacred scripture.

Daniels and Mayhew joined that week's guest stars, Redd Foxx and Kris Kristofferson, the latter still mega-hot from the critical and commercial success of the previous year's sensation, *A Star Is Born.* For the *Star Wars* production number, Kristofferson would be Han Solo and Foxx would be a sort of floating narrator. "I'm Luke and Marie's Leia, with the bagels on the side of her head," recalls Donny Osmond. "My brothers were dressed as stormtroopers dancing, and I'm dancing around R2-D2, and there's C-3PO and Chewbacca's there, and I'm thinking, 'This is probably one of the coolest finales we've ever done.'"

Likewise, not only was Jay Osmond having a blast but that day he finally crossed a threshold and became terribly proud of their show. The jury was still out as to whether the Brothers (as they affectionately refer to themselves) had made the right decision to leave their other personas behind to join Donny and Marie. However, on *this* day, Jay truly believed they had made the right call.

However, Kermit Eller, who was cast as Vader on the show, says it almost didn't happen. "There was a freak-out on the show," Eller recalls. "The producers wanted to have Darth Vader saying certain things." Eller says they surreptitiously went around and hired voice actor and bass singer Thurl Ravenscroft. One of the most recognizable voices in TV, film, and commercials, Ravenscroft was best known for voicing Tony the Tiger for Frosted Flakes, as well as being the uncredited vocalist on the song "You're a Mean One, Mr. Grinch," from the 1965 holiday cartoon classic *How the Grinch Stole Christmas*.

"They were gonna do all sorts of weird lines . . . I remember that," Eller recalls. This prompted the dedicated Lucasfilm employee to inform the show's liaison, Miki Herman, that the producers were giving Darth Vader comedy lines to read. The original plan was that Lucasfilm would have control over the lines that were being said by Vader, Eller adds; and now, on hearing what was happening, they hit the roof. "They jumped all over that," he says. However, Eller felt that if Lucasfilm wanted to protect the integrity of these characters, "[They are] not going to put them on a singing and dancing variety show, because that's what they do." He adds, "You're not gonna interrupt the *Donny and Marie* show for a presidential debate."

Unlike everyone else who seemed to be having fun with the production number, comedian Paul Lynde was distant and moody. In his memoir, Anthony Daniels recalls that Lynde was to play "something Tarkinish"—a reference to the Death Star's commander, Grand Moff Tarkin. "He seemed a bit put out," he remembers. "It was quite evident he felt that the whole *Star Wars* team was upstaging him."

Eller says he tried to engage Lynde in conversation, with no luck. "He was just such a nasty person. I was like, 'Do you wanna run any lines?' And he goes, 'Just leave me alone.'"

If Lynde was a tad irritable at the time, ABC had just downgraded him to a regular on *Donny and Marie* after his own short-lived series tanked in the ratings and was abruptly canceled. Since ABC still had to pay out the remainder of Lynde's contract, the network relegated him to *Donny and Marie*, meaning he would continue to receive his leading-star salary but would have to be part of the show's supporting cast.

One of the memorable moments of the number is Kristofferson's entrance as Han Solo, emerging with Chewbacca from a *Flash Gordon*–era rocket ship. Kristofferson wears a leather outfit with sunglasses, looking less like Han Solo and more like a cartoonish Hell's Angel, belting out a reworded version of Sly Stone's "I Want to Take You Higher." According to Donny Osmond, "In some of the footage we had to cut away from him to Marie and me to cover up all the bad lip-synching."

Kristofferson singing to Donny and Marie that he wanted to take them "higher" created some controversy. "People have tried to overanalyze that," Donny recalls. The reference would likely have been controversial on *any* family program at the time, but considering the Osmonds' strict Mormon opposition to the use of alcohol or illegal drugs, it seems even more scandalous—even if it pales in comparison to what would be considered risqué today. "It was a song and it was a parody," Osmond says. "It was just music. Get over it."

At one point in the number, Donny, Marie, Mayhew, and Daniels were to follow Kristofferson up a ramp toward the rocket ship. After they all enter the rocket, they turn and wave goodbye while the hatch closes. As Daniels remembers, the spaceship "was a little more frail than even I had imagined," leaving them all in the dark. The abrupt closure immediately caused the rocket's makeshift roof to fall on top of them; a second or two of this collapse can be seen in the far top edge of the frame of some surviving video footage on YouTube.

"Nobody got hurt, because it's cardboard," Donny recalls. Daniels remembers that "everything went black. There was a brief silence, then Threepio's 'How...interesting' made everyone laugh."

Further challenging for Daniels was the final dance number, for which he was surrounded by a dozen "beautiful blonde-haired stormtroopers." His challenge was "not bumping into them, or not getting into the wrong place and having them bump into me. . . . I was never sure if Threepio should be bopping along with this strange assemblage. It all seemed rather undignified—a foretaste of the embarrassment I would suffer on a forest moon, in the distant future." The latter was perhaps a foreshadowing of the Holiday Special.

"You can't imagine that happening in 1981," explains Jason Lenzi. "*Star Wars* couldn't have gone *near* a show like that in '81, but in '77, everyone's going, 'I don't know what this is or how big it's gonna get, but yeah, take it—go put it on a T-shirt, put it in your show, do a dance with the stormtroopers . . .'"

And dance they did. Miki Herman supplied Imperial Stormtrooper outfits for Jay, Merrill, Wayne, and Alan, the latter of whom was given the job of teaching some coordinated dance moves to his three brothers. *Donny and Marie's* on-staff songwriter, Earl Brown, rewrote the words to Smokey Robinson's "Get Ready," and the foursome became the highlight of the show, blasting onto the stage and offering *Star Wars* fans their first opportunity to witness dancing stormtroopers.

Donny Osmond has nothing but fond memories of the shoot. "I think that one of the coolest moments my brothers ever had in show business was transforming stormtroopers into vaudevillian dancers," he recalls. "That was one of the funniest moments of my life because I thought the stormtroopers were these evil, horrible robots, [and] the music starts and they're dancing. I'm trying to hold it and trying not to laugh and thinking, 'How in the world is George Lucas allowing this to happen? That's just so far from the movie.'"

He acknowledges that *Star Wars* devotees would squirm today if they saw their revered characters put in such utterly ridiculous situations. "We broke a lot of rules," he says. "Dancing stormtroopers? We broke that rule. There was a shot of Chewbacca with his arm around Darth Vader. How does that happen? Just having Chewbacca and Darth Vader as pals, I'm sure the George Lucas people—including George himself—are scratching their heads, saying, 'Why did we let that happen?' because that's not going to happen in this whole saga—they're archenemies … but I guess on *Donny and Marie*, everybody was friends."

Jay Osmond says, "Being in Donny and Marie's show, that was a strange time for the Brothers. The stormtroopers bit was the only thing I thought the Brothers did on a finale that was classy and cool."

Lenzi disagrees. "The *Star Wars Holiday Special* is *Citizen Kane* compared to that *Donny and Marie* thing," he remarks. "I mean, that's truly trainwreck sort of television." Nonetheless, ten days after the Pryor show with the "Star Wars Bar" parody aired, the second season of *Donny and Marie* premiered to spectacular ratings. As Donny points out, the show had the demographics that Lucas wanted, and "through research, he was right. They had the entire family watching the *Donny and Marie* show. George wanted to tap into that magic."

While Lippincott and others had hoped that some TV viewers would go back to the theaters that week, no one expected the huge spike it created. "When that *Donny and Marie* show aired and everybody saw *Star Wars* characters . . . they went back to the theaters," recalls Osmond. "I'm still waiting for those residual checks from George Lucas for that, but he's never called me."

Lippincott and Lucas's "September surprise" for Frank Wells was complete. Lippincott had also negotiated for Lucasfilm and Fox to produce a behind-the-scenes documentary about *Star Wars*. The one-hour television special, *The Making of Star Wars*, was narrated by William Conrad (TV's *Cannon*) and aired on ABC during prime time in the same week as *Donny and Marie*.

Whether it was Donny and Marie, Richard Pryor, Wolfman Jack, Dinah, Merv, or Mike Douglas—or R2-D2, C-3PO, and Darth Vader having their footprints enshrined outside Grauman's Chinese—Lippincott's campaign wound up having a huge effect on the film's receipts at the box office.

Miki Herman directly credits these appearances for the box-office spike *Star Wars* enjoyed. "The public appearances helped the ticket sales," Herman recalls, "and [Lucas] liked that. That was a very positive thing, and a positive reason to keep doing as many [TV projects] as deemed possible."

One by one, these appearances not only helped bring people back to the movie theaters for a second, third, and fourth time, but for Lucas and

Lippincott they also helped create a positive view of the television medium, which was normally trashed by the types of film auteurs in Lucas's world. This positive attitude toward TV variety specifically would wind up leading to Lucasfilm's desire to produce its own special.

"I probably owe George Lucas a huge apology if I was in any way responsible for *that*," offers Osmond.

It's unknown whether Wells ever reacted at all to Lippincott's "September surprise." Wells left Warner Bros in 1982, and a few years later he was recruited by Disney to become its president and chief operating officer. He worked alongside chairman and CEO Michael Eisner through one of the company's most successful eras.

Wells's escape from his business life was extreme mountain climbing. He had a personal mission to climb all of the Seven Summits—the highest mountains on each of the seven continents—and had climbed all of them except Mount Everest in Asia. He had come within three thousand feet of that summit when he had to turn back as a result of bad weather.

He died in a helicopter crash at Easter 1994 while encountering bad weather on a heliskiing trip in Nevada. He was sixty-two.

* * *

Variety shows did not only appear in the form of weekly series. The three networks also regularly aired standalone variety specials. Among the most prominent were the infamous Bob Hope specials NBC had been broadcasting for five decades. Aside from hosting his own series in the 1960s (*Bob Hope Presents Chrysler Theater*), he would wind up hosting more than 250 standalone specials for the network.

During the time of *Star Wars'* initial release, Hope was averaging a half-dozen specials a year. Though he was far from a critic's darling, his conservative political leanings always gave him a base and kept him on television.

"The Bob Hope specials were always scary," recalled Gilbert Gottfried, reflecting on the Hope of that era. "At that point, his eyesight . . . I mean, forget cue cards. They would write out his jokes on the side of a building."

Hope's specials were quite formulaic. The show would start with a politically driven monologue, which took over an hour to shoot and was subsequently edited down to about ten minutes for air. He would normally bring a few of his guests out to do one-on-one interviews, as well as a sketch or two—normally a parody of something in the news.

Producer Elliott Kozak and specifically Bob Mills, who joined Hope as a writer during his older years, always pushed the old-timer to do a vaudeville number, whether his partner was eighty-two-year-old George Burns or eight-year-old Joey Lawrence. "We encouraged him to do it because the audience loved to see him doing it," Mills recalls.

By the mid-1970s, however, his tap-dancing skills were questionable. Instead, he could *sand* dance—where a dancer sprinkles sand on the floor that subsequently replaces the louder tap noise with a quieter, refined audio effect. Known as the "soft shoe," it was a way for tap dancers to reduce the heavy-handedness of thunderous dance moves and create a more elegant version of a dance (as Fred Astaire delicately did in *Top Hat*). However, the soft shoe wasn't designed to be used for dancers that can no longer tap effectively, to just add sand audio effects while feigning partial dance moves. The latter simply sends a message that this sand dancer can no longer handle the physical requirements of actual tap dancing. But this is what Hope's producers wound up settling for, and it subsequently became a staple of his specials in the 1970s and beyond. Suddenly, it seemed like every other special featured "Tea for Two," and Hope himself had sprinkled enough sand on the floor of NBC's Stage 2 that they could have shot a Frankie and Annette film on it.

In the fall of 1977, Kozak booked Mark Hamill for Hope's annual Christmas special. Hamill participated in a one-on-one interview with Hope, as well as a *Star Wars* parody featuring Perry Como as "Luke Sleepwalker" and Olivia Newton-John as "Princess Olivia." Hope appears as "Barf Vader," whose spaceship has gobbled up Santa Claus, leaving Christmas in jeopardy.

To this day, Bob Mills remains quite proud of the writing of this bit. "This is the worst thing that's happened since the Planet Pluto got fleas," he says, quoting Newton-John forty-five years later. Hope's Barf Vader also sings a send-up of Cole Porter's "You're the Top," which Mills can still recite from memory: "I'm the pits, I am cold linguini / I'm the pits, I'm an *Idi Ameanie* / I'm a lunar louse who will blow your house to bits."

Toward the end of the sketch, Hamill surprises the crowd by entering as Luke Skywalker, which Mills says brought the house down. "The studio

Mark Hamill was booked on Bob Hope's 1977 *All Star Christmas Comedy Special*, where he did a one-on-one interview with Hope and appeared in a sketch parodying *Star Wars* with special guest star Olivia Newton-John. *Courtesy Hope Enterprises*

audience went buggy to see Mark Hamill in the flesh because he was one of the biggies in [*Star Wars*]."

"Did you bring the Force?" Hope asks, to which Hamill responds, "You better believe it—the Los Angeles *Police* Force. Now, you're all under arrest for malicious mutilation of a marvelous movie."

Mills says that, while rehearsing the sketch, Como came over to him with a question. Often, guest stars would ask for a line to be rewritten, so Kozak always required the writers to be at rehearsals. "Is this based on a movie or something?" Mills remembers Como asking. "I said, 'What?' And he says to me, 'It's getting so many laughs and everything, it must be a real popular movie or something.'"

Mills told him it was based on *Star Wars*, to which Como responded, "What's *Star Wars*?"

Mills was aghast. *Star Wars* was in its sixth month in theaters and had recently surpassed *Jaws* as the highest-grossing film of all time. Not to mention, Como was *in show business*.

"Perry," he said, "it's the biggest thing to hit theaters since *Gone with the Wind*. Everybody's talking about it. There are lines around the block."

"Well, you know, I play a lot of golf," Como replied. "And by the time I get home, my wife has usually watched the news. So I miss a lot of this stuff."

The most memorable part of the special has to be Hope and Hamill getting locked in a toy store. They sample various costumes and try on outfits from "The Bob Hope Vaudeville Kit" ("complete with vegetables," Hope quips). The kit includes hats and canes, which Hamill and Hope put on and then start a soft-shoe routine. In the midst of the number, Hamill shouts out, "Look, Ma, I'm dancing!" to which Hope responds, looking down at his feet, "The jury's still out."

Even the Force couldn't help *this* bit.

The Bob Hope All Star Christmas Comedy Special aired on December 19 to typically high numbers for a Hope holiday special, but it didn't create the same spike for *Star Wars* in the theaters as had been seen the week after *Donny and Marie* and *The Richard Pryor Show* aired. Although there had also been a significant spike during the Thanksgiving holiday weekend, by December the film's receipts were finally starting to drop. By January 1978, *Star Wars* was in half the theaters it had been in the previous month.

Nonetheless, once again, *Star Wars* had been part of a highly rated variety show on a major national network; once again, the appearance gave the whole television genre a positive spin in Lucas's eyes. He and Lippincott had found a way to use the often-trashed medium to their advantage.

Kenner hadn't bought TV ads during the Hope special because, again, the toys had still not arrived at the toy stores. However, if they could keep the interest alive in *Star Wars* until the following holiday season, the toys would certainly be available by then. Next holiday season, they could appear on another Christmas special, and they had built up enough contacts at the networks to make sure they could be booked on a halfway-respectable special the next year as well. There were other stars who hosted Christmas specials at the time—Bing Crosby, Dean Martin, Julie Andrews, Perry Como—but Lucas had other ideas.

CHAPTER 4

TAKING THE DIVE

FOR MANY YEARS, the period from Thanksgiving through the end of January was often referred to by TV freelancers as "The Dead Zone." If you were unemployed at Thanksgiving, chances are you wouldn't be hired until February. No shows were sold during the holiday season, and most wouldn't start staffing until after the National Association of Television Program Executives held its annual conference in late January.

Gary Smith and Dwight Hemion—whose production house was one of the busiest in Hollywood—appreciated the break. Smith–Hemion Productions was arguably the gold standard of production companies in town; Hemion was the creative force behind the camera, while Smith was the dealmaker and entrepreneur of the two, "and when they got together, it was magic," according to Steve Binder, one of the top television directors in the industry.

They had just returned from London, where they had produced a fairly challenging Bing Crosby special. David Bowie—mostly as a favor to his mother, who adored the old crooner—had agreed to make an incredibly rare and uncharacteristic performance on Crosby's 1977 Christmas special. According to Ian Fraser, it had been Smith and Hemion's idea to leapfrog three generations to have seventy-year-old Crosby sing a duet with thirty-year-old Bowie.

Bing Crosby's Merrie Olde Christmas was taped in September 1977 at the historic Elstree Studios in London, the site of filming for movies like *2001: A Space Odyssey*, *The Shining*, and *Indiana Jones and the Temple of Doom*—and coincidentally the same complex where Lucas had shot all of the Death Star interior scenes for *Star Wars* the previous summer.

At the time, Bowie was about as huge as a rock star could get. Critics raved about his concerts, as did those fans who had been able to see him live. But these were the years before MTV, and those who hadn't seen him live were left to their own imaginations.

It might have been part of an informal strategy to tone down his persona a bit. After all, Bowie had just gotten off an incapacitating drug addiction—as well as claims of making pro-fascist comments. He had also just starred as an alien in Nicolas Roeg's *The Man Who Fell to Earth*. Adding to the various personas he took on throughout his recording career—from glam-rocker Ziggy Stardust to the schizophrenic Aladdin Sane to his dystopian-era Halloween Jack to the dapper Thin White Duke—fans were desperate to see what the real David Bowie was like for a change.

The original plan was for Bowie and Crosby to sing "Little Drummer Boy." However, Fraser recalled, "David came in and said, 'I hate this song. Is there something else I could sing?' We didn't know quite what to do."

The shooting schedule was rejiggered; director Dwight Hemion began working with Bowie on taping his new single, "Heroes," while Fraser—along with writer Buz Kohan and composer Larry Grossman—found a piano and tried to salvage the song. "We decided the best way to [save] the arrangement was to do a countermelody that would fit in between the spaces and maybe write a new bridge and see if we could sell him on that," he recalls. Within an hour, he says, they had written an original melody, "Peace on Earth," and found a way to bridge the two songs, creating a "mashup" decades before the technique became routine. They brought it to Bowie, who liked it, and, after he rehearsed it with Crosby, they went ahead and recorded it.

Kohan wrote some idle chit-chat about holiday traditions and their favorite Christmas songs to help assuage the general uneasiness of the duo. "Bing loved the challenge," Kohan says, "and he was able to transform himself without losing any of the Crosbyisms—that relaxed feeling of the atmosphere that he would always create whenever he was on camera."

Mary Crosby, Bing's daughter, says that the two legendary musicians developed an instant respect for each other. "They sat at the piano, and David was a little nervous. Dad realized David was this amazing musician, and David realized Dad was an amazing musician. You could see them both collectively relax, and then magic was made."

On Bing Crosby's 1977 Christmas special, David Bowie sang the amazing duet "Peace on Earth / Little Drummer Boy" with the legendary crooner, creating one of the greatest holiday moments ever recorded for television. The special was produced by Smith–Hemion Productions, who within months would begin preparing for an even bigger holiday TV project. *Photofest © CBS*

Bowie recalled that although Crosby's voice was in tip-top shape, his mental acuity wasn't terrific. "I was wondering if he was still alive," he said in a 1999 interview. "He was just . . . not there. He was not there at all. He had the words in front of him. [*In a deep Bing voice*] 'Hi, Dave, nice to see ya here . . .' And he looked like a little old orange sitting on a stool [because] he'd been made up very heavily and his skin was a bit pitted, and there was just nobody home at all, you know? It was the most bizarre experience."

Afterward, Crosby referred to Bowie as a "clean-cut kid" and a "real fine

asset to the show. . . . He sings well, has a great voice, and reads lines well."
He also added, with a bit of premonition, "He could be a good actor if he
wanted."

While Fraser, Kohan, and Grossman were proud of the finished product,
they were quickly on to their next project before the Crosby special had even
wrapped. "We never expected to hear about it again," Kohan says. Six weeks
after the duet was recorded, Crosby died of a heart attack. The special was
aired posthumously that November in the US, and on Christmas Eve in the
UK, and was introduced by Crosby's wife, Kathryn.

For the next few years during the holidays, radio stations would play
an off-air version of the song—until 1982, when RCA Records formally
released it as a single. Twenty-two years later, *TV Guide* would include the
Crosby–Bowie duet as one of the twenty-five best musical moments ever
televised. And, within a few months, this exact same production team—from
the executive producers to the musical directors to the technical directors—
would be starting work on a new CBS television special for George Lucas.

* * *

Actor Seth Green is the genius behind the stop-motion animation series
Robot Chicken, and he became friends with Lucas after the two decided in
2007 to co-produce a few *Star Wars*–related episodes of the show. Another
collaboration followed five years in the form of an animated parody series,
Star Wars: Detours, though to date Disney has yet to release any of the more
than three dozen episodes they produced together.

Throughout the time they spent together, Green was relentless in asking
Lucas about why he had agreed to do the Special. He learned that by late
1977, when Lucas had begun pre-production on *The Empire Strikes Back*, he
was already getting pressure from Fox, who didn't think they were going to
be able to keep fans' attention through the sequel's release date, almost three
years away. "There was so much pressure in between *Star Wars* and *Empire*,"
Lucas told Green. "The way that executives thought about the audience [was]
that everyone would just forget *Star Wars* was a thing. 'The audience . . . they
just can't be depended upon,' so you gotta make some other kind of short-
term *Star Wars* content. What kinds of TV shows can you make on the kind
of budget it takes to make *Star Wars*? And they're like, 'A holiday special.'"

At the end of 1977, just a month or so after pulling off the extraordinary Crosby/Bowie duet, CBS approached Lucasfilm, wanting to do a special. As Miki Herman recalls, "Originally it was going to be an hour long, and it was going to be a variety show. And so that sounded like a good idea."

It seemed logical not only to Herman but also to Craig Miller, who was in tune with the audience as Lucasfilm's director of fan relations at the time. "Charley Lippincott and George [Lucas] wanted to keep *Star Wars* in the public mind. They wanted there to still be that interest in *Star Wars* as a property, and Lucasfilm said, 'Yes.'"

Julie Welch, daughter of *Special* producers Ken and Mitzie Welch, explains that variety shows were the norm at the time. "The idea now seems crazy. But at the time it didn't seem that weird. That's the kind of show lots of folks were doing, and *Star Wars* could do no wrong."

CBS wanted to do a "kind of a bastard *Star Wars* movie," says Bruce Vilanch, but have the [production] values of the traditional variety television special in it. "This was not going to be a great marriage."

Nearly half a century later, it's easy to pass judgment as a "Monday-morning quarterback" on the network's decision to mingle *Star Wars* with variety television, but CBS was seeing the tremendous success that competing shows were having with *Star Wars* actors and characters, so it struck while the irons were hot.

"It's more egregious now, looking back, than it was at the time," says Kyle Newman. "It was a very normal way of getting it out there, and *Star Wars* embraced that opportunity." Newman adds that these variety-show appearances were very early in the life of *Star Wars*, and fans back in 1977 didn't have the attachment issues that they have now for the franchise: "These characters weren't embedded in our consciousness the way they are now. We'd met them once in one film. It's not like we'd gone on a nine-film adventure with R2-D2. We'd seen them once, and that was the only voice we knew."

With the number of specials being broadcast around this time, the networks routinely tasked independent companies like Dick Clark Productions, MTM Enterprises, or in this case Smith–Hemion Productions with actually producing them. For example, the executives at CBS's specials department, Fred Rappaport and Bernie Safronsky, would pay a "license fee" to a production company like Smith–Hemion to produce and deliver a show.

Throughout the 1960s, '70s, and '80s, the top TV production company in the industry was Smith–Hemion Productions, led by producer Gary Smith (*right*) and director Dwight Hemion. They won a total of twenty-four Emmys, producing specials for such top-tier talent as Barbra Streisand, Paul McCartney, Elvis Presley . . . and George Lucas. *Smith–Hemion Productions*

"All the variety shows, whether they were ninety minutes or two hours or one hour, they had different license fees," explains former ICM agent Richard Brustein. Smith–Hemion produced what he calls "very, very high-end variety. Smith and Hemion, we always knew, got very high license fees in order to produce their high-end shows." Although the company produced the show, it was the network's responsibility to make sure that they delivered something close to what was agreed upon in the original pitching phase of the project. (Rappaport declined an interview request, and Safronsky did not return calls.)

For the *Star Wars Holiday Special*, CBS again went to Smith–Hemion. The company's résumé was filled with critically acclaimed specials it had produced for the biggest stars in the industry, including Barbra Streisand, Julie Andrews, Frank Sinatra, Mikhail Barishnikov, Paul McCartney, and dozens of others. Its reputation was flawless. "They had ninety-two Emmys, and they were famous for doing really classy shows," says writer Bruce Vilanch, who worked on several specials for them, including the *Star Wars Holiday Special*. "I mean, a whole bunch of really good stuff."

Veteran cameraman Larry Heider separates Smith–Hemion from the rest of the production companies of the era: "They were considered to be the cream of the crop for doing a really tasteful and different kind of TV show. They emerged right away as the premier production company. If you had anything, any big project, whether it was an award show or a variety show, or a special of any kind involving music, they were the guys to go to. They were the gold standard, and that lasted for well over twenty years."

Steve Binder, one of the top TV producers and directors of that era, agrees. "Dwight was known for his visual art. Gary was known for his salesmanship, his entrepreneurship, and the combination was magical."

Bob Newhart had also worked with the duo, starting back in the early 1960s, when they were producing *The Perry Como Show*. For Newhart, "Dwight and Gary, they're incredible producers, and [their shows are] beautifully directed." Even he doesn't have an explanation for the outcome of the *Star Wars Holiday Special*: "The bottom line is, yes, they are so talented it's hard to believe that they couldn't have produced something that was sensational."

By 1978, Vilanch was starting his fourth season writing for *Donny and Marie*, but he wanted to do more freelancing around town, which led him

When he was booked on the Special, Bruce Vilanch had already become a fixture in variety TV, writing for such series as *The Brady Bunch Variety Hour* and *Donny and Marie*, and one-offs like *The Paul Lynde Halloween Special*. He would eventually become a much-requested writer for the Academy Awards and a regular celebrity guest on *Hollywood Squares*. *Photofest © Miramax Films*

to take short-term gigs at such off-the-wall variety shows as *The Paul Lynde Halloween Special* and *The Brady Bunch Variety Hour*. He soon got a call from his agent, ICM's Dan Stevens, with an offer to write for the Special.

"Where do I sign?" Vilanch recalls asking Stevens. Years later, he fondly reflects, "And it was fun from the beginning."

In addition to Vilanch, the producers hired Lenny Ripps and Pat Proft, a young comedy-writing team who had worked on such shows as *The Redd Foxx Show* and *Shields and Yarnell*. The two had been singled out because of their experience with the latter, a short-lived prime-time series starring a young couple whose specialty was mime. Shields and Yarnell were most known for the Clinkers, a robotic couple whose amazing mechanical moves were a huge hit when they appeared on shows like *Sonny and Cher* and *The Mac Davis Show*.

But why would writing for mimes help Ripps and Proft with this current gig? Rumor had it that Lucas's story was centered around Chewbacca's family, a bunch of grunting, nonverbal Wookiees. "It was not a problem," Ripps recalls. "Listen, I worked for Mac Davis. So I could write for any big hairy creature."

When Ripps's agent called with an offer to write for the Special, he was ecstatic, thinking that the job would generate annual royalties for him for the rest of his life. "We thought that this was going to be one of the great annual re-run shows, like *The Charlie Brown Christmas* [and] *The Grinch That Stole Christmas*." He and Proft hoped that the program "would run every year for an eternity . . . as it turned out, this eternity was a different reality."

At the time, ideas for specials were pitched without the elaborate sizzle reels or pitch decks that are standard in the industry today. Dealmakers like ICM TV variety agent Elliott Kozak would routinely pitch ideas to the heads of specials at the networks. Kozak was not a writer or a producer at the time, just an agent trying to create projects for his clients.

"How about for Dorothy Hamill we do *Romeo and Juliet on Ice?*"

"That works," the network would respond. The show was sold right over the phone, and details were discussed at lunch the following week.

Actor Lance Guest confirms that from the late 1970s through the early 1980s, television executives pitched ideas over the phone and at happy hours. "[Producers were] able to make a one-line pitch on a cocktail napkin, [where] somebody takes it and goes, 'Okay, we can do this. We're making a deal right now. Here it is,' after three or four vodkas or whatever . . . people were fast and loose, like, 'Okay, let's throw some money behind you.'"

Agent Richard Brustein explains that pitching projects—especially TV variety specials—was easier during this time period. Networks were always looking for quick, silly ideas for variety shows, especially during the summer, when fewer people were watching. Plus, they ran their dramas, situation comedies, and variety shows once, and then repeated them once, but they would rarely get a third run.

"They would try to come up with inexpensive ideas to use as filler [during the summer] so they could look like they were producing new stuff," Brustein explains. "Networks had to maintain their momentum. They can't just drop off the face of the earth during the summer, so they had to maintain some kind of level of 'newness.' The way they looked at it, they could save some money because, during those days, I think it was a hundred thousand dollars they had to pay for a third run."

So, instead, they experimented with low-cost variety series. The networks had little to lose from testing some talent in their own "summer replacement" shows. While shows hosted by Helen Reddy and the Manhattan Transfer bombed during those '70s summers, Sonny and Cher, Mac Davis, and Tony Orlando and Dawn flourished. The experiment not only saved the network money by not senselessly airing a variety show for a third time but also used the time slot to experiment with new talents, several of which—like Sonny and Cher—would go on to practically *own* the TV variety genre.

It was almost as if there was a contest between producers and networks for who could come up with the silliest ideas. "There was a lot of freeform creativity going on," says Guest. "It was definitely a period of time when there was a kind of 'anything goes' aspect to television comedy."

The specials might have been crazy and off-the-wall, but the magic was in the simplicity of the idea, Vilanch explains: "*Wayne Newton at Sea World*: 'Wayne, meet Shamu. Kids, let's do a show.'" In addition to the Holiday Special, audiences in the late 1970s would also be offered such rich variety as *KISS Meets the Phantom of the Park*, where the four masked musicians join forces to thwart an evil plan to clone everyone at Six Flags Magic Mountain. Just before that, viewers were given Ringo Starr in a wacky version of *The Prince and the Pauper*, where the former Beatle switches place with Everyman "Ognir Rrats" and mingles with guest stars John Ritter, Art Carney, Vincent Price, and even Carrie Fisher.

But the wackiest of the period has to be *The Telly Savalas Show*, which Kojak's alter ego opens with scantily clad backup dancers and a rocked-out original number, "Who Loves Ya Baby?"

In these early moments of the Special's inception, it was hard for people to understand why Lucas was risking his good name—as well as the reputation of his new franchise—by doing a television special.

Vilanch strongly believed that since Lucas was about to start shooting *The Empire Strikes Back*, he wanted to be sure the *Star Wars* fans were still hungry for another serving coming their way in a few years: "*Star Wars* had kind of petered out a little bit, and he was concerned that there be a momentum, that there be a 'stirring of the pot' to make sure people were still aware of the franchise. There weren't that many franchises in those days. *Star Wars* was only really the second blockbuster. I mean, *Jaws* was the first one, and then *Star Wars*."

But many don't buy that take—especially Blast from the Past store owner Larry Ross. "[They say] it was to keep the brand alive," says Ross, rolling his eyes at the absurdity. "In retrospect, it is exceptionally foolish, because the brand was not going to die. It was very, very popular. But somebody, somewhere said, 'You know, if we don't give them something, they're going to forget about us.' . . . Not possible, but they didn't see it at the time."

Jonathan Rinzler wrote more than two dozen behind-the-scenes books about film franchises like *Star Wars* and *Indiana Jones*. He adamantly disagreed with those who insist that because of *A New Hope*'s amazing box-office numbers, Lucas had money to burn on a sequel.

"It's real easy for us to look back and go, 'George Lucas, he had it made,' [because] he'd made this huge juggernaut. But that's not the way it was . . . everything was up in the air and up for grabs." Lucas was under unimaginable pressure, investing all of his *Star Wars* profits into the sequel with no assurances he would get any of it back. "There was no guarantee sequels made any money. Most sequels did not," Rinzler added, referring to the recent disappointing follow-ups to *Jaws* and *The Exorcist*. "Most franchises died a pretty quick death."

At the time, however, Lucas's potential *Star Wars* franchise was in a unique position. Rinzler pointed out that, by the late 1970s, most other franchises had been initially adapted from books—Peter Benchley's *Jaws*, William Peter Blatty's *The Exorcist*, Pierre Boulle's *Planet of the Apes*, Mario Puzo's *The Godfather*, and Ian Fleming's 007 series—"whereas *Star Wars* was a lot inspired by stuff wholly out of George's head. He was completely responsible for what usually is [solved by hiring] a bunch of writers, and you have a writer's room and run it like that. But he couldn't do that."

* * *

One of Lucas's prerequisites in doing the Special was that he wanted a colleague of his from USC film school, David Acomba, to direct it. Smith and Hemion agreed to this arrangement, even though it was very rare for Hemion

David Acomba (*right*) wins the "Best Feature Film" award at the 1973 Canadian Film Awards for *Slipstream*. Lucas, who went to USC with Acomba, made a rare request of Smith–Hemion: for the legendary Hemion to step back and allow Acomba to direct the Holiday Special. *Photo by Reg Innell/Toronto Star via Getty Images*

to step back and let someone else sit in his director's chair: he had always been the eyes of the team. But the easygoing Hemion—who would eventually win eighteen Emmy awards in his illustrious career—didn't feel the need to push back against Lucas. He'd served as an Air Force belly gunner on bombers in the Pacific during World War II. He knew how to choose his battles.

However, when David Acomba walked into the Smith–Hemion offices to begin directing the Special, he was not just another pimple-faced, spoiled film-school graduate that Lucas had met at USC. In his young life, Acomba had already garnered significant success in film, receiving international critical acclaim as well as several top directing awards.

Acomba was born and raised in Montreal and came to the US in the early 1960s to attend Northwestern University in Illinois. After graduating, he returned to Canada and created a niche in the Toronto musical community, directing such films as *Welcome to the Fillmore East* (with Van Morrison, Albert King, and the Byrds) and *Mariposa: A Folk Festival* (with Joan Baez and Joni Mitchell). Both were well received by critics: the *New York Times* described the former as "fresh and innovative," while the *Toronto Globe and Mail* called the latter "a beautiful film. ... To watch it is to be reminded of the deft strokes of a master bricklayer, who can put together a wall with motions that would seem more appropriate to a painter, but with results delightfully tangible and pleasantly rough-textured to the touch."

In 1967, Acomba came to Los Angeles to begin film school at USC, where he crossed paths with Lucas, Lippincott, and Kurtz. He disliked the experience tremendously. Anxious to move on with his life, he crammed three years of work into eighteen months, got his master's degree, and returned to Toronto. In 1973, he won a Canadian Film Award for producing and directing *Slipstream*, and afterward was asked to film George Harrison's 1974 *Dark Horse* tour with Ravi Shankar, though the resulting footage was never released. Between that and the *Star Wars Holiday Special*, Acomba was a director for the BBC series *Camera and the Song*.

From the beginning, the plan was always to incorporate music into the Special. In fact, according to Acomba, Gary Smith had referred to the project as "*Showboat* in Space."

Hearing that Lucas and Smith–Hemion would be turning this amazing film into a musical was the first of many red flags for Proft. "My thinking was it would be dumb to do things that aren't in *Star Wars*," he recalls. "It would really diminish the *Star Wars Holiday Special* if all of a sudden it turns into something that isn't even *Star Wars*. I mean, *Star Wars* was never a musical. It was an adventure."

But Proft was a young writer and probably not confident about making his opinion known. In fact, music would not only be included but would be a large part of the Special, as evidenced in a treatment that was found in Ralph McQuarrie's archive after his death. Who actually wrote the mysterious treatment has long been debated, but most, including Kyle Newman, feel that, "when reading it, it does feel decidedly Lucas. When you look at those old Ralph McQuarrie concept pieces, it makes sense that George would've floated this five-page treatment to his key collaborator on *A New Hope*."

In the treatment, Lucas writes of a "Starship Musica" that travels from planet to planet as a sort of Outer Space Peace Train that "celebrates the spirit of life and brotherhood." The treatment also mentions that "Wookiees enjoy the beat of rock and roll, and the sequence might feature that kind of group."

Even though Hemion had directed his share of specials featuring such legendary rock artists as Paul McCartney, Lippincott wanted to push the limits of the traditional TV special: "We wanted something that was going to make us different in variety shows. We didn't want the same old, same old, which is why David Acomba was brought in."

In the beginning, Acomba's enthusiasm was infectious. "He was adorable," recalls Vilanch. "He had curly hair and he was bright-eyed, and he could play Pippin. We all liked him a lot." But, he adds, "He was also very unlike everyone else who directed this kind of stuff."

Two more key hires were show-business veterans Ken and Mitzie Welch, who—among other things—had been credited with helping launch the career of a young Bob Newhart. They had worked on dozens of musical specials for such A-list talent as Barbra Streisand and Julie Andrews and had songwriting gigs on *The Garry Moore Show* and *The Carol Burnett Show*. "I just saw two people who, for the most part, loved what they did," their daughter Julie recalls. "They were in an interesting position, working together as a married couple. My dad was a little bit more the technician and my mom a little bit more of a passionate sort of storyteller. They really poured their heart into things."

The Welches would eventually receive credits as writers, composers, and producers on the Holiday Special. Smith and Hemion often delegated top producing responsibilities, so their role was to help ensure the Special stayed on track. To Vilanch, who had heard Acomba's stated desire to make this variety show different than anything he'd ever seen before, it made sense to have some experienced prime-time television people, like the Welches, to help him. "They were [hired] because there had to be professionals who had done this kind of thing before, who knew what the requirements were to get the show done. Otherwise, it would have never been done."

In terms of specific expertise, the Welches could write their way out of a paper bag. However, while they were award-winning songwriters with dozens of variety shows under their belt, they had no experience producing a show, much less actual show-running. But there was no chance that Smith and Hemion—even with the dozen or so shows they were juggling at the time— would back off the production and leave them as the showrunners, solely in charge of delivering such a unique and challenging show.

Would they?

More generally, two worlds—Acomba and Lucas from film and the Welches and Vilanch from TV variety—were being suddenly and violently thrust together. As a result, the script suffered. In Lucas's recollection, "It just kept getting reworked and reworked, moving away into this bizarre land. They were trying to make one kind of thing and I was trying to make another, and it ended up being a weird hybrid between the two."

In a 2008 *Vanity Fair* article, Frank Digiacomo explains the huge generation gap between these two worlds, as well as the difference between the perfectionism of a film director and the budgetary concerns of the Smith–Hemion staffers. Acomba, he adds, was "a product of rock 'n' roll and the rebellious milieu of '70s filmmaking that had also shaped Lucas," while "the producers, and to a lesser extent the writers, hailed from the song, dance, and shtick era of Establishment American TV, which paid heed to advertisers and Standards and Practices."

So, while Acomba was looking forward to shooting Jefferson Starship, channeling his experience working with rock legends like George Harrison, Van Morrison, and Joni Mitchell, the Welches were writing a song hearkening back to the nihilism of Bertolt Brecht and Kurt Weill for Bea Arthur to sing. A match made in heaven, it wasn't.

* * *

To say George Lucas hated Hollywood is an understatement. So he must have seemed dreadfully miscast when he visited the Sunset Boulevard offices of Smith–Hemion Productions of his own accord, as he did in the spring of 1978. Driving eastward from the beach, he would have to meander through the ritzy, exclusively residential areas of Santa Monica and Westwood, through Dead Man's Curve—a paddle tennis court short of the Playboy Mansion—through Beverly Hills, to the infamous 9220 and 9229 office buildings. Standing on opposite sides of Sunset Boulevard, the fifteen-story behemoths were like huge doors that announced your arrival to West Hollywood—and, after that, to Hollywood. The twin buildings were home to producers, personal managers, publicists, record companies, and talent agencies—as well as medical facilities that took up half of the available offices. "You'd share the elevator with gorgeous models with their headshots and people who were about to have a root canal," Vilanch recalls. "It was the kind of building that nobody knew what we were doing. We were shrouded in secrecy, not even a name on the office door."

Mike Erwin, a stage manager for the Special, had first heard that Smith–Hemion was going to be producing some sort of *Star Wars* project from Wenda Fong, one of the company's lead staff producers. He had never really believed it until, "one day, all of a sudden, George Lucas walked in with a whole phalanx of suited-up people. I thought, 'This is pretty cool that we're gonna be known for that famous thing—the David Bowie and Bing Crosby duet . . . then all of a sudden we're gonna jump to the *Star Wars Holiday Special.*' [I realized] we're gonna take another step up. We're gonna have a jump in *elitism.*"

Erwin wasn't being naïve, he was being optimistic. He had no reason to doubt the ability of his company to produce a *Star Wars* special. Heck, they had just brought Bing Crosby and David Bowie together. And, with the team Smith–Hemion had assembled for *this* Special, there was no doubt in *anyone's* mind—at that point in the process—that they could hit this one out of the park.

About a dozen staffers assembled in the office's rear conference room to welcome Lucas's entourage. According to Erwin, Vilanch, and production coordinator Elle Puritz, the Smith–Hemion reps included Acomba, Ken and Mitzie Welch, Ripps, Proft, and musical director Larry Grossman. Most likely, producer Joe Layton was also there, along with associate producer Rita Scott and writers Rod Warren and Buz Kohan. The Lucas "phalanx" that Erwin remembers likely included Lippincott, Kurtz, and Herman.

As Vilanch recalls, two other key people were there as well: "Gary Smith and Dwight Hemion, who were actually *allegedly* producing it—but they didn't *really* produce it. [Recently] I was looking at the credits on the show, and I saw it was a Smith–Hemion Production. I don't remember them being there [most of the time], but they were at the beginning when I thought about it."

That summer, Smith and Hemion were up to their ears in specials. Most production companies as large as theirs couldn't get into the weeds with each project, so instead had to step back and oversee them from a distance, rotating from production to production, spending less time on tried-

and-true projects and more time on the more unusual ones that included relatively new directors and producers. That year, aside from the *Star Wars* project, they were in line to direct and produce *Cinderella at the Palace* and the *Kraft 75th Anniversary Show*, as well as specials for Lucille Ball, Shields and Yarnell, Steve Lawrence and Eydie Gormé, and Ben Vereen, as well as Christmas shows for both Mac Davis and the Rockettes.

Although Vilanch held Smith–Hemion in high regard, he admitted "this wasn't exactly in their wheelhouse," which could be one of the reasons they delegated most of the duties to the show's producers, Joe Layton, the Welches, and Acomba, who seemed to be acting as Lucas's eyes and ears.

In Vilanch's memory, Smith conducted the meeting and introduced everyone. It is all but impossible that Smith wouldn't have taken a moment to brag about the Bing Crosby–David Bowie duet that would have aired months before to huge critical acclaim. It is also hard to imagine Grossman and Kohan not mentioning—either on their own or after Smith asked them to give a quick account of it—the legitimately fascinating story of how the duet had been pitched, rejected, rewritten, re-pitched, and eventually recorded, all within a few hours. Lucas no doubt would have thought that if you were indeed looking for clever and inspired writers who could work well with talent—and produce amazing heartwarming holiday moments for the coveted family audience—Smith–Hemion would surely be the place.

However, it should be noted that Grossman and Kohan were never actually hired for the Special, only Ian Fraser—the third and least involved of the trio of songwriters and musical directors who'd tweaked and reimagined the Crosby–Bowie number. Did Smith and Hemion use Grossman and Kohan to reassure Lucas over any potential concerns before swapping in the Welches, who had just become available after their ten-year gravy train, *The Carol Burnett Show*, ran out of steam and stopped production?

Either way, Lucas's idea of focusing the story around nonverbal characters that don't speak any discernable language immediately raised some flags. Associate producer Rita Scott recalled that this concept floored the production team. "I remember that Dwight Hemion and Gary Smith both said, 'That's going to be close to impossible to do.'" They pressed Lucas: "'They don't speak English?' and George said, 'No, they will just, uh, use their grunts, their Wookiee language.'" According to Scott, "Everyone kinda jumped in as gently as they could," all explaining how difficult that would be to accomplish.

Vilanch immediately warned Lucas of the problems: "I said, 'You've chosen to build a story around these characters who don't speak.'" As Vilanch would later note, "There was no way it could be done. There was nothing you can do with that. It featured the Wookiees; they were the stars of the story, and the Wookiees speak no known language. They sound like fat people having orgasms."

Lucas also emphasized that he didn't want any English dubbed in during post-production, and he also did not want subtitles used in the show, Vilanch recalls. "This was in an era when producers wouldn't use subtitles because they had concluded most of America would not read them, because they didn't go to subtitled movies." It was rare that a foreign film like Lasse Hallström's *My Life as a Dog* (1985), from Sweden, could sneak its way into the hearts of American audiences, in Swedish with subtitles—and even *that* film was eventually re-released theatrically in the US overdubbed in English.

Of course, that has all changed now. Most of the recently released *Star Wars* projects are subtitled, in Vilanch's words, "because they're speaking Tatooine-ish or Interplanetary Whatever-it-is. . . . Having been able to use subtitles would've been a lot easier because we could have had the Wookiees interacting more." But that option was off the table, and Lucas—despite pleas from Vilanch and other experienced television writers and producers who begged him not to go ahead with this concept—would not be persuaded. Instead, he pressed forward with his decision. In Vilanch's view, he had "what a director needs to have, which is this insane belief in their personal vision, and [that] he was somehow going to make it work."

Thirty years earlier, the producers of *Lassie* had used a creative device that allowed the dog's feelings and intentions to be understood by the audience: Lassie would run over to its human owner and start barking. "What's wrong Lassie?" the owner would ask. After Lassie barked again, the owner would indirectly translate for the audience: "Oh, there's a fire at the hospital, Lassie?" It's a technique that Lucas used in *A New Hope*, whether it was Han Solo communicating with Chewbacca or Luke comprehending R2-D2. The writers of the Special now needed to create a similar type of device to help the audience comprehend the grunts of Chewbacca's Wookiee family. As Ripps explains, "In silent movies, there were at least titles. So you could see what people were saying and thinking. We didn't have that. It all had to be done through mime. That becomes more of a challenge if you can't see somebody's face and their joy or sorrow or whatever they're feeling."

That's when they came up with the idea of the Great White Hunter, Vilanch recalls. "There should be someone who is the liaison between the Wookiees and the English-speaking world." The term "Great White Hunter" evoked big game hunters from the Western world who came to Africa to profit from the sale of ivory. It seems as though Lucas and others liked the idea of a sophisticated adventurer who could understand the Wookiee language, but they didn't like the negative connotation of the "Hunter." The character was eventually changed to a "Trader."

According to the original treatment, the Trader is "folksy and kind" but not interested in the "Life Day" festivities at the heart of the story because he has no family, and "commercialism is prohibited . . . so there's nothing in it for him." Instead, the treatment describes the Trader taking his ship to Tatooine's infamous Mos Eisley cantina, where he will spend the holiday drinking with his friends.

Chewy's family are big clients of the Trader, who delivers merchandise to their home on the planet Kashyyyk on a regular basis. "[He] understood the Wookiee language, and he could translate so the audience would understand what they were talking about," Herman explains. In the final version of the script, the Trader—ultimately named Saul Dann—knows the family so well that he seems to enter their home whenever he wishes, like a Kashyyykian version of Building Superintendent Dwayne Schneider from *One Day at a Time*—or, more accurately, a yet-to-be-conceived Kramer from *Seinfeld*.

"Life Day" is a holiday that Lucas invented, and Chewbacca getting home to celebrate it with his family is the main thrust of the Special's story. "The whole 'Life Day with the Wookiees' was something that George took very seriously at the time," said Jonathan Rinzler. The story also gave him the opportunity "to expand the *Star Wars* universe in his first major visual expansion. George didn't choose the storyline lightly."

Indeed, Lucas might have been holding on to this Wookiee storyline for quite a while. In July 1976, as author Alan Dean Foster was working on the novelization of *Star Wars*, he had a brainstorming session with Lucas and Lippincott that was recorded on audio tape. Years later, Lippincott transcribed the tape.

In the meeting, Lucas revealed to the others that he had conceived of a literary device to open his film. "I had an idea—as a joke—which usually ends up being my best ideas. I was thinking of how to start the film in a knoll-like, hobbit-hole kind of thing. And you go in and there's a Wookiee family. Mama Wookiee, Papa Wookiee, and Baby Wookiee . . . and Daddy Wookiee was going to sit down the baby Wookiee on his knee and tell him the story." But, he adds, "I don't know whether we dare try it. It might be interesting. I thought of doing it in the movie, actually, and then I chickened out."

"It's a lovely idea," Foster told Lucas, "but it's sort of distracting."

Undeterred, Lucas continued pitching the idea, explaining that he was concerned that the story might become typecast as hard-core science fiction. "I want to try to get the thing out of the science-fiction thing and more into a fantasy kind of thing, because I think, more than anything else, that's where our trouble is going to be. No matter what we do, no matter what we write, it's still going to be a science-fiction thing. But if we try to take the edge off the thing, I think it will help us."

To do that, Lucas suggested this "big old journal" have "a big, fuzzy storybook quality" to temper the "hard-edged steel sort of science fiction." He imagined the older Wookiee telling the baby, "Well, now, Uncle Chewbacca brought this back from his adventures, just before he died."

"What do you think of something like that?" Lucas asked Foster, who said he would give it a try.

"Look, if you don't like it, I can rewrite it," Foster told Lucas. "We're only talking about a couple of pages here. At the very worst, you can always start on page four."

Foster still vividly recalls the discussion. "I didn't think it was a good idea. And I tried to . . . do a little sidestep. I thought it would go away, and it did. So I never had to write it. I never had to deal with it."

Kyle Newman says that, in the long run, they didn't use that Wookiee storytelling device story element in Foster's novel, "but that idea remained in [Lucas's] head, and it seems that it was the seed for the Holiday Special."

As for the Wookiee holiday, Life Day, as it's described in the original treatment, "For one day each year, the galaxy celebrates the spirit of life and brotherhood with a festival."

"It was the biggest day of the year, and that's pretty much what I knew about the story," Ripps recalls. "It was kind of a Wookiee Rosh Hoshana."

Vilanch adds, "[Lucas] thought it would be like a later Festivus-for-the-rest-of-us from *Seinfeld* would be, but not so much."

According to the treatment, this jubilee is designed to unite the galaxy, to the chagrin of the Imperial authorities, who "cannot cancel it for it is not illegal, but the [Empire] would prefer the galaxy split: the more it comes together it would help the rebel cause." Further, we learn it is Kashyyyk's turn to host the Life Day celebration, and Chewbacca—"the most noted of the Wookiees," because of his recent heroics helping the Rebel Alliance—will be honored at the festival.

One of the enduring fan controversies from *A New Hope*—apart from the question of whether Han or Greedo shoots first at the Mos Eisley cantina—is that after Chewbacca helps blow up the Death Star, he doesn't receive a medal from Princess Leia at the end like Luke and Han do. In the words of historian Brian Ward, "You give Han Solo a medal and you give Luke Skywalker a medal, but Chewbacca only gets a chance to stand up on the platform and roar?"

Lucasfilm's Miki Herman knows the controversy well, and she's been pelted with questions about it for decades. "George's answer to that was, 'Wookiees don't want [one], he didn't want a medal. Chewbacca deserved a medal, but he didn't want it.' That's what George said . . . but his reward was that Han would take him back to his home planet for Life Day."

Indeed, in Lucas's treatment, Luke, Leia, and Han accompany Chewbacca home, and he arrives safely in the first act of the story. However, in the final Ripps–Proft version of the script, it is Han alone who accompanies Chewbacca. They are delayed by Imperial forces, creating concern among Chewbacca's family as to whether he will get there in time for the festival, or even return at all.

Ripps was overwhelmed not only by how detailed the story was but by how familiar the characters seemed to Lucas: "To George Lucas, this was real . . . 'This is what happened. This is how they live. This is who they are.'

Lucas would not allow the producers to use subtitles or overdubs for the Wookiees' nonverbal language, which created stress for the writing staff as to how to make the story comprehensible. *Clockwise from top left:* Peter Mayhew as Chewbacca; Mickey Morton as his wife, Malla; Patty Maloney as his son, Lumpy; and Paul Gale as his father, Itchy. *Photofest © CBS*

He was kind of like a reporter, sharing with us a world that we didn't know about, that he knew lots about.

"You have to remember," Ripps adds, "he had come up with at least a dozen stories. So he knew what this was about." As a result, Ripps and Proft were not shy about pummeling Lucas with questions: "What do they do? How do they talk? How do they communicate? How do we create them in a way that you think is authentic?"

Ripps and Proft spent one entire twelve-hour day with Lucas, who went over the story as he saw it. "That was worth everything," Ripps recalls. "He was the most intense, most focused person I had ever met. I mean, we were so into it that I forgot about lunch, and that's infrequent for me."

One concept that Lucas was adamant Ripps and Proft incorporate into their story was the "good versus evil" theme he had begun in *A New Hope*. Now, on Kashyyyk, the Wookiee civilization is being terribly oppressed by the Empire. Proft recalls Lucas emphatically describing the stormtroopers as the villains: "Think of them as Nazis, and the Wookiees as the Jews, basically . . . being persecuted by these [storm]troopers."

Ripps does not remember the "Nazis vs Jews" subplot that Proft recalls. In his view, Lucas saw the Special "as two things: first of all, that life-affirming experience of the whole universe coming together. And second, it's a good way to sell toys in between movies. This show, among other things, was meant to keep that consciousness alive. It was meant to sell product."

Nonetheless, for Ripps—who like Proft was at the beginning of what would become an illustrious screenwriting career—Lucas's creative drive was like a bolt of energy that had been infused in him. "I mean, it was really enthralling," he recalls. At moments like this, any fear Ripps had had previously about successfully completing a *Star Wars* story for television disappeared. "One of the most attractive things about anybody is passion, and he had such passion that it was inconceivable that we couldn't do it."

However, Ripps soon realized, "As it turned out, it was *very* conceivable."

During that initial meeting, Ripps recalls, Lucas took out a pad of paper and asked how long a TV special was. "Sixty minutes," they responded—CBS had not yet offered to extend the program to two hours—so Lucas numbered two pages from one to sixty, one number for each line, and explained that all they had to do is come up with one thing to happen in every minute of the story.

"He was breaking down the story into time, not into story," Proft recalls. "It was like, 'We open with the five-minute thing here, and then we do a ten-minute thing here . . . I need five minutes here of this. I need ten minutes here of that. I need fifteen of this.' I mean, it was never about the story itself, but how it fits into this time[line]."

Lucas also explained the backgrounds of the main characters, in case they wanted to incorporate those elements into the Special's story. One specific backstory regarding Han Solo caught the two off guard. According to Ripps,

Left to right: director Irvin Kershner, producer Gary Kurtz, Lucas, and screenwriter Lawrence Kasdan on the Hoth set of *The Empire Strikes Back*. Now that the second movie—which he fully funded with his *Star Wars* revenue—was beginning production, Lucas was spending no time at all on the Holiday Special's sound stage. *Terry Chostner/Photofest © Twentieth Century Fox*

Lucas "said that Han Solo was married to a Wookiee, 'But we can't say that, because people wouldn't accept it.'" Back in 1998, Proft corroborated Ripps's claim, but he has since forgotten the incident. However, an early draft of a *Star Wars* script, dated January 28, 1975, supports Ripps's statement. After Han meets Luke and Ben at the cantina, he invites them back to his home, where he is greeted by a female "fur-covered creature" named Oeeta.

Meanwhile, Lucas was into pre-production for *The Empire Strikes Back*, and script issues for the film were seriously jeopardizing his timeline. Because of this, he was spending less and less time in the Smith–Hemion production offices, and he could only be reached by phone. Acomba—in whom Lucas had tremendous faith—was his eyes and ears at the production office.

With the Special's first day of shooting looming, Ripps and Proft forged ahead to finish *their* script on time. "We wrote a version without the variety parts," Ripps explains. "The variety parts we left blank. Most of our work was with the Chewbacca stuff."

The "variety parts"—the songs and comedy sketches that the Wookiees weren't in—would be written by Bruce Vilanch, Rod Warren, and Mitzie Welch. Among their contributions would be the two Harvey Korman sketches (a Julia Child parody, and an instructional video Lumpy uses to help build a mini transmitter) and a general outline for a scene in Saul Dann's trading post with Lev Mailer (playing an Imperial Guard), which was ad-libbed nearly in its entirety. Ripps notes that he and Proft could have helped write the other sections, "but these people were heavyweights, and our job was more these silent bits, and trying to create some kind of continuity, trying to create a story."

Besides, Ripps and Proft had enough on their plate. Not only did they have to write a story that—no matter what caveats were being given—was going to be compared to *Star Wars*, they were tasked with coming up with one that would allow Chewbacca's family to remain largely stationed at their treehouse home, whose set was already costing Smith–Hemion a pretty penny. The original treatment idea of the traveling Spaceship Musica was overreaching, budget-wise—and, ideally, the producers hoped *not* to have to move the large costumed characters to and from additional locations, whether they be on Kashyyyk or Tatooine.

The solution that emerged was a series of communication devices that allowed actors to share scenes with characters in different areas of the galaxy who were actually being shot in other areas of the soundstage. According to Vilanch, the idea for these devices actually originated with Lucas, who during their initial meeting brought with him a makeshift prototype of his proposed virtual-reality helmet and explained how he envisioned it fitting into the story.

"It was like a little helmet," describes Vilanch. "You could wear it as a hat. I mean, it looked like a frisbee that was juiced up, just to show the principle of it." This would be a gift that the Trader would bring over on his many visits to the Chewbacca household. "[Lucas] wanted to explain the concept, and how real it could be, and how real it would look when he actually had them built for the show."

Vilanch says that Lucas had designed this to help realize different characters' dreams. And they all had dreams: Chewbacca's son dreamt of being an acrobat, so the acrobats and tumblers would entertain for him. The Imperial Guard dreamt of escaping his mundane life, so a rock band would perform for him. And, of course, the grandfather dreamt of a beautiful woman who would serenade him. Why try to transport Itchy to another location when he could simply create the magnificent Mermeia—soon to be played by Diahann Carroll—in his head?

* * *

The variety scenes that took place outside of the Wookiee household were the natural destination for the guest stars who were a mainstay of television specials. As Vilanch explains, CBS liked these "openings" because they could serve as promotional opportunities: "If you had a show on CBS, even if you couldn't sing and couldn't dance, they would put you on *The Carol Burnett Show* because they wanted to plug your show—*Mannix*, or *Cannon*, or something like that." In Julie Welch's recollection, "You'd give them a list of folks you wanted, and they would come back and say 'yea' or 'nay,' sort of like, 'Here's our list, take it or leave it.'"

Back in this era, a larger percentage of television and film stars arrived in Hollywood with more rounded backgrounds, and having some sort of singing and dancing chops was pretty much the norm, Welch explains. Film stars were no exception. Although she was quite the cultural icon, Raquel Welch's popularity had waned significantly since the late 1960s, when she starred in such time-stamped films as *Fantastic Voyage* and *One Million Years B.C.* By the late 1970s, she had transformed from a 1960s poster child to a halfway-legitimate song-and-dance performer, parlaying those basic singing and dancing skills Julie Welch describes into the TV variety world rather effortlessly. It is highly likely that Lucas saw her 1970 CBS special, *Raquel*, where she performs a sultry "space dance" in a sort of bikini space suit. She recorded the number in front of the Ruta de la Amistad, or Friendship Route—futuristic-looking sculptures that had been commissioned for the 1968 Summer Olympics in Mexico City. (Coincidentally, that show was directed by choreographer David Winters, and the space suit itself was designed by Bob Mackie; both would soon be part of the Special's crew.)

In the original treatment for the Special, Lucas actually envisioned "guest star" Raquel Welch as an Imperial spy who accepts a mission from the Empire to infiltrate the Rebel Alliance. Once on board the alliance's "Peace Train," Welch "starts vamping the Starship commander to gain his confidence." R2-D2 and C-3PO see this and, observing protocol, tell the commander he must report it to Luke. However, the Commander is enjoying the attention, back at home in her own kitchen.

C. Raquel has arrived on board the Starship Musica, and in the midst of the final preparations, she starts vamping the Starship commander, to gain his confidence. R2 and 3PO observe this, and since they are not programmed to know about what she's up to, they tell the commander they must report it to Luke. The commander, who rather enjoyed Raquel's attention, reminds them that they know nothing about the ways of a man and a woman.

D. Now that Malla and Chewie know where Lumpy is, Chewie gets the Trader on the wall ___

Discovered among the belongings of conceptual artist Ralph McQuarrie was a five-page treatment for the Special. In it, Raquel Welch is cast as an Imperial spy who boards the Rebel Alliance's starship and "vamps" for the commander in order to distract him. Although there is no name on the treatment, many say it resembles Lucas's style. *Courtesy of the Ralph McQuarrie Estate*

and he tells the two droids they know nothing about the ways of a man and a woman. The treatment continues with Welch finding Lumpy on board; she tells him a story, "with dance and gestures, about what drives a spaceship" and "dances her way into the power-supply room and screws everything up."

"I think the Raquel Welch idea was something that probably sprang from George's fascination or imagination," *Fanboys* director Kyle Newman surmises. "It definitely wasn't so much of a TV-friendly name for 1978. So I feel like [choosing Raquel Welch] was intrinsically George. It wasn't something that was cutting-edge or relevant, and definitely not for young audiences. *Star Wars* had so many young fans at the time . . . maybe that was a ploy to get some of the parents to sit down with the kids to watch the Holiday Special."

Lucas would have been thirty-four at the time the treatment was written, which would explain the choice of Welch, who was the sexpot of *his* generation. However, by 1978, the infamous *One Million Years B.C.* posters featuring Welch that had hung on the walls of college dorms had been taken down and replaced by ones of Farrah Fawcett. (The *Charlie's Angels* poster princess couldn't sing or dance, though, which would have been a huge prerequisite for the Special.)

Neither Ripps nor Proft recalls even seeing the original treatment that included this preposterous scene with Welch. The only thing remotely close to this character in the Ripps–Proft final script would be Mermeia—a "holographic water creature," according to the online *Star Wars* resource Wookieepedia, who worked as a "private entertainer." Most importantly, she was to be the virtual fantasy of Chewbacca's father, Itchy.

Of several names that were batted around at the time to play Mermeia, Cher was on the top of the shortlist. She was one of the biggest stars at CBS and a perfect casting decision for this sultry role. The producers reached out to her and even hired her renowned wardrobe designer for the Special—the "Sultan of Sequins" himself, Bob Mackie.

To put it mildly, Mackie is a cultural icon. A member of the TV Academy Hall of Fame, he made a huge mark designing dresses for the stars of television—and, in the process, created a style all his own. There were no limits to the outrageous outfits he would design for Cher, his most famous client, who always pushed him to keep taking risks with her dresses. Her annual appearances on the Oscars red carpet became media events of their own, as both fans and reporters waited anxiously to see her in the latest Mackie original.

However, Vilanch says that they weren't able to coordinate with her schedule, so she fell out. "It was supposed to be Cher, but Cher suddenly couldn't do it," Vilanch recalls. "She'd had a little surgery, and she couldn't do it."

Whatever the reason, the producers now had quite a problem on their hands. Mackie had already designed and produced the dress, so they were in quite a bind—stood up at the dance with a Bob Mackie original in hand, looking for a name talent who could sing and who had Cher's unique physique, so as to fit into the dress.

Potentially among those in the running to replace Cher was Jefferson Starship's lead singer, Grace Slick. According to a wire story published a few weeks after the Special was broadcast, there was a reference to a "dress that Bob Mackie had designed for Slick" on the set of the Special.

When asked about Slick, Mackie does not recall any costume being specifically designed for her. But then suddenly, during the interview, he remembers he was asked to do *another* design for the special that was never actually created. "I have another sketch that was obviously done for the same character, but [was for] a dancer…maybe [Mermeia] was [originally] gonna sing *and* dance. I don't know."

His assistant retrieves it from his storage, and—unlike Mackie's other sketches for the Special—this particular one does not include the name of the actor on it. While the legendary designer has an impeccable memory for someone in his mid-eighties, he does not recall the name of the dancer.

Mackie holds up his two forty-year-old sketches—one clearly identified in writing as Diahann Carroll, and one of a "mystery dancer"—and compares the differences. Although they both have water-themed outfits, Carroll's dress is clearly not for dancing, "just a simpler, more of a gown kind of version." On the other hand, the dress for the dancer is more open and has less fabric. However, it is likely that this is the original sketch for Mermeia, made long before Carroll was booked, possibly with the idea that the water creature would be dancing as well.

Also, the dancer has significantly lighter skin than the sketch of Carroll. Mackie acknowledges that it still could have been Cher or Slick. "That looks kind of like Juliet Prowse, but I don't think it is," Mackie says.

As he looks again at his mysterious dancer, Mackie cannot believe that it *wasn't* intended for Cher: "This was an outfit, obviously, that was designed for Cher. It's very, very naked and see-through, but not so naked you couldn't put it on television, although sometimes we came perilously close in the naked department."

Whomever Mackie's mystery Mermeia was, Vilanch recalls the moment when Diahann Carroll finally arrived to save the day. To put it simply, she fit into the dress, and she was available. She was booked immediately.

Acomba pushed back: "Why is Diahann Carroll in this?" The response he was given was, "Because of the name, and the network wants Black people." Acomba said he recalled there was some controversy about the cast of *Star Wars* not having any diversity. He thought to himself, "What do we do with Diahann Carroll?"

Oh, how they would find a place for her.

Carroll—a successful actress, singer, and activist—had carved out an illustrious career in film, television, and the theater, shattering racial barriers along the way. Specifically, she holds a place in history as the first African American to win the 1962 Tony Award for "Best Actress in a Musical" for her role in *No Strings*. Six years later, she received the Golden Globe Award for "Best Actress in a Television Series" for playing the lead in *Julia*, a part she would be forever identified with throughout her career. After years of breaking racial stereotypes for African Americans in the industry, she spent the latter part of the 1970s performing on prime-time variety television with such stars as Sammy Davis Jr., Bob Hope, and even Telly Savalas.

Little did she know, back then, that by agreeing to this appearance, she would subsequently become by far the most controversial and talked-about portion of one of the most critically maligned specials in television history. One more for the record books.

While the producers were searching for a replacement for Cher, CBS had opened the doors to its collection of television stars. Earlier that year, Carol Burnett had ended her eleven-year run on *The Carol Burnett Show*, leaving her sidekick, Harvey Korman, free. Bea Arthur had just left *Maude* after six seasons and was also available, as was Art Carney (famous for playing Ed Norton in *The Honeymooners*), once NBC stopped production of *Lanigan's Rabbi*, where he played a police chief who partners with his rabbi to solve local crimes.

In short order, Korman, Arthur, and Carney were all booked for the Special, with rehearsals scheduled to begin in mid-August.

In the opinion of former Lucasfilm receptionist Mick Garris, Smith–Hemion's first mistake was including CBS's older talent in the Special: "Yes, they were TV stars, but they were the elderly audience. It just seemed like the worst fit in history."

Garris was right: CBS's audience skewed toward older adults. It was far less octogenarian than that of NBC—the home of Hope, Johnny Carson, and *Little House on the Prairie*—but ABC virtually *owned* the youth demo with a slew of teen-friendly hits like *Happy Days*, *Laverne and Shirley*, *What's Happening*, *Welcome Back Kotter*, and *Good Times*. CBS's more mature programming included shows like *All in the Family*, *Maude*, and *60 Minutes*.

Radio personality Mo'Kelly understands the geriatric booking of these older comedians. "This is 1978. Not everyone got *Star Wars* at that point. It was still a burgeoning franchise. I suspect [the producers are] thinking, 'The young people already get *Star Wars*.' But, if you have some bona-fide stars, that will help people to want to tune in."

Even the writers themselves were questioning the choice to book these older comedians. "If someone was telling you you'd be doing a *Star Wars* special," says Ripps, "you probably wouldn't think that Maude would be one of the guest stars."

Gilbert Gottfried never understood the casting. "When you think *Star Wars*, the first name that pops into your head is Art Carney," he drily lamented, mocking the show's creative decision to integrate Carol Burnett–type schtick. "When Harvey Korman and Harrison Ford did those sketches together and they'd break each other up, that was so funny. And then, at the end, when Chewbacca came out and said goodnight to the audience and pulled on his ear and you never really knew why, but something about it is definitely *Star Wars*."

In addition to the fact that Arthur, Carney, and Korman reached a much older demographic for the show, the Lucasfilm contingent was promised *A-level* stars for the Special, as opposed to these guest stars who were all considered television veterans. According to Herman, "The talent was supposed to be the caliber of Cher, Mikhail Barishnikov, and Ann-Margret. That was the people that they had hoped would be on the variety show."

While the producers were under the covers with CBS booking their octogenarian talent, Acomba was on a completely different mission. He thought Arthur, Carney, and Korman were immensely talented, but he agreed with Garris and Herman about the generation gap. Acomba wanted to bring some "fresher"—code for "younger"—faces to the show, so he spent several evenings scouring local clubs for stand-up and improvisational comedians, perhaps someone that could fill the important role of the Trader.

After visiting some of the top comedy clubs in Hollywood, he checked out the Off the Wall improvisational group, who performed on the second floor of a dance studio in West Hollywood. Although alumni John Ritter, Garry Shandling, and Chevy Chase had all left the group by then, the ensemble still boasted a stellar cast. On that summer night in 1978, Acomba would probably have seen such future celebrities as George Wendt (pre-*Cheers*), Jim Belushi (pre–*According to Jim*), and Paul Willson (pre–*Office Space*), but in his memory, he was mesmerized by one specific cast member who was stealing the show. He was likable and energetic, and he did a variety of different accents and voices. His name was Robin Williams. He had been a member of the ensemble for barely over a year but had already become the unofficial star of the show.

Off the Wall's founder, Andy Goldberg, says there was a lot of buzz about their group but that Williams was building a following all his own. One night, he recalls, he was excited to see legendary producer Norman Lear in the audience. During intermission, Lear came up to Goldberg, who thought he had finally made it.

"This is it," Goldberg thought to himself. "I'm about to be discovered."

Lear smiled and shook Goldberg's hand. "Boy is that Robin Williams funny," he told him.

"It was certainly not what I was hoping to hear from him," Goldberg recalls, "but I had to agree. Robin was faster and funnier than anyone I had ever seen."

Acomba had the same reaction to Williams, and after the show, he went backstage to meet him. "I was totally knocked out," he recalled. "I met him and said, 'This is amazing, you would be perfect,'" probably envisioning him in the Trader Dann role that would eventually go to Art Carney.

Acomba says he asked Williams to come to the Smith–Hemion production offices to meet the Welches. "I presented him to Ken and Mitzie, but they wouldn't see him," Acomba said. "They said, 'No, no, no, we don't want new talent . . . we've got to have names.' So all these people that I had been seeing got nixed."

Coincidentally, Williams had just shot a pilot for a sitcom that also had a sort of space theme to it. Its network premiere was just two months away. On September 14, Williams's sitcom, *Mork and Mindy*, premiered on ABC to record numbers. It was a smash success, and ABC immediately ordered a season of the show. Williams became not only an immediate star but a household name, never looking back once for not being considered "name talent."

* * *

And, as they say, "for the kids" . . . the producers booked Jefferson Starship. It was a pretty sweet booking: in February 1978, the band had released the album *Earth*, which resulted in two Top 20 hits, "Count on Me" and "Runaway." After a spring-summer tour of the US and Europe, they would return home and record a new song written by lead guitarist Craig Chaquico. They would then be taping a lip-synched performance of "Light the Sky on Fire" for the *Star Wars Holiday Special.*

Chaquico has suggested that the band's booking was the result of someone at the studio being a huge fan. However, knowing the actual booking processes of 1970s variety shows, it was more than likely the producers knew next to nothing about the band, and that they were actually hired as a result of their space-related name.

"It is possible that they only booked us because we were called Jefferson *Starship* and had a song called 'Hyperdrive,'" admits keyboard player Pete Sears. "So it's possibly that ... it's probably *actually* that."

If there *was* a reason for the booking beyond the name of their band, it very well could have been front man Kantner's obsession with science fiction. In 1971, he had released a solo album, *Blows Against the Empire,* which by his own admission was derived from the works of science-fiction author Robert A. Heinlein. As obscure as the subject matter was, the album still went gold.

With the booking of Jefferson Starship and Diahann Carroll—as well as Arthur, Carney, and Korman—and the script close to being completed, the Special was getting closer to starting shooting. On the network side, the advertisers had bit hard on the one-hour *Star Wars* biscuit, prompting CBS to come back to Lucasfilm and ask to increase the show to ninety minutes. Lucasfilm agreed, but then, soon after, CBS came back again, asking to extend it to two hours. Lucasfilm again agreed.

This increase in the Special's overall running time would give Smith–Hemion additional funds, but it also meant the writers would have to create about forty-five minutes of additional content. Lucas had already met with the writers, and the story they'd knocked out was only an hour long.

* * *

At this point, Lucas has another mission that wasn't going to be as easy as he had imagined. He and Kurtz were saddled with getting commitments from the main cast of the film, and getting the three lead stars—Hamill, Fisher, and Ford—would take some work. Kurtz had been given the arduous task of negotiating with them individually to appear, and he acknowledged that begging was involved. Hamill and Ford had both done work on dozens of TV shows—everything from *Ironside* to *The Partridge Family*—but they had both worked hard to make their way *out* of television. In the 1970s, film actors were more reluctant to make appearances on the "boob tube," with many considering the medium beneath them.

Ford had made something of a name for himself in *American Graffiti* as the enigmatic Bob Falfa, who cruises into town looking to race the so-called fastest driver on the boulevard. However, the father of two was still having to take on carpentry jobs to supplement his acting work right up until his Han Solo gig. From his 1968 film debut as a bellboy in *Dead Heat on a Merry-Go-Round* to *Star Wars* in 1977, Ford spent most of those years as a television workhorse, appearing in about two dozen series that included *Gunsmoke, Dan August, Dynasty, Kung Fu, The Rookies, Petrocelli, The F.B.I., The Virginian*, and *Love, American Style*.

Since the release of *Star Wars*, Ford had also been the busiest of his co-stars. But it hadn't been back-to-back hits: the movie *Heroes*—in which he co-starred with Henry Winkler and Sally Field—was released at the end of 1977 to mixed reviews and certainly less box office than expected. But things were looking up for the soon-to-be Indiana Jones. He had just wrapped *Force 10 from Navarone* with Robert Shaw, and Coppola's Vietnam epic, *Apocalypse Now*, which he had filmed before *Star Wars*, finally looked like it would be released the following year.

Ford claimed in a 2011 interview with the *Irish Cinema Times* that he was *required* to appear in the Special: "It was in my contract. There was no known way to get out of it." When the reporter asked if he had seen the Special, Ford responded, "No, I was there, man. I didn't have to see it."

In an Associated Press interview at the time of the broadcast, Ford clarified that he had caveats to his appearance, saying he left the singing to Fisher. "I don't sing, I don't dance, and don't ask me."

However, Hamill says that when he was asked to appear in the Special, he turned it down, saying, "I'm *not* under contract." (It is not clear whether Ford has exaggerated his commitment to Lucasfilm out of embarrassment for participating in the Special, or whether he meant he felt obligated to Lucas for casting him in *Star Wars*, and that refusing a favor to him so soon after the film's tremendous success would be considered ungrateful.)

Like Ford, Hamill had done his share of television shows, starting at the age of twelve on *General Hospital,* and followed by appearances on *The Bill Cosby Show, One Day at a Time, Medical Center, The F.B.I., Room 222, Cannon, Night Gallery,* and *The Streets of San Francisco.* Just prior to *Star Wars,* he had completed filming a TV movie starring Don Johnson and Robert Forster in which he plays a psychotic, knife-wielding teen. IMDB.com describes the plot: "Matt and Scott are two detectives trying to catch a crazy guy who has a beef with a country singer. Banks's problem with country singer Wes Collins is that Wes punched him in the face when he was a baby. Banks is now intent on getting revenge for this by killing Wes. Only Matt and Scott can stop him."

Adventuring back into prime-time television would not be easy for Hamill. From the start, he hated the script, which he has said also required him to sing. "I remember when I read it, I said, 'This is awful. Why are we doing this?' And I said, 'I'm *not* doing this.'"

Although he notes that he doesn't like to bring up "family dirty linen," he explains that, in his opinion, the Special was "just not *Star Wars.* So I don't care. I love the Jefferson Starship. I love Beatrice Arthur and Art Carney. But what the heck does that have to do with our movie?"

Hamill only reconsidered appearing on the show once he got a phone call from Lucas himself. "I said, 'It's terrible, it's some mishmash. It's not *Star Wars,* it's like a Bob Hope special or something.'" Lucas reminded him that by the time the Special eventually aired, "we would have been in movie theaters [on and off] for almost a year and a half. It opened in the summer of '77. This is fall of '78." He added there was great demand for *Star Wars* toys, but they wouldn't be available until that holiday season, and that the Special was "just a way to keep the merchandising fresh in people's minds." This would also reassure Fox, which was concerned about fans losing interest in the three years between *A New Hope* and *The Empire Strikes Back.* After all, even though Lucasfilm was bankrolling *Empire,* Fox would still be ponying up some cash for its promotion and distribution.

"It's really a favor for me . . . ," Lucas admitted to Hamill.

Ultimately, Hamill gave in.

"Well, all right," he told Lucas, "but I'm not singing."

"I personally love to sing," he later noted. "I did a Broadway musical, but

I didn't think it was right for Luke to sing. Carrie had a wonderful voice, and Carrie did a great job."

Some have theorized that Hamill's initial concerns about appearing in the Special had nothing to do with the script but were because he was in the midst of a difficult recovery. On January 11, 1977, near the end of principal photography for *A New Hope*, he had been in a serious car accident along the Antelope Valley Freeway in California, probably somewhere between Santa Clarita and Barstow. As he recalled a year later, "I was speeding, going too fast, and what happened, I think, was that I tried to negotiate an off-ramp and lost control, tumbled over, and went off the road."

The impact resulted in Hamill's face slamming into the steering wheel, fracturing both his nose and his left cheek, which required reconstructive surgery using cartilage from his ear. When Hamill woke up in the hospital, he knew that he had hurt himself "very, very, very badly but wasn't really sure. Then someone held a mirror up to my face, and I just felt that my career was over."

A week later, as *Star Wars* animator Peter Kuran recalled, Hamill was recovering and shooting last-minute pickups for *A New Hope*. Kuran was assigned to deliver Hamill back and forth between his home on the beach and the Antelope Valley. "He had a pin in his nose that was there to hold it in place," Kuran recalls. "He would pull the pin [with his finger] and shift his nose back and forth on his face. He laughed so hard. It was gross."

After *Star Wars* was completed and released, Hamill made appearances on talk shows like *The Merv Griffin Show* and *Dinah!* where he certainly looked different, but not to the extent that he would on the Special.

"One of the biggest reveals for the *Star Wars Holiday Special*, for me, was seeing my hero, Luke Skywalker, on my small-screen TV," comedy writer Anthony Caleca recalls. "The only trouble was, I didn't know who that was when I saw him."

His appearance baffled many. "It was jarring to me," recalls Mo'Kelly. "It was distracting to me. Carrie Fisher looked like Carrie Fisher, Harrison Ford looked like Harrison Ford, but Mark Hamill did not look like Mark Hamill."

Hamill's appearance—with its conspicuous, heavily layered makeup—is still a topic of conversation among fans and critics. Mo'Kelly clarifies that it wasn't just the facial makeup. "It was heavy on mascara. It was heavy on blush. It was heavy on everything." He acknowledges that sometimes makeup is used to exaggerate a performer's features, but it seems like these makeup artists changed and distorted his features in a completely different way. Hamill's makeup, he adds, "didn't *accentuate* anything. It *changed* everything."

There are competing explanations as to why Hamill was wearing so much makeup. In the Blu-ray commentary for *The Empire Strikes Back*, Lucas says that, after the accident, he knew that Hamill was going to look different in the sequel. Many believe that the idea to open the film with Luke getting attacked by a Wampa snow monster was partially to explain Hamill's reconstructed face, allowing the audience to slowly adjust to his new look.

However, that assumption has been countered by Lucas himself, who elsewhere has said that the reason for the Wampa attack was to start the film off with some suspense, not to camouflage Hamill's face. He has also said that in the years between *A New Hope* and *The Empire Strikes Back*, there was a change in Luke's character: "My feeling was, some time had passed, [the *Star Wars* characters] had been in the Rebellion fighting, that kind of thing, so the change was justifiable."

Richard Woloski, who co-hosts the podcast *Skywalking Through Neverland*, believes that the actor's look in the Special had absolutely nothing to do with the car accident. "The makeup artists were trying to match Hamill's actual complexion in *A New Hope*," he suggests. "After working under the hot sun in Tunisia, he became very tan . . . I think [the Special's] makeup artists got notes on how they did Hamill's makeup but didn't factor in that the Holiday Special was being shot on videotape, which captures light and images infinitely different than film."

Bonnie Burton wrote and edited for Lucasfilm but has also spent many years performing in film, television, and theater. She has the most likely explanation for Hamill's excessive makeup, pointing out that, at the time, variety shows "felt like they were written, created, and maintained by people who do Broadway shows." Joe Layton had been a Broadway producer, and Ken and Mitzie Welch started out in musical theater. "When you have musical theater people in charge of something, they use that background for when they create television. . . . They're gonna cake it on a lot more in *theater*."

Joe Layton (*center*), shown here directing *Two by Two* on Broadway in 1970, was hired as a producer, having partnered with the Welches for years. He went back and forth between Broadway and variety TV, specializing in directing and choreographing divas like Barbra Streisand, Cher, Diana Ross, Bette Midler, and Raquel Welch. *Photofest*

Carrie Fisher, meanwhile, had actual showbiz blood in her veins as the daughter of Debbie Reynolds and Eddie Fisher. A few years before *Star Wars*, she had made something of a name for herself in a small but memorable part alongside Warren Beatty in Hal Ashby's *Shampoo*. But, like her co-stars, she was hesitant to participate. One piece of lore that has often been shared about the Special is that Fisher had a serious singing career in her sights, and that she was so determined to bring it to fruition that she told the Special's producers that if they gave her a singing part, she might be amenable to the idea. However, although this claim was promulgated for years, it has been countered by both Mitzie and Ken Welch—the actual producers of the show. They insisted that Fisher did *not* ask to sing, and that, "in fact, she resisted" the concept when it was eventually proposed.

Fisher is not on record giving her own version of this, but the Welches' contention makes sense, since TV variety casts are usually required to sing, and Hamill and Ford were certainly not going to go down that road. It makes more sense, then, that the producers *needed* her to sing, so they asked her to.

Besides, the Fisher that most people knew was not a scheming, driven person desperate to risk everything to make it in Hollywood. She was born into the industry, and once she achieved mega-success from *Star Wars* and became an actual celebrity in her own right, she did everything she could to *destroy* that star persona. She was actually more of an "anti-star" than anything, not scared to say something that might offend others or, God forbid, jeopardize her standing in the industry. She always seemed more than willing to jettison her stardom out the escape-pod hatch rather than do something that went against her core beliefs. Far from a sell-out, she was real—and she didn't seem to be even remotely thrilled to have the opportunities she had in show business that today's actors would die for.

Anthony Daniels and Peter Mayhew would require less convincing, and from early on they were amenable to flying in from London to shoot the special. Daniels had already had his first taste of American television as part of the *Star Wars* segment on *Donny and Marie*. In London, he worked as a stage and radio actor—and a busy one at that, having won the annual Carlton Hobbs Award for most performances with the BBC's Radio Repertory Company. He had been fairly grateful when he was cast in *Star Wars*, so when the request came down the pike to participate in the Special, he signed on immediately. This is not to say he wouldn't eventually come to despise it viciously, however.

Peter Mayhew seemed genuinely flattered by the request. Following his death in 2019, Harrison Ford praised Mayhew for his "great dignity and noble character"—qualities that can be found in a 1998 interview he gave twenty years after the Special's only broadcast: "It was a wonderful surprise, coming when it did, and to suddenly get an invitation to become part of a show which benefitted the Wookiee family and showed where they lived was marvelous."

"An *invitation*," Mayhew called it, echoing Daniels's gracious acceptance of the offer, as opposed to how Hamill, Fisher, and Ford responded to it. Maybe it was a British thing. Either way, all of the main cast members were now booked, and the producers were finally ready to start shooting.

CHAPTER 5

INTRODUCING BOBA FETT

ONE PART OF the Special would be created largely apart from the rest of the production, creatively, logistically, and geographically: an animated segment that is widely considered to be the best part of it.

In the initial meeting between Lucas and the production team, Vilanch recalls him telling the group that he had come up with ten *Star Wars* stories and was planning on making six movies. There were four other stories that he wanted to produce a bit differently, "and one of them was *Boba Fett*."

In fact, the development of this animated segment goes back even further than that. According to LucasBooks' Jonathan Rinzler, Boba Fett originated as a character that was being developed for *The Empire Strikes Back*. "They needed a new character [for the franchise]. They needed it to be a kind of super bad guy, and so George's original idea was to do a 'Super Stormtrooper.'"

Scott Kirkwood, the man behind www.starwarsholidayspecial.com, explains that this Super Stormtrooper was a sort of "elite version . . . like the Green Berets of stormtroopers. They were basically 'shock-troopers,' and they had this all-white outfit with all extra weapons and armor that was different from the regular stormtroopers."

However, the alterations made to this outfit would prove too costly for Lucas, considering he didn't want just one of them—he wanted a small army. So, Lucas decided to have the film's art director (and future filmmaker) Joe Johnston and concept artist Ralph McQuarrie modify their "shock-trooper" design. "And, once they decided to change this character, it became the concept for Boba Fett," says Kirkwood.

"The character went through several incarnations," Rinzler explained, until finally, "Lucas decided that—in terms of the story he was working out—Boba Fett being a bounty hunter would make much more sense." So, Lucas changed the character "from working uniquely for the Empire and made him more like a mysterious Clint Eastwood bounty-hunter character—somebody who could kind of stand up to Darth Vader in the film. And so it was excellent from a storytelling point of view."

However, as Vilanch recalls, Lucas had still not fully fleshed out his character—much less figured out how he would fit into the story of *The Empire Strikes Back*. So, when Lucas was in the midst of sketching out the Special with the writers, he thought, why not make Boba Fett's story into a "mini adventure" and somehow shoehorn it in?

"They were doing this holiday special, and there wasn't much of our involvement," Lucas said in a recent interview. "But I came up with the idea of, why don't we take the Boba Fett character and put him in that—make a little movie out of it."

Ultimately, Lucas decided to make a shorter animated sequence featuring Boba Fett and offer it exclusively for the Special. Ripps and Proft would then be saddled with having to figure out a creative way to insert this isolated story into the Special. This would offer audiences a sneak preview of a brand new character eighteen months before Boba Fett's big-screen debut—a move that would relieve the pressure Lucas was feeling to keep *Star Wars* alive until the release of *The Empire Strikes Back*.

Acomba, being a Canadian native, knew of a Toronto-based animation studio, Nelvana, and showed Lucas the holiday film they'd created the previous year, *A Cosmic Christmas*. Lucas was impressed and had Fox reach out to Nelvana to see if they would be interested in producing a ten-minute animated Boba Fett segment for the Special.

In January 1978, Nelvana co-founder Michael Hirsh got a call from Fox, asking if he would be interested in coming out to San Francisco to pitch for the gig. The three Nelvana founders discussed the job—which was budgeted at somewhere between $75,000 and $100,000—and, knowing they would probably barely break even, still decided to rub a couple of nickels together and see if they could afford to send Hirsh to San Francisco to pitch their production company directly to Lucas.

When Hirsh and his colleagues said they were broke, they meant it. Nelvana's animation studio was not exactly a hub for glitz and glamour. It was a small start-up that consisted of a half-dozen animators and a director, with offices on one of the upper floors of the Terminal Warehouse in the harbor-front area of Toronto, right off Lake Ontario.

"They had some sort of smelting business going on," Nelvana animation director Clive Smith recalls of his office neighbor. "It just happened to be right next door to us, a guy who did gefilte fish or something—some horrible thing. Once a month, he'd come and process some of this product, and the smell was absolutely hideous."

Hirsh flew to San Francisco and rented a car to get to Lucas's digs in San Rafael. He was given specific directions to a shopping mall, then told to call the office from a payphone. Then someone flagged him down and escorted him through a storefront entrance. On arrival there, he was told that the editors were working on a sequence for *The Empire Strikes Back*: "They said, 'Close your eyes and we'll walk you back.'"

Hirsh followed the directions, only to learn that Lucas had changed plans and had gone home early. So, Miki Herman escorted him to Lucas's house, which Hirsh immediately identified from the World War I–era cannon in the front yard.

Lucas took Hirsh to his car and suggested lunch at Taco Bell. The nearly penniless Hirsh was feeling quite stressed, and he hoped Lucas wasn't expecting this potential vendor to buy him lunch, even if it was just Taco Bell.

To Hirsh's delight, however, Nelvana was offered the job, meaning they had beaten out the likes of animation heavyweights Fox and Hanna-Barbera. Lucas told him he'd chosen Nelvana because he loved supporting independent filmmakers—and the fact that they were working not in Hollywood but in Toronto only solidified his choice. He knew that larger outfits typically sent their animation requests overseas, and he liked that the film was going to be completely produced in Toronto.

Lucas had already sent Nelvana a ten-page treatment for a cartoon called "The Story of The Faithful Wookiee," which would eventually become a sixteen-page script. As with the rest of the Special, the cartoon's main plot originated with Lucas. In it, Luke and the droids are searching for Han and Chewbacca, who have gone missing, when they crash-land onto a planet. After meeting Boba Fett, they discover that Han has been infected by a "talisman virus" that renders him comatose, and soon Luke becomes infected as well. Boba Fett, Chewbacca, and the droids manage to secure a serum that cures them, but soon they learn that Boba Fett has been secretly working for the Empire. Once our heroes discover this, he makes his escape by jetpack.

Special writer Rod Warren had taken Lucas's treatment and was isolating which specific scenes they wanted animated so that animation director Clive Smith and his crew could move ahead and attempt to meet their challenging deadline. Ripps and Proft soon found a way for the cartoon to be semi-organically incorporated into the story: while the Imperial stormtroopers and guards are searching the home of Chewbacca's family, the lead guard orders Malla to keep her son quiet. She gives Lumpy a small video player, equipped with headphones, which allows him to watch the cartoon. "It was like a little viewing thing, like—what do you call it?—it's like a Game Boy or something like that, which hadn't been invented yet," Clive Smith recalls. "She gives her son this little toy, and when he plays it, this animated piece that we did is dropped into that toy."

However, it looked like Nelvana had potentially bitten off much more than they could draw. Not only was Smith given the shortest turnaround he'd ever been given for a project, but Lucas wanted them to animate his cartoon in a very specific way: he wanted Hamill, Fisher, and Ford depicted "loosely enough that they would not look like human actors rotoscoped but also carefully enough that they would not look like grotesque caricatures," Smith said in a 1998 interview. The animators' biggest challenge issue was that he was an original character without much of a reference. They would have to make sure that the costume designers for *Empire* were in alignment with the way Nelvana was depicting him.

Smith was a huge fan of the second-hand look of *Star Wars*, particularly its "roughness": "I love the fact that everything was beaten up and lived in. We wanted to get that kind of real-world quality into the animation, too, and not make it too pristine."

Conceptual designer James Carson, who worked on *Star Wars Episode VIII: The Last Jedi*, calls the style of that film "a kind of a junkyard brutalism," noting the "heavily recycled, worn-out look" that Tatooine became known for. "It could be symbolic for the result of the Empire's oppression on the tiny planet that left most of its population to scavenge for what they needed, doing whatever they could do to acquire parts for their kludged-together weapons, hardware, and transportation—giving all of the objects on the planet a used, makeshift look."

When Luke sees the Millennium Falcon for the first time, he cries out, "What a piece of junk!" Han then explains his ship's true strength: "She'll make point-five past light speed. She may not look like much, but she's got it where it counts." Translated: *Don't judge a book by its cover, Skywalker.*

Herman, as the liaison between Lucasfilm and Nelvana, was given explicit directions from Lucas that the cartoon should be drawn in the style of Moebius. Moebius was the pseudonym for Jean Giraud, the late French illustrator whose combination of psychedelic fantasy and surrealism helped launch a modern sci-fi movement in the late 1960s. Although he also gained notoriety creating conceptual designs for such visually striking films as *Tron*, *Alien*, and *The Abyss*, illustrating comic books was where he made his mark in modern art.

Carson describes Moebius's style as being somewhat influenced by Japanese art of the 1800s, specifically Katsushika Hokusai's 1831 drawing "The Great Wave," calling it "highly stylized" and "dominated by a strong use of shapes. Every so often, someone comes around who breaks conventions, and that's what Moebius did in the late '60s. He took art to another level."

Lucas was a huge fan of Moebius—so much so that, ten years later, he asked the legendary artist to work with him on his 1988 fantasy film *Willow*. "In all his drawings, Moebius demonstrates a command of many disciplines in art," Lucas writes in his foreword to *The Art of Moebius*. "He is a master draftsman, a superb artist, his vision is original and strong. Since first seeing the Moebius illustrations in *Heavy Metal* years ago, I have been impressed and affected by his keen and unusual sense of design, and the distinctive way in which he depicts the fantastic. Perhaps what strikes me most of all his work is its sheer beauty—a beauty that has always given me great pleasure."

Back in Toronto, Smith needed no schooling on Moebius. Every teenager who read *Heavy Metal* magazine dreamt of creating art like his. Smith was already a huge fan and was heavily influenced by Moebius's lengthy comic-strip series *The Airtight Garage of Jerry Cornelius*, considered by many to be the high point of his career. "It was a beautiful style," Smith recalls. "We kind of based the visuals, the imagery, on that. And that wasn't dictated to us. We didn't get any kind of particular direction for how [Lucas] wanted to go with it visually. It worked very well because it was simple [and] had kind of a comic-book quality to it, kind of a flat quality to it, which was nice." Many feel that the decision to draw the Boba Fett adventure in a Moebius animation style was the key to its eventual critical success.

Because of the tight deadline for this animation project, Smith and his right-hand layout artist, Frank Nissen, needed to simplify the artwork. Whether the art for this cartoon was derived from a photo, a sketch, a drawing, or a real-life object, they needed to streamline their drawings by limiting the number of lines they were using. The more lines the animator had to draw, the longer the project would take to animate.

Nissen says the illustrators from Lucasfilm sent up drawings of the cartoon's main characters—Han Solo, Princess Leia, Luke Skywalker, and Chewbacca—so that they could begin "interpreting" them and transforming the film's real-life cast members into drawings. For each image they sent, they also included a short paragraph describing each character.

Apparently, Lucasfilm's initial biography for Boba Fett explained that he was a bounty hunter and that he was "scruffy and beat up," so Nissen added dents to his armor and various scratches on his helmet. He also felt inspired to add a string of Wookiee scalps over Boba Fett's shoulder.

Nissen updated the character write-up to include background information on those Wookiee scalps, explaining that, at some point, Boba Fett would have come across some Wookiees "that he had to do away with, and his way of commemorating his victory is to have a piece of Wookiee scalp." Nissen then sent it, along with the other character drawings and mini-bios, back to Lucasfilm.

A few weeks later, Nissen says, the drawings were sent back to him with revisions, including the one of Boba Fett, which had been "cleaned up. No dents, no scratches, no scuffs, no Wookiee scalps."

Lucasfilm's revised write-up for the character also omitted the fact that he was a bounty hunter. "They took that out, for whatever reason," says Nissen, who thought, above everything, that they were passing up on a good storyline. "*Star Wars* is an amalgam of so many things. One of the things is, it's a Western. It's a Western in space. So, to give up this bounty hunter thing, I thought, 'Man, they're really passing up a good thing here.'"

Nissen spoke with Hirsh, who was Nelvana's liaison for the *Star Wars* project. Nissen told him to tell Lucasfilm that "the coolest part about him is that he was a bounty hunter. So I harassed Michael, and I can only assume that he must have talked to them, because the next time that all the stuff came [back], he was a bounty hunter again."

Of course, what Boba Fett is most known for is his accessories—specifically his weapon. And Boba Fett's was quite unusual. Some would describe it as a ray gun. Some might call it a stun gun.

Nissen says that a writer never offers visual details about something as specific as the type of weapon Boba Fett would use, so it wasn't described in the script he was given. In this case, he adds, the writer was basically asking the designer to create it themselves. "Scripts never articulate that kind of detail," explains Nissen. "Probably all the script said was, 'Boba Fett stuns [a] creature.' But what the gun looks like is entirely up to me."

These are the kinds of opportunities, Nissen adds, where he and other artists can get really creative and push the boundaries. "I gotta design a weapon," he continues, "but obviously it can't look like anything everybody's familiar with, because they don't wanna do that. So I had to sort of think about what can I do that will look like a weapon, have all the attributes of a weapon, yet look different. So I came up with the idea of, instead of one muzzle, there's two muzzles. That's essentially how it sort of came about."

The final version of Boba Fett's gun resembles a tuning fork more than anything, but thanks to the ever-present Moebius influence, Nissen and his crew managed to create the coolest-looking double-muzzle tuning fork ever toted by a bounty hunter.

In addition to the sketches and write-ups of Boba Fett that Lucasfilm was sending Nelvana, they also sent an eight-millimeter black-and-white video shot in *Star Wars* sound designer Ben Burtt's backyard. In the video, Burtt introduces the character, which is sound editor Duwayne Dunham in a prototype of the original Shock Trooper suit. Burtt interviews Dunham, testing the outfit's exterior speakers, as well as showing various high-tech accessories included in the uniform. "So, based on [that] footage—that kind of slightly out-of-focus and jittery footage—we came up with the design [for Boba Fett]," says Smith.

Nelvana's depiction of the characters, particularly Boba Fett, would all need Lucas's approval. Nowadays, sending images to one another is effortless. Forty-five years ago, however, Smith had to send the team's most recent artwork in hard copy via US Mail or FedEx, or bring it to Lucas in person. So, Smith pinned their storyboard frames around their storyboard room, then shot each one with a 35 mm camera to subsequently create a film strip that could be easily run through a projector.

Smith and Hirsh flew down to Los Angeles to present the current storyboards to Lucas and the Smith–Hemion production team. "That was sort of my first one-on-one meeting with George," Smith recalls. "That was where I met George, and I met the whole gang—the whole group, everybody. We were in this room with about ten or fifteen of them." Smith recalls also meeting Ben Burtt, Ralph McQuarrie, Miki Herman, and Charley Lippincott on that occasion. Considering the lack of crew from the Special in attendance, it's very likely that this "show-and-tell" presentation took place months before most of the crew was even assembled, likely in the late winter or early spring months of 1978.

Smith began describing the story frame by frame, "trying to read the nuances in this room of silent people and stone faces, not knowing if I was winning or losing. I kind of stood nervously for an hour with my overheating projector. I mean, I was just sweating. You know what it's like talking, giving a presentation, and you're getting no feedback? You don't know what they're thinking, whether they're thinking, 'Oh my God, who is this person?'"

After the final frame, Smith says, Lucas stood up from his seat and applauded, which allowed everybody else in the room to breathe. "He loved it," says Smith, adding that Lucas had no major notes and seemed to like everything they were doing. From that point on, Lucas backed off and allowed them to complete the cartoon on their own.

Soon after that, Hirsh booked a half day at a Los Angeles recording studio to record the voices of Hamill, Fisher, and Ford, who all arrived together for the session.

Hirsh admits that he struggled a bit when recording Fisher and Ford, claiming they both had flat voices. "That's what you get with Han Solo—you get this voice of quiet resignation," he says. When he asked both to provide alternative takes of some of their lines as an option in the post-production process, "Harrison and Carrie both said, 'Look, I've given you Han Solo, I've given you Princess Leia. That's the voice. That's the take.'

"They knew their characters," Hirsh adds. "I was fine with that because none of the lines in the [cartoon] really depended upon their dramatic reading."

Hamill was different. He had done voiceover work as a child actor, and he knew that giving alternative takes with different inflections would provide more options for the director.

"Mark Hamill had done voices as a kid and really loved doing them," Hirsh says. "So he gave me multiple takes. He understood what I was going for, because, in animation, a lot of the acting comes from the voice. I had all these [alternative] readings from Mark Hamill because he was prepared to do take after take to get the nuance. And [his] character frankly had more lines in the [cartoon]."

Hirsh adds that Hamill seemed more invested in the process. "Luke is a guy who's much more of an excited kid," he adds. "You know, enthusiastic. Carrie and Harrison left very quickly. Mark, who loved to do voices, just stayed, and we chatted and talked about animation."

Like a kid in a candy store, Hamill stayed for several hours, picking Hirsh's brain with the enthusiasm of someone whose career would mysteriously move from television and film acting to a new world of voiceover—and faster than even he expected.

By September of 1978, Lucas was curious about the Boba Fett character Nelvana had designed. He had figured out a way to insert the bounty hunter into *The Empire Strikes Back*, though he would be far from a significant character. The film designers had added a poncho to the costume, which gave the bounty hunter a more mysterious look—a nod to Clint Eastwood's "Man with No Name" gunslinger from the trio of Sergio Leone spaghetti Western films of the 1960s.

At the time, Lucas was living in the small town of San Anselmo in Marin County, which held an annual county fair that featured a parade. Lucas had offered to have Darth Vader walk in the parade and then decided to have Boba Fett walk alongside him. So, on September 24, 1978—two months before his animated debut in the upcoming *Star Wars Holiday Special,* and two years before his film debut in *The Empire Strikes Back*—Boba Fett made his international debut in this small town in Northern California.

According to Dave Filoni, who oversees all of Lucasfilm's animation projects, "It's hard to imagine a local parade where *Star Wars* characters— not just like people in costumes [but] the actual screen-used costumes—are walking down the street . . . but that's exactly what happened."

There exists at least one surviving home video of the parade, showing children ecstatic at the sight of this mysterious associate of Darth Vader, not knowing who he was at all. "It was a strange sight, because Boba [Fett] hadn't been put on film yet and become well known," says Burtt.

Lucasfilm senior writer Pete Vilmur describes the parade appearance as a huge success: "Vader was a known quantity at the time, but the fans definitely responded to Fett."

Boba Fett's inclusion in the Special would become its one saving grace.

CHAPTER 6
TAPING BEGINS

AS THE HOT summer days began to beat down on the crew, whether they were working at Smith–Hemion's Sunset–Doheny offices, rehearsing at the Methodist Church in Hollywood, or building the massive set at Warner Bros Studios in Burbank, everyone was hoping things would settle a bit once taping began. A steady hand at the wheel would soon be somewhat of a luxury for these captive crew members.

However, the sudden and unexpected departure of Charley Lippincott, who had steered Lucas and company into producing this Special, jolted many. Although he had been there from the beginning, he had been having issues with the new corporate atmosphere at Lucasfilm, and things had finally come to a head.

In the latter part of 1977, with *Star Wars* still occupying theaters, the company definitely needed a more finely tuned organizational structure. The scrappy startup was now expanding in several different directions, and Lucas was up to his ears in projects. Pre-production for *The Empire Strikes Back* was taking up most of his time, but he was also producing the sequel to *American Graffiti* and developing a script for *Raiders of the Lost Ark* with Steven Spielberg, as well as supervising his newly created Industrial Light and Magic visual-effects division, which was being bombarded with business.

Lucas had hired Charles Weber, a real-estate specialist, to be Lucasfilm's new CEO. Weber, who had little or no entertainment experience, immediately recruited Sid Ganis and Susan Trembly from Warner Bros to run Lucasfilm's new marketing and publicity department, which cut significantly into Lippincott's responsibilities. "When he went to work, Charley was the biggest

Star Wars fan in the world, and he thought he had the best job in the world," says Lucas biographer Dale Pollock. However, "I think in his time there, that turned into something else that was *not* the best job in the world."

Weber's current online biography for NOVA Filmhouse claims that in his three years at Lucasfilm, the company grew from two people to over four hundred employees. Kermit Eller was there. "I watched the corporation happen," he recalls. "It was a little plucky band of like seven, eight people that were Lucasfilm, basically. Then they started making a lot of money and expanding and . . . they just hired a whole bunch of people that came in and said, 'Obviously your success is because of my efforts.'" The original half-dozen were soon deemed "irrelevant baggage by the time the new arrivals got in and start[ed] putting their stamp on everything. These same [original] staffers used to joke about how the Rebellion had become the Empire," Eller adds. "That's exactly what happened."

One early Lucasfilm employee questions Weber's math, however, as he clearly recalls being part of a large contingent of employees long before Weber was even hired. Either way, Lippincott longed for the pre-Weber days, when he worked with a smaller group of creatives, all dedicated to the success of *Star Wars*. It wasn't *like* a family, it *was* one: editor Marcia and George Lucas were a couple; Kurtz's assistant was his sister-in-law; Lippincott's girlfriend, Carol Wikarska, was head of publications, and his neighbor was their editor.

In those days, Lippincott practically ate and slept *Star Wars*. Pollock describes him as "The *Star Wars* Guy . . . that's how he was known. And so, once that possibility existed where he wasn't going to be that anymore, that was a major issue for him. I think it's why he turned bitter and resentful."

One would think that having a moniker like "The *Star Wars* Guy" would be flattering at the offices of Lucasfilm, particularly in the summer of 1977, just months into the jaw-dropping run that *Star Wars* was on at the time. But for Weber, Lippincott's association with *Star Wars* dated him. "I think the company outgrew him," Weber explains of Lippincott's sudden marginalization. "Lippincott was an outside person. He was never part of the corporate structure."

Referring to the vice president of advertising, publicity, promotion, and merchandising for the Star Wars Corporation—a man who two years earlier had left working for Alfred Hitchcock to join Lucas's grassroots efforts—as an "*outside person*" seems outrageously dismissive. But while Weber acknowledges that Lippincott was "very good," he describes his responsibilities as just being those of "a PR guy" whose input was not needed much anymore.

To Lippincott, it seemed a few people were attempting to lessen his massive accomplishments by redefining his wide range of responsibilities for the years he worked at Lucasfilm to those of a mere publicist. After he died in 2020, his widow, Bumpy, took over his Facebook page, posting pictures and other film memorabilia. She also likely posted the following comments under there: "A *Publicist* does not pitch SW to Fox Board of Directors to get budget approval," and "A *Publicist* does not go to NY Toy Fair and pick merchandise to license." Also posted: "Charley would roll over in his grave if his legacy was only 'Star Wars Publicist.'"

Former Lucasfilm SVP Sid Ganis, who would stay at the company for seven years, counters Weber's rewriting of history, specifically his lessening of Lippincott's long list of responsibilities. "That's not fair, because Charley Lippincott, as I understand it, was really very close to George and his thinking. So 'just a PR guy' is not fair. I know he was much more able and sophisticated in the world of media in those days to be dismissed."

It would be pretty outrageous for anyone to dismiss Lippincott at that point of *Star Wars'* trajectory, particularly the CEO at the time. The comic deal with Marvel and the novelization by Ballantine were strokes of genius; Lippincott skillfully negotiated both media moguls to publish their *Star Wars* content one month (Marvel) and six months (Ballantine) before one fan had even seen the film.

In fact, this "PR guy" was so involved with the creative aspect of *Star Wars* at that early time frame that the novel's ghostwriter, Alan Dean Foster, referenced him in the novel. At one point, Chewbacca is concerned that Han Solo has gotten lost while being pursued by evading stormtroopers on the Death Star. Han defends his skills.

"Of course I can find the ship from here—Corellians can't get lost."

There comes another, slightly accusing growl. Solo shrugs.

"Tocneppil doesn't count. He wasn't a Correllian. Besides, I was drunk."

Tocneppil was certainly not a Correllian. It was Lippincott's last name spelled backward.

According to Weber, Lippincott's role became redundant after he hired

Ganis and Trembly to oversee Lucasfilm's marketing and publicity. "[Now] we had our own merchandising department. We had our own publishing department. I mean, we were rolling."

Lippincott was fully aware that Lucasfilm was successfully "rolling" after the success of *Star Wars*. Prior to Weber's arrival, nearly all of the advertising, publicity, promotions, publishing, and merchandising for *Star Wars* was being done by Lippincott and his ex-girlfriend, Carol Wikarska. (According to Lippincott, this was a relationship that he sacrificed for the film: "I was young and at the point of my life where *Star Wars* meant more to me than my girlfriend.")

Soon, Lippincott's responsibilities were being taken away from him. According to a source who worked with both men at Lucasfilm (and who asked not to be identified), Weber arrived telling Lucas that Lippincott didn't know what he was doing and that he'd signed a merchandising deal with Kenner Toys too soon, costing the company millions of dollars in profit. Weber made it known that "if only he'd been there, he would've made much better deals for George on all the licensing and everything. And there would've been so much more money."

According to this source, instead of just letting Lippincott go, Lucasfilm's management chose a more humiliating approach, slowly peeling off most of his duties and giving them to Weber's newly hired people. Subsequently, he was also stripped of the many job titles he had worked day and night to earn.

Finally, when the man who has been credited with creating the initial buzz for *Star Wars* was left without any significant role at the company, he accepted 20th Century Fox's offer to supervise the marketing of its new science-fiction film, *Alien*, which was filming in the UK.

The man who was at least *partially* responsible for making Lucasfilm a mother lode of revenue also left without any significant financial compensation for himself, just a pocketful of war stories.

Weber lasted two more years before Lucas fired him in 1980. When Lucas initially hired him, he had told Weber he had no interest in increasing his overhead; he just wanted Lucasfilm to be able to finance and produce independent films. However, when Weber then asked Lucas for $50 million to invest in other companies—suggesting he sell Skywalker Ranch to help raise the revenue—an infuriated Lucas fired him and then let half of the Los Angeles office go.

According to biographer Pollock, Lucas's career is full of people leaving his projects feeling bitter and resentful: "He tends to use people up and move on." Pollock cites Gary Kurtz, who would part ways with Lucas after *The Empire Strikes Back*, as another example of someone who really left "feeling that he had been screwed, shafted, pushed out of the picture. ... You see these bodies all through Lucas's career."

The victims of Lucas's imperial entanglements also include *Star Wars* digital-effects guru John Dykstra and associate producer Jim Nelson. Dykstra was notoriously behind on the ILM effects (although he won an Oscar for producing them), and Lucas felt Nelson did not deserve an AP credit, saying he didn't contribute anything artistic to the film and would instead be listed among less-important positions.

Lucas also had a falling out with his former agent, Jeff Berg of ICM, over *The Empire Strikes Back*. Berg had represented Lucas for several years and negotiated his *American Graffiti* deal for Universal, as well as the *Star Wars* deal with Fox, which allowed Lucas to retain half of the merchandising rights and all of the sequel rights.

For *Star Wars*, ICM received its standard ten percent of Lucas's gross earnings, which was almost $5 million in commission. Lucas had no issues with ICM continuing to collect commissions from that deal, but since he was no longer using them as his agent, he didn't feel they were owed anything on the sequel. Although Lucas says he was happy with Berg, he was reportedly frustrated that Berg didn't pressure Fox hard enough for the sequel rights to *Star Wars*, which he says he acquired on his own through his friend Laddie, who now, more than ever, was Lucas's biggest cheerleader at the company.

The dispute escalated into a lawsuit that was eventually sent to arbitration. In 1980, a decision was made in Lucas's favor, setting a precedent throughout the industry. Former ICM agent Richard Brustein says that the decision resulted in losses in the tens of millions for ICM and dramatically changed the way contracts were written, how clients were represented, and how projects were pitched to networks and studios throughout the industry.

Lucas's grudges are not limited to disagreements he had over *Star Wars*. He held resentment toward the executives behind his previous films, *THX*

1138 and *American Graffiti*. While he was shopping *Raiders of the Lost Ark* to studios, Lucas reportedly would not pitch to Universal until its production chief, Ned Tanen, apologized to him for editing four minutes out of *American Graffiti*. He did the same to Ted Ashley, making him apologize for gutting five minutes out of *THX 1138* before he would even begin to entertain discussing *Raiders* with Warner. "Lucas had a very Old Testament view of not forgiving," Kurtz said. "Once he was wronged, he would always remember it."

Ashley was not the only *THX 1138* collaborator Lucas held resentment toward. "Lucas felt that Coppola just rolled over and did whatever Warner Bros wanted him to do," Pollock says. "And that's really, frankly, why [years later] Lucas did not want him involved with *Star Wars*. If that had been a good relationship and Francis had fought for the film, Lucas would've not needed to hire Gary Kurtz—he could have hired a simple line producer." And, of course, this is not to omit the disdain for—and subsequent retaliation against—Warner's Frank Wells.

However, of all Lucas's imperial entanglements, the lawsuit that resulted from comments he made about the Kenner Toys deal forged by Lippincott and former Fox VP Marc Pevers is one of his messiest. While being interviewed by Pollock for his first biography, Lucas called Lippincott and Pevers's Kenner Toys deal a "stupid decision" that had lost him "tens of millions." These claims subsequently appeared in Pollock's book, *Skywalking*, following the publication of which Pevers sued Lucas and others for libel: in his view, Lucas was claiming that the deal was his fault, even though Star Wars Corp. had signed the contract. After three years, Lucas eventually settled out of court.

Lippincott was another victim, but he chose not to enter into the libel lawsuit against Lucas, instead holding in his bitter resentment for decades. However, as time went on, he learned through public disclosures that Lucas and Kurtz had given out shares of *Star Wars* profits to other collaborators such as composer John Williams, sound editor Ben Burtt, and the law firm of Pollock, Rigrod, and Bloom.

By 2015, Lippincott had decided he could not hold back anymore. "I'm ambivalent about my work on *Star Wars*," he wrote on his blog. "On one hand, I'm proud. On the other hand, I'm bitter. The more I read of *Star Wars*' financial success, the bitterer I get. I know people who have been able to retire off of points from a successful film who did less than I did. . . . I know, had I been given my due for building the *Star Wars* franchise, I would be eating better than instant noodles."

However, Lippincott also indicated that the money was less important to him. His most prized asset—to *him*, anyway—was the unrevised history of *Star Wars* that he was collecting, preserving, and sharing with fans all over the world. In his separation agreement, Lippincott said, "All *Star Wars*–related papers and materials were to have been returned to Lucasfilm." This included potentially thousands of pieces of original artwork, sketches, illustrations, promotional posters, scripts, letters, and agreements in Lippincott's possession.

However, after he abruptly left Lucasfilm to start his gig on *Alien*, he neglected to pack up his office, so it was packed up for him and placed in an offsite storage facility separate from the Lucasfilm property. In Lippincott's view, this inadvertently created "The Lippincott Archives," whose contents he maintained from 1978 until his death in 2020.

For years, Lippincott had insisted he was supposed to be paid residuals on Jonathan Rinzler's book *The Making of Star Wars*, to which he allegedly contributed elements. Since he had never received any payments, many advised him to go after Lucasfilm—now a division of Disney—for money he was owed on the book. However, going after the residuals could have meant losing the archives.

That wasn't an option for Lippincott. The current history of *Star Wars* has been written under the watchful eye of Lucasfilm, and Lippincott was concerned that its true history might never get told. "Lucas's ex-wife Marcia can be written out of history," Lippincott blogged in 2015. "His former producer Gary Kurtz can be written out of history. *I* can be written out of history." Up until now, he noted, he had lived without any additional financial benefits or rewards from the work he did on *Star Wars*. "So I can die without them."

However, Pevers says that before *Star Wars* was released, Fox *did* give Lippincott a bonus for his merchandising efforts. Just before the release of the film, Pevers says, Lucas's attorney, Jake Bloom, called him to ask if Lippincott could receive some additional compensation for handling product approvals and servicing licensees. According to Pevers, Bloom had initially suggested giving ten percent of all *Star Wars* merchandising revenue to Lippincott. Pevers liked Lippincott immensely and wanted to make sure he was paid fairly, but he thought it a tad excessive to give him ten percent of all the licensing revenue, *in perpetuity*. Pevers also wondered whether Lucas would approve.

After crunching some numbers, Pevers estimated that the initial revenue from *Star Wars* would be about $750,000, so he amended Bloom's offer by making that the *ceiling*. This would limit Lippincott's earnings to ten percent of the first $750,000, as opposed to making Fox–Lucasfilm his lifetime benefactor.

Pevers called up Lippincott and offered him the money as a bonus, asking him to choose between taking the $75,000 in payments or in a lump sum. Lippincott chose the latter and picked up his check at Fox. Many years later, when Lippincott was blogging about never receiving any bonuses for the extraordinary revenue he made for Fox and Lucasfilm, Pevers reminded him of that one-time payment from 1977. However, the sweat equity Lippincott had spent generating billions in *Star Wars* revenue for Lucasfilm was far, far greater than $75,000.

The relationship between Lippincott and Lucas continued to cool over the years—particularly after Lippincott began his relentless anti-Lucasfilm blogging campaign. However, after his death, Lucas publicly recognized him for changing the film business by bringing the fans directly into the marketing process. "Charley was one of the founding pillars of the *Star Wars* films and phenomenon," Lucas said in a press release. "[He] was the one who said early on that 'we can make this work' and was the first person to both develop *Star Wars* licensing and engage with the fans. He had insights into marketing and public relations that were truly unparalleled."

Mark Hamill wrote, "When it came to marketing a movie no one was interested in, his out-of-the-box ideas showed everyone how it could be done. We had so much fun on the 1st world tour . . . imagine trying to explain that movie to someone who had never seen it!"

* * *

As troubling as Lippincott's departure from the Special was, another key figure was increasingly absent, someone even more vital to the project: Lucas himself, who had silently slipped out the back door and had not been seen or heard from for a while.

At the time, Kurtz blamed Lucas's absence on him being swamped with several film projects—and, in his defense, he was indeed quite inundated. *The Empire Strikes Back, Raiders of the Lost Ark*, and *More American Graffiti* were all pulling Lucas farther away from the Holiday Special. Commitments like these took away his focus and were one of the main reasons why Charles Weber had been hired.

"We knew that we were not going to spend any more time with [Lucas]," Ripps recalls. "I mean, he had much bigger fish to fry."

Vilanch thinks that although Lucas had serious time constraints, the real reason he left was because he was uncomfortable working in the TV variety genre. "I don't think George realized that he picked the wrong format in which to do these stories. That wouldn't happen today. But then, forty years ago, this was the style. And so it was executed by people who did these things all the time."

Ripps says he didn't think Lucas expected the Special to be "so much of a traditional variety show," adding that he didn't have the time or the interest to learn about it. When they were assembling the plot with Lucas, he adds, "it never occurred to [us] that Harvey Korman and Bea Arthur and Art Carney were going to be in it."

Lucas had not formally quit, per se, but Vilanch says that by the time shooting had begun, he had "detached himself from the show because he suddenly realized what it was going to be. I don't think he ever envisioned a show with guest stars and numbers. I think he envisioned a show where a team was going to write original material and all the songs were going to be organic, and he didn't realize it was going to become what it became. And so he just got outta Dodge."

* * *

Warner Bros has been shooting films on its massive studio complex—referred to at the time as the Burbank Studios—for over a hundred years, starting with just a few soundstages and expanding to become one of the largest studios in the world. In 1935, the company began construction of what is now referred to as Stage 2; dozens of movies and television shows would be shot there, but one of the most infamous is Brian De Palma's legendary turkey, the 1990 adaption of Tom Wolfe's bestselling novel *Bonfire of the Vanities*. The film, about Wall Street in the 1980s, lost a staggering $31 million and was such a disaster that the cinematic catastrophe *itself* became a bestselling book by Julie Salamon called *The Devil's Candy: The Bonfire of the Vanities Goes to Hollywood*. De Palma, obviously not sensing he was propelling a Titanic at the time, had invited Salamon to follow him around on set, resulting in a lurid first-person account of the excesses and chaos of the film's production. It came close to replacing Michael Cimino's *Heaven's Gate* as the shorthand for expensive, large-scale projects doomed to fail because no one had the business acumen to keep the budget under control.

If you believe in curses, just ten years before *Bonfire*, Smith–Hemion leased the same stage to shoot all of its scenes for the *Star Wars Holiday Special*.

The first day of taping on Stage 2 was August 22, 1978. While several rehearsals by the guest comedians—Bea Arthur, Harvey Korman, and Art Carney—had taken place in the Smith–Hemion offices, other acts, like the holographic circus performers, had rehearsed at the Hollywood United Methodist Church, just north of the infamous Hollywood and Highland intersection.

When stage manager Mike Erwin walked in on that first day, he couldn't help but notice Acomba. "There was this sort of a frenetic guy with long, wild hair jumping around," Erwin recalled. A fellow stage manager, Peter Barth, filled him in: "That's our director," he said, adding an eye roll. Acomba's manner caused a bit of confusion, as most of the personnel were used to having the elder, stoic Hemion at the helm. "[Hemion] was like a Buddha of directing," Erwin said, "and he always had people surrounding him, waiting for morsels of wisdom."

One of the things that struck Erwin immediately about Acomba was that no one was paying attention to him. "He was kind of bouncing off the walls. He was just amped, you know—overzealous. 'Frenetic' is the best word for it. He was like an atom or something, bouncing around. He just came in and started idea-throwing, and idea-throwing doesn't really work."

The first scene scheduled to be taped that morning was "The Gormaanda Show," a sketch written by Mitzie Welch (and most likely punched up by Rod Warren) that featured Korman as a four-armed alien version of Julia Child. Costume designer Bob Mackie says that Gormaanda's look was adapted from Mother Marcus on *The Carol Burnett Show*, "a big Jewish mama with big boobs and a funny character."

Bob Mackie, the costume stylist for both *The Carol Burnett Show* and the Special, said that Harvey Korman (*left, with Burnett*) "loved to dress in drag." He adds that the alien Julia Child character Korman plays in the Special was very similar from his recurring role of big-bosomed Mother Marcus in Burnett's show. *Author's collection*

According to Wookieepedia, Gormaanda is a four-star-rated TV chef who authored the book *Travels with Gormaanda: Cooking in the Core*. (The name Gormaanda derives from the word gourmand, which means "a person who is fond of good eating, often indiscriminatingly and to excess.") She is known for her unabashed excitement and for working so rapidly that all four of her arms are needed to prepare each dish.

"Harvey Korman is in a purple dress with silver hair and four arms," comedian Taran Killam says of the Gormaanda scene, "and that's still not the most weird thing that's happening in this film." Assisting Korman in the bit was the actor Mickey Morton, who was also scheduled to play Malla as well as the bouncer in the cantina scene the following day. Morton stood behind Korman and fed his arms under the comedian's shoulders to help create the four-armed cooking creature.

After Korman was shot as Gormaanda, the footage would then be played back on a television set in the Wookiee kitchen, so that Malla—and other viewers at home—can cook along with her. On this day, Gormaanda would be showing Kashyyyk households how to make "Bantha Surprise" (as a reminder, banthas are the large, furry mammals with spiral horns ridden by Tusken Raiders on the planet Tatooine in *A New Hope*), while Malla desperately tries to keep up with the manic preparations.

For Korman, playing a female character was a joy. "Harvey would wear anything I'd put on him," recalls Mackie, who had previously spent over a decade designing Korman's wardrobe at *The Carol Burnett Show*. "I mean anything and everything. He did like to get into drag because he was so good at it . . . he was so funny. You know, if you do drag and you're not funny, forget it."

The Special was one of Korman's first television appearances since Burnett had put the brakes on her variety show earlier that year. Like some of the greatest comedic talents, he had started out in the early 1960s in dramatic television, specifically on such shows as *Dr. Kildare*, *The Untouchables*, *Perry Mason*, and *Route 66*. One of the first roles Korman had as he transitioned into television comedy was as another alien: the voice of the Great Gazoo in the animated prime-time series *The Flintstones*.

During his eleven years on Burnett's show, Korman won four Emmy Awards for "Best Supporting Actor in a Musical or Comedy Show." He then catapulted to working in film, winning over audiences with brilliant comedic roles. "Mel Brooks adored him," Mackie recalls. "He put him in everything he could"—most famously as the evil Hedley Lamarr in *Blazing Saddles*.

Mitzie Welch, who had written dozens of parody songs for Korman on *The Carol Burnett Show*, had been intimidated at the prospect of writing actual comedy for him. "We tried the cooking thing, and I thought, 'Oh my gosh, this isn't going to be funny enough.'" However, the Gormaanda sketch would wind up being one of the more appreciated moments from the Special. When asked recently for something positive she remembers about the Special, Miki Herman cites the Korman bit as being her favorite, referring to Gormaanda's "stir, whip, stir, whip" technique: "Sometimes, when I'm cooking, that does come to mind. 'Stir, whip, stir, whip' . . . that is kind of unforgettable."

The Korman bit was also supposed to be one of the simpler scenes to shoot: one person, one camera, one angle. After all, they had scheduled to shoot it in the morning, giving Acomba the majority of the day to work with the circus tumblers and acrobats, whose hologram scene was likely to be far more complicated to shoot. However, the Korman shoot ran long, and it subsequently pushed back the whole day.

If there hadn't been such an ungodly cost for going into overtime, there would be nothing wrong with a comedian like Korman showing off his amazing improv skills and breaking up the crew members who were enjoying the show. On *this* set, however, there were approximately one hundred members of IATSE—the International Association of Technical Stage Engineers—who were working under a union agreement that assigned severe penalties to productions for late or missed lunches and breaks. But surely professionals like the producers for Smith–Hemion wouldn't wind up accruing overtime penalties.

Or would they?

★ ★ ★

Once Acomba had finally finished the Korman bit, he was ready to start shooting the two jugglers, the gymnast, and the ringmaster that choreographer David Winters had recruited. The Abderrahman family's Wazzan Troupe would be shot after that, so they were excused for lunch, the producers promising they would start shooting by 1 p.m.

"We'd have lunch, and lunch came and went, and then it was three," recalls Antar Abderrahman. "Then it was five, and it just kept getting pushed back more and more and more."

The Abderrahmans had been in Las Vegas, performing with a traveling circus, when their agent called with a last-minute offer to appear on the Special. The circus's promoter gave the family permission to leave for a few days, so they all flew to Los Angeles to shoot their segment.

While the Abderrahmans had been working professionally as a family for several years, the other four performers were a potpourri of varied talents. Winters had put out an open call for acrobats to audition for him at the Bel-Air Hotel. He asked candidates to perform a prepared routine and he subsequently hired four of the dozens that had auditioned.

Winters would also be directing the specific segment, which would appear in holographic form, similar to the scene in *Star Wars* where C-3PO and Chewbacca play a chess-like board game on the Millennium Falcon. The circus performers—with the help of advanced visual effects—would be shrunken and performing on a platform for the exclusive pleasure of Chewbacca's son, Lumpy.

Before the late 1970s, editors created effects like this using a Chroma-key system that allowed you to extract an image, manipulate it by reducing or enlarging it, and place it anywhere within the frame. "The Chroma key was an imperfect visual effect," says Newt Bellis, who owned several editing facilities from the 1970s through the 1990s and whose company, MVS Television Complex, supplied the Special with all of its camera, sound, lighting, and editing equipment. "It would add a blue wave or a halo around the keyed-out image, and the viewer could tell the effect was being keyed. That ruined the illusion."

Bellis explains that at the time the Special was taped, the Ultimatte was the new kid in town. A precursor to modern-day blue- or green-screen technology, it "was digital, and so it gave you a much sharper key." Joe Layton had located an Ultimatte system that the Special could use, which gave the producers the ability to maneuver the circus performers into any background they desired, but much more cleanly than ever before.

Winters was something of a legend by this time. He was most noted for appearing as A-Rab in the theatrical and film versions of *West Side Story*, but he had also danced regularly on such weekly variety shows as *Hullaballoo* and *Shindig!*, as well as choreographing such popular musicals as *Pajama Party* and *Viva Las Vegas*. (He also directed and choreographed the Raquel Welch "Space Dance" number that might very well have inspired Lucas to include her in the Special's original treatment.)

The Hollywood press was also well acquainted with Winters. A few years earlier, he had been the live-in boyfriend of the adult film star Linda Lovelace, right in the midst of her *Deep Throat* fame. In fact, Yuichi Sugiyama, who performed as the ringmaster acrobat in the Special, knew Lovelace very well through appearing in past projects with Winters. The two had initially met while Winters was producing the stage show for Alice Cooper's *Welcome to My Nightmare* tour, for which Sugiyama had been one of the dancers.

When all nine of the performers arrived in the morning, they were met by Mackie, who showed them the costumes he'd designed for them. Beverly Abderrahman, the mother of the Wazzan Troupe, wasn't thrilled with her 4 a.m. call time, but her attitude changed when she arrived on the set. "They

Choreographer David Winters had become quite the hit among Hollywood photographers when he started dating adult film star Linda Lovelace a few years after she appeared in *Deep Throat*. The two dated for about two years; Lovelace later spoke out about pornography and the abuse she suffered in the adult film industry. *Photo by Ron Galella/Ron Galella Collection via Getty Images*

had big posters of the drawings of the costumes. It was fantastic! And *Bob Mackie was there*," she recalls, drowning in schoolgirl enthusiasm. "I was thrilled."

However, Mackie's presence didn't eliminate the stress from what would become a terribly exhausting shoot. "It was a very long day," recalls Wazzan daughter Alisa Abderrahman. After her early morning arrival, she was immediately led to a room for extensive hair and makeup to be applied. "I had very, very long, big, big hair. So I was in the chair for a couple hours, getting pin curls. And then I believe we had to have circles of black around our eyes for the costumes." In the end, this lavish attention to detail wound up being just another excruciating waste of time, as their faces were not visible in the final cut anyway.

Other than there being two jugglers, a gymnast, a ringmaster, and a family of five tumblers, Mackie had not been given any information about the characters. "It's like an inspiration thing," he says. "You just sort of think, 'What would be really fun? What would I like to see?' It's all in the fun." When he finally got a chance to read the script and learn a bit about what they were planning to do with these characters, he was inspired. "The minute I saw that, I thought, 'I know what I want to do.' I knew they were going to be reduced small, but I didn't want them to look like little shrunk humans. So they didn't look like that. They looked like creatures, and that was kind of fun."

One of the standout aspects of the performers' costumes was Mackie's choice of colors. To offset Tatooine's grimy, recycled look, Mackie wanted to go in a completely different direction, offering modern, vibrant colors for the circus characters. He wanted effervescent hues to counteract the heavily rusted *Star Wars* palette, which was "all grays and taupes and browns and beiges, and a little black. Basically no color, really . . . I guess, in space, they don't have color."

To get the costumes to jump off the screen, he used bright, Day-Glo colors: "Pinks and lime greens and Kelly greens and oranges—those would sure stand out." The outfits for the Wazzan Troupe were in matching hot pink. Being costumes for acrobats, they had to be quite stretchable, so he made them out of spandex. "[Everyone] that had to wear this stuff was very comfortable. Nobody complained ever, which was kind of a good thing."

Sugiyama's ringmaster was the first individual costume that Mackie designed, and it was one of his favorites. He wanted to have "this kind of Asian half-man, half-bird kind of situation," he recalls. "He had this big tail that he could move around like a whip, and he had all these pheasant feathers that were dyed this green color." Although the ringmaster character was half-bird, he was no pet. "He's still a warrior," Mackie explains. "They're all warriors of a certain kind." Sugiyama was very aware of Mackie's stature in the industry and honored to be wearing a costume he had designed. The outfit was fairly comfortable, he recalls, with only one issue where the extravagant costume presented difficulties. Searching for the perfect word, he finally finds it, eking it out in his broken English: "Bathroom."

The original plan called for Sugiyama to enter and then introduce the other acrobats individually. However, it is likely that the language barrier complicated that portion of the segment. "The ringmaster was so great and he was so good, but between you and me, I don't think he spoke a word of English," says Stephanie Stroher, who played the gymnast. Sugiyama's pronouncements would be cut in post-production and replaced with electronic scoring by musical director Ian Fraser.

Acomba had just begun shooting the hologram segment and was already several hours behind schedule. Some of these performers would not be available to return the following day to finish the scene, so Rita Scott and line producer Monroe Carol—charged with trying to keep this already out-of-control production under control—crossed their fingers and forged ahead, urging everyone to move quickly through the scene, which subsequently resulted in an avalanche of crew overtime.

Shooting the jugglers was quite challenging. Referred to as the Reeko Brothers in an early script, they were known professionally as the Mum Brothers, and they were encountering some issues with the costumes. "They were doing all this fancy juggling, and their goggles—which looked really dashing—were fogging up during the performance, and they couldn't see," says Stromer. "Although the costumes were great . . . their glasses fogging up made juggling significantly even more challenging than usual."

Although they all had some sort of issue with the costumes fitting correctly, they all paled in comparison to Stroher's.

Mackie knew that these performers would be performing physically challenging stunts—and inside a hot soundstage—so his first priority had been to ensure they could take in air properly. "The hats almost completely covered their faces, [except] the noses were exposed, the mouths were exposed. The bottom parts [of their faces] were just painted on so they could really breathe." As for the actual outfit, Mackie's design for Stroher was a bodysuit covered in a layer of black elastic, with silver buttons holding it together. "Anytime [the gymnast] moved, the elastic would move with [her], and it would stay in place," he explains.

However, Stroher says that despite how great the costume looked, it was terribly uncomfortable. "I complained to [Mackie] about it and he complained to me back, more or less [saying], 'If you were [a] professional, you'd have on certain underclothing.' And I'm like, 'Well, what is that?' He goes, 'You need to be wearing a G-string.'" Still confused, Stroher asked

Mackie again: "What's that?" She had just graduated college a few months earlier, and she would learn more as the day progressed. "I learned a lot," she recalls, laughing. "But ... too late [for] that day."

Stroher—whose character was formally referred to in an early script, rather inexplicably, as "The Great Zorbak"—was a three-time All-American gymnast when she auditioned for Winters. Just a few years earlier, she was the highest-scoring US performer in the 1973 World Games in Moscow, and she had led Southern Illinois University to the AIAW National Championships in 1974 and 1975.

In her early twenties at the time, she was asked to execute a short routine on the uneven bars. Winters had been arguing with Acomba over the gymnastic sequence for quite a while, according to both Alisa and Antar Abderrahman. Seemingly neither Winters nor Acomba was satisfied by Stromer's performance. "They just kept asking her again and again and again," Alisa recalls. "'Fifty-two takes on this one, let's try it again.' Just hours and hours, over and over. ... She was thoroughly exhausted."

Stage manager Peter Barth says there seemed to be no end in sight for this segment: "It just went on and on and on." Acomba continued to ask for additional angles to be shot, further extending the allotted time for the shoot. Omar Abderrahman found the amount of time spent on it "amazing": "Just the amount of takes that they took, and the amount of different setups that they had. I mean, they had a camera on a crane, they're doing high shots, low shots, tight in, back out, [this] angle, that [angle]. The coverage"—a film and TV term for shooting an ample number of angles of a scene to assure there is enough footage for the editor to work with in post-production—"was outrageous."

Omar was also mindful of the time. "Then it was six [o'clock], and it just kept getting pushed back more and more and more," he recalls.

"We're going to get to you, hang in there," the producers kept telling him.

"And we hung in there," he says.

A few hours earlier, the crew had gone from time-and-a-half overtime to double time. Omar Abderrahman recalls that "the crew was loving it because they were making a ton of money ... I think it was ten or eleven at night before they actually finally got to our segment." His sister Alisa remembers it being later—"around midnight"—when it was their turn to perform. Considering their day had begun at 4 a.m., that would mean that just this group of acrobats had been on the clock for over *twenty hours*—not to mention the hundred or so union members working on the same timetable.

Once Acomba was ready to shoot the family, Alisa recalls, "We just got in there and got out. I think we did it in about seven minutes." Compared to the conductor, gymnast, and juggler foursome that Winters had slapped together, the Wazzans were flawless professional performers who had been closely working together their entire lives.

Rita Scott did not allow for any additional angles to be shot; Acomba had covered enough, and they called it a day. The earlier call time that the acrobats had been given for their extensive makeup would turn out to be fruitless, as there was no time left in the budget for Acomba to shoot their close-ups.

One of the reasons for this specific scene ranking among fans' worst in the Special is the score. Composer Ian Fraser, fresh from co-writing the "Peace on Earth" portion of Crosby and Bowie's "Little Drummer Boy" duet, does not exactly shine here. "What better testament to the mastery of John Williams than whoever scored this entire holiday special," Taran Killam remarks. "Because somebody came in with a new Casio synth sound, and they're like, 'You gotta let me flex this out, you guys . . . I'm telling you it's gonna be timeless!'"

Earlier in the day, producer Ken Welch had approached the Wazzan family and asked if they had been told the context of the scene they were shooting. "Up until then, we really had no idea what this, our segment, was even about—let alone the whole show," says Omar Abderrahman.

Welch told them that the scene was largely influenced by the 1940 film *The Thief of Bagdad*, a critically acclaimed magnum opus that at the time had been at the cutting edge of film technology (Roger Ebert compared it to *The Wizard of Oz* for its striking look and groundbreaking visual effects). At one point in the film, the toy-obsessed Sultan of Basra opens up a large cabinet, revealing a music box with six miniature tumblers inside, performing human pyramids. Welch explained that their family would be performing in a similar fashion and, thanks to the Ultimatte visual-effects system, they would all become miniaturized images as well.

The Abderrahman patriarch, Antar Sr., got very excited as he listened to Welch describe the 1940 film. What Welch was not aware of was that the Wazzan Troupe had been performing for many generations, going back to the turn of the century. Antar Sr. revealed to Welch that not only did he know the film, but that *he himself* had been the youngest of the six acrobats in *The Thief of Bagdad*, appearing in that scene with *his* parents and siblings nearly forty years earlier.

It is noteworthy that Welch acknowledges that this acrobat scene was inspired by *The Thief of Bagdad*, since another scene from the film looks very much like it could have been modified for the Special as well. The villain in the film, Jaffar (played by Conrad Veidt, who the following year would reach tremendous fame playing Major Heinrich Strasser in *Casablanca*), creates a seductive "silver maiden" to tempt the Sultan. The maiden, played by British actress Mary Morris, is dressed from head to toe in silver, except for her face and hands, which are painted blue.

By comparison, Korman's Gormaanda character wears a purple outfit from head to toe, except for his face and hands, which are painted in a darker hue of purple. However, more striking is that the Silver Maiden has *multiple arms* as well (six—two more than Gormaanda's four). The two remarkably different scenes are also shot similarly, using additional people to sit or stand behind Korman and Morris, feeding their arms under their shoulders to create the multi-armed effect. It seems quite unlikely that if the Welches drew inspiration from the acrobat scene in *The Thief of Bagdad* they wouldn't also have seen this extraordinarily unique scene twenty-five minutes later in the film and created the Gormaanda character—especially considering Mitzie Welch wrote the segment herself.

Assistant art director Leslie Parsons estimated that the first day's shoot ran to "twenty-one or twenty-two hours." A few others have estimated the length at between eighteen and twenty-two hours. The one undisputed fact is that Rita Scott and Monroe Carol had likely never experienced a television director like Acomba in their entire careers, and this was just the first day.

CHAPTER 7

THE PRESSURE COOKER

ON THE SECOND day of shooting, cameraman Larry Heider came to work quite exhausted from the long night before. He had just spent over twenty hours shooting tumblers in hot pink costumes, jugglers, and a gymnast—not to mention a cross-dressing Harvey Korman with four arms.

This was not a typical TV variety special, and it certainly wasn't *Star Wars*.

This was not the type of television variety Heider was used to shooting. Even though he had just been nominated for an Emmy for his camerawork on a Neil Diamond special for Smith–Hemion, he had pretty much just started his career (which, when he eventually retired, garnered him a staggering fifty-seven Emmy nominations and fifteen wins). But that morning, as he walked through the sound stage, he immediately recognized the cantina bar set from the film. He didn't have access to a script, but he soon learned this was going to be a musical number.

"It clicked," Heider says. "Okay, now we're in Smith–Hemion's world. We're doing a musical now, and we know how to do this. So this shouldn't take very long. This should go pretty well."

What Heider didn't yet know was that this scene was much more than just a song. On paper alone, the cantina bar was expected to be by far the most difficult scene to shoot. It included Bea Arthur as Ackmena the Barkeep; Harvey Korman as her eleven-fingered admirer, Krelman (his second role in two days); and about three dozen extras wearing various alien costumes with either constrictive masks or complex makeup.

There was a tremendous number of different elements in just this scene alone. The script called for Korman to flirt with Arthur; Arthur to reject Korman's advances; Arthur to flirt with a giant rat; Korman to drink via a hole in his head; the cantina band to perform; Imperial authorities to announce a curfew via a wall speaker; Arthur to ask her customers to leave; some guests to be ejected; Arthur to announce "last call"; Arthur to sing and dance with customers; and Arthur to lead the patrons out of the bar.

When the edited Special finally aired, this scene would clock in at over twenty minutes. Acomba had one day to shoot it all. If there was any gambling going on in that cantina bar, most of them were likely betting against the house.

"For our purposes, the place was run by a very strong, forceful presence," Vilanch recalls. "Bea Arthur in her Statue of Liberty period." Arthur had wrapped up six seasons of playing the title role in the critically acclaimed series *Maude*, through which she had become not just a respected comedian and actress and a whopping television star, but also a political activist. She, Norman Lear, and Alan Alda were the leading Hollywood liberals who were not the least bit shy about speaking out for equal rights for women and protesting against the Vietnam War. There wasn't a female comedian on television at the time with anywhere near the amount of brass chutzpah that Arthur had. Vilanch loved the idea of her playing a tough-as-nails barkeep. "She was so strong. I could see her: 'You with the seven arms, put that down...'"

Bob Mackie had taken his time designing costumes for the characters played by Arthur and the other guest stars. "These were new characters for *Star Wars*, and for those people that just love *Star Wars*, that was important. Whoever designed *Star Wars*, it had kind of a fairy tale, medieval quality, and yet very futuristic at the same time. You have to understand what they wore and why. So, the characters that we made up for the show—the Art Carneys, the Harvey Kormans, and the Bea Arthurs—had to fit into that atmosphere."

Mackie always took creative liberties with his designs. In this case, he says, Arthur was "thrilled" when she first saw his sketch of the barkeep costume he'd designed for her. "Visuals are very, very important, especially in television," Mackie says. "When you did those shows, you could kind of stir people's minds up by what you put people in. You could tell them about the character before they even opened their mouth."

While most people were aware of Arthur the actor, fewer knew she could sing. Before winning over television audiences in the 1970s, however, she had slayed crowds on Broadway, winning a Tony Award for "Best Actress in a Musical" as Vera Charles in *Mame*, as well as playing Yenta the Matchmaker in the original *Fiddler on the Roof.*

Mitzie Welch had worked with Arthur before and knew her singing ability: "We knew we had Bea as a guest, and we knew how to treat her singing, because a lot of people don't even know she sings, and she loves to sing."

Arthur wanted to do a number. "It was in her proviso," Vilanch recalls. However, deciding on the music for her to sing would be quite a challenge. Her choice was "The Alabama Song," a nihilistic piece filled with dark themes of sex and alcoholism from the 1930 opera *Rise and Fall of the City of Mahagonny*, with lyrics by Bertolt Brecht and music by Kurt Weill. In the opera, it is sung by a group of prostitutes and depicts the decadence of pre–World War II Germany, which, Vilanch remarks, is "not exactly what you want on the *Star Wars* Thanksgiving holiday weekend show."

"[The producers] didn't want to piss her off," Vilanch explains, "so they finally went to the Brecht estate" to seek permission, but the estate "was not interested in having the song on the *Star Wars Holiday Special*. They were very serious." So the Welches began writing one. They reread the scene and then wrote "Goodnight, but Not Goodbye," a wistful and nostalgic sing-along for these tavern dwellers. It was in the vein of "Those Were the Days," the 1968 chart-topper written exclusively for Mary Hopkin by Paul McCartney, although the Welches also included some signature riffs from John Williams's iconic cantina-bar music from *Star Wars.*

Vilanch describes the new composition as an "up version" of "The Alabama Song," and everyone seemed to like it. The question was, would Bea?

"This is the right song for Bea," Mitzie kept telling her husband on the drive over to Arthur's home to audition it for her. "We knew it was right for her," Ken recalled. "But Bea is very particular and difficult about material." Fortunately, Arthur was bowled over by the song. "I remember that she just loved it," Mitzie recalled. Ken added, "We played the song and she cried. She was very moved by it."

Music producer Jeff Babco calls the song "a haunted musical treasure": "the minor harmony is so Yiddish ... and the tempo is pretty darn slow. Even the cantina band part seems slowed down, like it's at the wrong speed."

"That song is so deliciously '70s," says action figure designer Jason Lenzi. "The lyrics are so sad, so sentimental, so saccharine-drenched ... 'You're such a dear friend / You know I'm here, friend / Is that a tear, friend?' Really? But Bea Arthur really delivers it with such sincerity, she sells it."

Babco agrees that her "Is that a tear, friend?" line to the bouncer "is so earnest, her face sells this final morsel of sincerity, and I think therefore we buy the whole *Star Wars Holiday Special* in this one moment."

Music fans of the 1970s wholeheartedly embraced schmaltzy melodramatic songs like these. There was a tolerance and frankly a huge *market* for these overly theatrical, first-person narratives. Record buyers in that decade embraced such gloomy tales as "The Night the Lights Went Out in Georgia," "Cat's in the Cradle," "At Seventeen," "One Tin Soldier," "Seasons in the Sun," and—of course—the theme song to *M.A.S.H.*, "Suicide Is Painless." As musician Jeff Babko notes, "In the '70s, every song was *Brian's Song*."

In a 2001 interview, Arthur still remembered the production number, and particularly the song, fondly: "Harvey Korman and I were in a bar with aliens and strange looking people, [and I was given a] lovely piece written by Mitzie and Ken Welch."

Around the same time that the Welches had been writing "Goodnight, but Not Goodbye," Tom Burman was at work on the cantina patrons. Burman had started out in 1968 as an assistant makeup artist on *Planet of the Apes*. A decade later, when he was hired on to do makeup effects for the Special, his résumé was nowhere near its present-day length, but it still included work on *Close Encounters of the Third Kind*, *The Island of Dr. Moreau*, and *Invasion of the Body Snatchers*.

Burman's young apprentice and makeup-effects specialist for the Special was Rick Baker. Like Burman, Baker had also started out at *Planet of the Apes* before forging ahead with gigs on such films as the 1976 *King Kong*, *It's Alive*, and eventually *Star Wars*. He had helped create nearly all of the cantina aliens in the film, and Lucas had also asked him to create some new aliens for *The Empire Strikes Back*, which he had already begun building.

"[Lucas] had a whole bunch of new aliens, but he didn't want to use them on the show," Vilanch explains. "So we used remainder aliens. We went to the alien warehouse and pulled out the aliens that had not made the cut in the first two movies. And they were all [held together with] Elmer's glue and Scotch tape." In Vilanch's recollection, Acomba instructed the cameramen, "Don't go too close [on] any of them."

While working on the cantina scene, Burman and Baker remembered that they had built over a dozen large rats for the cult favorite *The Food of the Gods*, a movie about a strange substance that is emitted from the earth and that causes the rats and wasps who eat it to grow to massive size. Baker pulled one of the supersized rodents from cold storage and inserted it into their scene. According to Burman, the giant rat that they used might have been the prototype Baker had originally built for *Food of the Gods* director Bert Gordon, just to show him it could be done.

The rat wasn't just thrown into the cantina scene. During one verse of her song, Arthur winds up hanging out with it while it is operated from behind through a hole in the set's wall. The rat made such an impression during the scene that it has been formally identified by Wookieepedia as being a member of the Tintinna species and given the name "Rungs."

The rat wasn't the only one vying for Arthur's affection that day. The Krelman character played by Korman also comes into the bar that night to declare his love for her. "Harvey Korman is trying to pick up Bea Arthur, which is very disturbing," explained Gilbert Gottfried. In the process, he tries to embrace her, and he also exhibits a very unusual way of drinking. In Gottfried's description, "To somehow make the scene weirder, he has a hole in his head that he pours the drinks into. So, in the center of his head, he has what's either a mouth or a vagina . . .

"He's done a lot of great [things], that Harvey Korman. This wasn't one of them."

* * *

On this second day of taping, things got off to another delayed start—mainly as a result of the costumes. On the first day, the wardrobe, makeup, and hair folks had only Korman and nine acrobats to prepare. On the second day, they had Korman, Arthur, and about thirty other extras who all needed costumes and complex hair and makeup.

In addition to the makeup and hair issues, some of the costumes weren't fitting. "It took forever to get the costumes on all of these people," recalls Rick Wagner, who had been hired as an extra for the day. "They had to be refitted, and the wardrobe people were going crazy." It was a pretty thankless job for the backstage crew, who not only had to prepare each extra upon their arrival but also had to keep them touched up throughout the day.

One of those extras was Wagner, a dancer with quite a résumé. In the previous year or so, he had managed to appear in a slew of top-notch musical schlockers like *Roller Boogie* and *Sgt. Pepper's Lonely Hearts Club Band*. After his stint in the *Star Wars Holiday Special*, he would next appear in the 1980 Village People film *Can't Stop the Music*. You'd think there'd be some sort of an award for that.

When Wagner arrived at the set, he was handed a costume and told, "You're 'Walrus Man.'" He was excited, he says, as the character actually had one of the more significant roles in the original cantina scene in *Star Wars*. In the movie, Walrus Man approaches Luke and grunts. His companion translates for Luke: "He doesn't like you. I don't like you either. You just watch yourself." Obi-Wan Kenobi intervenes and tells the alien that Luke isn't worth the trouble. When the alien moves to attack Luke, Ben pulls out his lightsaber and shears off Walrus Man's arm.

After his arm is cut off by Kenobi, there is a shot inserted of the bloody arm on the ground with what seems to be a hand with human-like fingers. When Walrus Man first taps Luke on the shoulder, however, he seems to have a sort of hoof instead of a hand. Likewise, when he appears in the Special, he does not have hands, but hooves.

A likely explanation would be that it was a bit too early in the life of *Star Wars* to think Lucas cared tremendously about continuity. However, as the franchise's popularity would expand to an almost unhealthy level, soon there would be answers to even these obscure questions.

Jason Lenzi explains that things were far more different in the *Star Wars* zeitgeist between 1977 and 1980. "Back then it was a wilderness filled with insane ideas and everything wasn't 'nailed down' or canon. Greedo was the only guy in the cantina with a proper name," he says, noting that the rest of the denizens that Kenner Toys made action figures of had descriptive, almost generic names like "Snaggletooth" and "Hammerhead." Those two

ABOVE Charles Lippincott enlisted Mark Hamill to help promote *Star Wars* before its release through events like Worldcon (a.k.a. MidAmericaCon), held in Kansas City in early September 1976. Along with Lippincott and producer Gary Kurtz, Hamill participated in a Q&A session with sci-fi fans.
Jim Van Hise

LEFT Lucas's 1971 science-fiction film *THX 1138* was critically well-received but a commercial flop. Frank Wells's decision to pull four minutes from the final cut irked Lucas for years; he compared it to "having your finger cut off." © *Warner Bros*

The Future is here.

THX 1138

Warner Bros. presents THX 1138 · An American Zoetrope Production · Starring Robert Duvall and Donald Pleasence · with Don Pedro Colley, Maggie McOmie and Ian Wolfe · Technicolor® · Techniscope® · Executive Producer, Francis Ford Coppola · Screenplay by George Lucas and Walter Murch · Story by George Lucas Produced by Lawrence Sturhahn · Directed by George Lucas · Music by Lalo Schifrin

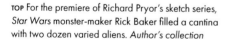

TOP For the premiere of Richard Pryor's sketch series, *Star Wars* monster-maker Rick Baker filled a cantina with two dozen varied aliens. *Author's collection*

ABOVE LEFT The hiring of writer/producers Ken and Mitzie Welch came as a shock to director David Acomba, who thought all hires, especially *producers*, would be run past him. *Courtesy of Julie Welch*

ABOVE RIGHT Lucas intended the segment on the hit family series *Donny and Marie* to help bring more people into theaters before *Star Wars* ended its run. The highlight saw Jay, Merrill, Alan, and Wayne Osmond dressed as imperial stormtroopers, performing a reworked version of The Temptations' "Get Ready." *Courtesy of Donny Osmond*

BELOW RIGHT A standard moment in most Bob Hope specials was the soft-shoe dance number. Mark Hamill, who had some dance experience, donned a hat and cane for *The Bob Hope All Star Christmas Comedy Special. Courtesy of Hope Enterprises*

TOP In the fan-favorite cartoon "The Story of the Faithful Wookiee," there is no explanation for the dark red strips that are hanging off of Boba Fett's right shoulder, but according to Nelvana layout artist Frank Nissen, they are wookiee scalps. *Author's collection*

ABOVE LEFT *Left to right:* co-founders Patrick Loubert and Michael Hirsh, layout artist Frank Nissen, and co-founder Clive A. Smith of the Toronto-based animation company Nelvana. Lucas loved their work so much that they would be hired to produce the *Droids* and *Ewoks* animated series as well. *Courtesy of Michael Hirsh*

ABOVE RIGHT To inspire the Kenner Toys designers, Lucas did a little show-and-tell display of his latest character, Boba Fett, at his home in San Anselmo, California in July 1978. He invited along VP of preliminary design Dave Okada (pictured with Lucas) and senior product designer Jim Swearingen, who would add Boba Fett to the list of action figures they were already working on. *Jim Swearingen*

ABOVE LEFT If there was an image that could convincingly suggest Raquel Welch as an Imperial spy, it would be the space dance from her 1970 television special *Raquel*. *Author's collection.*

ABOVE RIGHT The legendary Bob Mackie, who was gaining quite the reputation as the wardrobe designer for Cher and others at the time, was hired early on to design costumes for many of the Special's characters. *John Barrett/PHOTOlink/Alamy*

RIGHT An early Mackie sketch of the "water creature" Mermeia, a part that was eventually played by Diahann Carroll. Bruce Vilanch specifically recalls Cher being booked for the part before Carroll eventually took on the role; Mackie has gone back and forth as to whether he drew this sketch with Cher in mind. *Art by Bob Mackie/author's collection*

Diahann Carroll

Bea Arthur

BOB MACKIE

Art Carney

BOB MACKIE

Harvey Korman

BOB MACKIE

BOB MACKIE

THIS PAGE A selection of Mackie's sketches for the characters in the Special, from top left. As well as designing costumes for the characters played by Diahann Carroll, Bea Arthur, Art Carney, and Harvey Korman, Mackie also provided looks for the circus performers who appear in the hologram scene. *Art by Bob Mackie/author's collection*

ABOVE LEFT From the beginning, Harvey Korman hated the Special. He didn't understand the story or the characters he was playing, and he didn't remember much about the entire production when interviewed. The only positive memory he had was working with Bea Arthur: "I mean, we had fun. But I didn't know what the hell that thing was about."
CBS Photo Archive/Contributor

ABOVE RIGHT Art Carney (shown here with Patty Maloney as Lumpy) hoarded ice in his shower to keep his liquor bottles cool. Director Steve Binder said he had to schedule Carney's scene early in the day, as he felt that the actor started drinking around lunchtime. The crew was amazed that he continued to hit his marks every time.
CBS Photo Archive/Contributor

RIGHT Prop builder Ted Baumgart, shown here in his tiny version of the Millennium Falcon, was warned by his boss to "not get too involved here," as Smith–Hemion was crying poor because of its depleted budget.
Courtesy of Ted Baumgart

ABOVE Carrie Fisher as Princess Leia in the Special, with Anthony Daniels as C-3PO. At first, Fisher was hesitant about participating, but she agreed to appear out of a sense of obligation to Lucas. *Photofest*

LEFT Mark Hamill appears as Luke Skywalker (along with R2-D2, sans Kenny Baker), marking his first appearance in a *Star Wars*–related project since the accident he suffered in January 1977. Since then, Hamill had undergone major facial reconstruction, and the excessive makeup he wears for the Special has been a topic of discussion ever since its initial broadcast. *Photofest*

TOP Whoever recorded and then distributed a copy of the Special from New York's WCBS probably did not realize they were remaking the legacy of news anchor Rolland Smith. His "Fighting the Frizzies" tease became part of the Special's lore and turned Smith into a viral sensation. *WCBS-TV*

ABOVE LEFT The critical consensus on the Holiday Special remains grim, even for a famously geeky webcomic like xkcd. *Courtesy Casey Blair/xkcd.com*

ABOVE RIGHT Like Jon Favreau, *Guardians of the Galaxy* director James Gunn was a fan of the Special and created a Holiday Special for his own hit franchise. *Marvel Entertainment/Disney+*

were likely nicknames given to the characters by the creature team during filming, their names about as thoughtfully considered as "Bald Guy with the Red Sweater."

So, when Kenner expanded the initial action figure wave, that information was just passed along. Hence, Walrus Man probably looked like a walrus to the costumers on *A New Hope*, so he was named just that. And, for nearly twenty years, that's who they were.

However, during the franchise's resurgence in the late 1900s, Lenzi says, "suddenly everyone and their mother who had two seconds of screen time in that cantina had first and last names, professions, and Tolkien-esque backstories." Lenzi cites Walrus Man as a perfect example, explaining that he was now called Ponda Baba; the creepy dude with the scarred face he hung out with (who didn't even get an action figure way back then, much less a name) now went by Doctor Cornelius Evazan. He says Lucasfilm took the creative license to write even more of the duo's history. "We learned they were partners in crime, and Evazan had even tried to surgically replace Baba's missing arm, which is so ironic, since Walrus Man has the distinction of being part of one of the most legendary gaffes in *Star Wars* history."

The decision to give Ponda Baba a fingered hand—and not a hoof—was Lucas's. "Walrus Man had flipper-like hooves in the cantina," says Lenzi, "but when his severed arm is shown on the floor in the insert shot, it's got a five-fingered hand at the end. Lucas *ordered* that change for the insert because he thought there was no way for Ponda Baba to grip the blaster he threatened Luke with.

"That's the kind of hidden mythology in *Star Wars* that I love," he adds. "Half the time, they were just making it up as they went along."

Wagner had a real connection with his character, having recalled the bloody hand scene from the film. But he was even more excited that he would now have an added role. He had listed dancing on his résumé, so when the choreographer learned there was a short sequence called for in the script, he turned to Wagner and said, "You're going to be dancing with Bea Arthur."

While the writers of the Special probably thought this would make for a great TV variety moment, it is quite bizarre to see *dancing* going on at what Kenobi calls "a wretched hive of scum and villainy" in the first *Star*

Wars movie, before warning Luke they must be "cautious" when entering. There almost seem to be two different Mos Eisley cantinas—and the vibe in *this* cantina is far from dangerous, looking less like the film's cutthroat underworld hub and more like the tavern where Tevya and Lazar Wolf sing "To Life" in *Fiddler on the Roof.*

"Some things are so contradictory to the film that had just come out," says Taran Killam. "So, is *this* that cantina? Because [it has] all the same costumes and characters, [but it's] not at all dangerous, right? That is the purpose it serves in the film: This is the most dangerous place where arms are cut off, people are shot under tables—and, occasionally, Beatrice Arthur will break out into song."

While dancing with Arthur was an amazing opportunity, Wagner had not been told what style he would be doing. They seemed to be blocking the complicated scene as they went along, so he took a seat at the back of the bar next to the cantina band and waited until Acomba was ready for him.

Wagner says that Acomba's explanation of the move he needed to perform—which was to run across to the opposite side of the bar, grab Arthur's hand, and take her back to where the cantina band was performing—made it sound overly simplistic: "I mean, that's hard to maneuver, even without this mask on my face. I was just trying not to trip over the tables."

Acomba seemed oblivious to the physical challenges that the constrictive costumes had created for the extras. For example, Wagner's mask did not have openings where his actual eyes were located; instead, there were two holes located where his mouth was, causing him to have to basically look down to see forward. This made just *seeing* a challenge. Dancing? Good luck.

"I couldn't see Bea. And I don't have hands. I have hooves. I felt my way down and I just kind of grabbed her wrists as best I could. I just started doing a two-step because there was no mobility to do anything else. I'm just swaying back and forth to the music."

In addition to having limited visibility, Wagner's two-step was facing some additional problems: "Bea is a very large woman and has very large feet. I can't see where *my* feet are going, so most of the time I'm just stepping on her toes. She just kept going; she's a professional. I did apologize afterward."

At least Wagner had a chance to move, which is more than his fellow extras got. They were trapped sitting or standing in one place for nearly the entire shoot—which, of course, went long into the night, just as it had the previous day.

Wagner says there was also a complete disconnect once the extras were dressed and ready to be positioned on the stage. Which table would they sit at? Who would be having what drink? Who would be sitting where for the best camera angles? Apparently, none of this was laid out in advance, and Acomba spent half the day positioning the extras, directing each individual as to where they would be sitting and what they would be doing.

Usually, complex scenes like this are planned ahead of time, with the director normally delegating this responsibility to a producer, an assistant director, or a stage manager. The choreographer was actually on hand, but the general consensus was that Acomba didn't like to delegate and preferred to be on the floor, blocking things out himself. Vilanch explains that while most directors will spend *some* time on the floor to converse briefly with the actors, most of their time is spent *away* from the performers, "calling the shots" from either a glass booth situated above the set or from a remote truck. In effect, Acomba was basically doubling as a stage manager—and it was already causing stress on the set.

For the crew, it was quite a red flag to see Acomba on the set with the extras. Wagner said Acomba was quite particular about the way he wanted everyone in the cantina bar scene to be situated: "Everything that we did was through the eyes of the director. If you had one of the characters that had a bigger head that was sitting closer to the camera, it wasn't going to work, because he wasn't going to get the right angle or camera shot around that character. So, the larger characters were placed in the back of the cantina. But then, if the color schemes were wrong, David would say, 'No, no, no, that's not working,' 'You're blending in the background,' 'We can't see you, bring that character out here.'

"He was just pointing and directing," Wagner adds. "It was just mind-boggling. It just took forever, the switching everybody around."

Apparently, on a few occasions that day, things got very heated between Acomba and other crew members. As Wagner recalls, Acomba had "a little short of a temper, and it just was getting to be a little bit of a volatile situation." Producer's assistant Elle Puritz saw more of Acomba's temper than she wished; she later called him a "loose cannon" who could erupt at

As production began, video cameraman Larry Heider had just got a new 35 mm camera and was shooting stills behind the scenes. Here he captures director David Acomba (*right*), with Harvey Korman as an alien Julia Child. Acomba had a very different style than most TV directors. He spent most of his time on the floor, almost as an additional stage manager, to the irritation of many members of the cast and crew. *Photo by Larry Heider*

any moment and over anything." She added that Acomba and the Welches argued in front of the crew, often resulting in one of them storming off the set.

Heider says that Acomba wasn't the only person quick to anger that day, saying that Arthur was quite "cold and demanding." As the cameraman, he had a view of all sides of the situation. "When she was asked to do something a second time, she wanted someone to explain what was wrong. When the script wasn't making sense for her to say something, she had a hard time translating all of that. She was pretty much Maude."

* * *

As the shoot continued, another problem arose. It was one heck of a scorcher in the San Fernando Valley the week that these hundred or so people packed inside a Burbank soundstage to work on a musical variety show. The temperature outside had topped out at about ninety degrees that week, but inside it was over one hundred degrees and showing no signs of letting up. By the late 1970s, most southern Californians had access to air conditioning, but due to the noise that it created on the soundstage, it was not being used during tapings. Heavy klieg lights were also aimed down at these extras wearing masks, either burning their heads or literally melting the inside lining of their masks to their heads for several hours at a time. The extras' vision was also being obscured, as the sweat from the ungodly heat dripped from their foreheads into their eyes, the salt from which irritating and blinding them throughout the shoot.

In addition to masks, the costumes themselves weren't exactly built for comfort. Wagner describes the Walrus Man costume he was required to wear: "It wasn't just made with one layer of burlap. It was two, three, four layers of this stuff, like leather"—along with an actual leather jacket and a mask.

The weight of the costumes was also an issue. The Cowardly Lion costume that Bert Lahr wore in *The Wizard of Oz* weighed ninety pounds. The outfits that these extras were wearing couldn't have weighed much less. Most of them likely weren't auditioned for their strength and stamina to stand in an outfit like that for several hours at a time, much less move around in it as well.

The masks were extremely heavy, too, and most of them, like Wagner's, had only two very small openings to see through, located on the bottom of the mask. Breathing was an entirely different challenge. The masks the extras were given each had a tiny hole with netting over it, and that was their only source of oxygen.

"You could not breathe in these costumes, "Wagner recalls. "And that was all the oxygen you're getting inside your head, which is crazy. For maybe half an hour or an hour that would be fine, but all day sitting in that thing? ... So,

Shooting of the cantina scene started early in the morning and lasted until the wee hours of the following day. The extras who wore these alien costumes had to endure smoke effects, obstructive costumes, and a lack of air conditioning. *Photo by CBS via Getty Images*

you've got all of these people crammed into this space with these costumes on and these heads on with limited breathing, and it's getting progressively hotter in these outfits. We're under heavy lights, and at some point I'm going to get up and start dancing. And then they bring in a smoke effect, and it's not dry ice. This is not the dry ice that was refreshing. It was that chemical-burning, sulfur-smelling crap. You're sitting there suffocating, sweating. We were there for hours and hours and couldn't breathe, and you're breathing in this smoke stuff."

And that's when the extras started passing out.

Suddenly, an entirely brand new problem had manifested on Stage 2. The issue was not the show going into overtime anymore. Now it was life and death on the set of a TV variety special.

"The aliens kept fainting because it was, like, 103 degrees on the set," Vilanch recalls. "You put those heads on and it's kind of like waterboarding."

It was quite a dangerous shoot, says Mick Garris, who operated R2-D2 for the Special. "Here are a lot of inexperienced actors in suits for the first time, and they're on the verge of heat exhaustion. There had to be breaks in the shoot constantly—far more than anybody had anticipated—just for the safety of the actors in these suits." As Heider recalls, whenever they were starting to find their rhythm, they needed to stop to give the costumed characters a break. "We'd have to have the EMT guy come in and give them some oxygen."

Ken Welch said that Acomba was clueless about the level of heat that these costumed characters were withstanding. "We were shooting [hour] after [hour] with them," Ken added, "and David had no sense of the fact of their needs as human beings."

According to Mitzie, had she and Ken not stepped in, "We would've killed them."

Vilanch says it was not just a few characters that passed out. They were being carried out on a regular basis and immediately replaced with other extras. He compared this fairly smooth switcheroo with the slickness of a Disneyland parade: "Suddenly you'll see Dopey will do a face plant because they just can't take it anymore, and so Goofy comes running out. Snow White will go by, and she'll say, 'Dopey down, Dopey down,' and suddenly Pluto will come running out and start dragging Dopey off, and Goofy will appear to distract people . . . well, that's what it was like. [Bea would] be singing the song, and suddenly there'd be, 'Boom!' and somebody from some lost planet had taken a dive."

It was on this day that writer Pat Proft decided to cash in one of the few perks that came with the gig. His son, Pat Jr., was ten years old and, like every ten-year-old in the world at the time, a huge *Star Wars* fan. So Pat, yearning to be the coolest dad in the world, brought him to the set to watch that day's taping of the Special. However, it wasn't long before Proft and his son realized the immense pain the costumed actors were in. "People were fainting, and they were being dragged out lifeless and laying outside the sound stage, [EMTs] trying to snap them back into shape. And my son was there to see that, which was, you know, like, a little weird."

Mike Erwin could not believe how long and stressful the scene was to shoot. "It was just endless, and it wasn't even that good. Like, once you saw it, you went, '*Wow*, they could have done that in an hour or two.' It just wasn't worth everybody's pain and suffering to get it, and then the music that they played over and over and over and over again. Here's all these people all jacked up on blow and stuff and being nervous and everything, and they're playing that music all the time. It was pretty funny—I mean, in a sort of gallows way."

For the extras themselves, the shoot was quite a disappointment. They had signed on initially to be part of what they thought was some sort of *Star Wars* sequel, and they wound up feeling they were literally trapped in some sort of third-world torture chamber.

"It was pretty miserable to be there that length of time," Wagner says. As he points out, the delays resulting from Acomba's perfectionism were part of the problem. "I don't remember how long we went, but I do remember doing another take and then another take and another take, to the point where people were passing out and collapsing. It was exhausting. I just remember the discomfort and [thinking], 'When is it gonna end?' . . . It just wasn't a pleasant place to be. And then when you think you're wrapping, we're gonna do it one more time, one more time, one more time. By the time you finally took off your head and handed in your sweaty costume, you had had a very, very long, hard, sweaty day."

For one reason or another, the cantina bar scene that had been shot for *The Richard Pryor Show* encountered none of these problems. "I think, to [director] John [Moffitt]'s credit, that scene was blocked long before the extras were in costume," says the show's producer, Rocco Urbisci. This was standard practice, particularly when extensive costumes were being worn by the extras: the director and stage manager worked with the actors directly and marked the extras' positions on the floor with colored tape.

Urbisci has been on sets before where the executives or sponsors show up to watch a shoot and the producer wants the extras to be in costume, just for show. He would explain: "The person who's gonna be standing here in his jacket and jeans, or gonna wear a dress, is the same person. You don't know what the costume looks like? Well, they're gonna come out in costume. [We've] already blocked it, bro. Now, tape."

Although Acomba could be blamed for putting the show tremendously behind schedule, a larger and more important reason for the misery of the day's shoot was that Smith, Hemion, and their producers had not adequately prepared for the health and safety of these three dozen extras. They were used to staging far simpler song-and-dance numbers on a large, half-empty stage, where the need for oxygen was never an issue. Their specials starred Streisand,

Sinatra, and Sammy Davis Jr., not Witchie Poo and H. R. Pufnstuf.

In retrospect, everyone might have been in much safer hands with Sid and Marty Krofft at the wheel. They had made their careers creating larger-than-life children's shows where people had to wear even more constrictive, unwieldy costumes than the ones the Special's extras had to perform in.

Johnny Whitaker, who appeared as Jodie on the series *Family Affair* in the late 1960s, also starred in the Kroffts' costumed-character series *Sigmund and the Sea Monsters* in the early 1970s. One of his concerns had been the amount of time his co-stars spent in these costumes, specifically his dear friend, the legendary Billy Barty, who played Sigmund. "We would wait every single second that we possibly could to zip him up," Whitaker recalls, "so that he could take one [more] good breath."

Nowadays, Whitaker adds, the union is much more stringent in requiring productions to allow their actors and extras significantly longer breaks, and SAG–AFTRA issues huge penalties when those breaks are not given. "The actor's health and welfare is number one in importance. . . . There are rules and laws that must be abided by [to] protect the actor."

Rita Scott and the Welches were implementing additional breaks for costumed actors and extras. These unexpected delays would push the schedule back even further, holding Acomba's feet to the fire to expedite this challenging cantina shoot, which all on its own seemed to be jeopardizing the entire project, each hour depleting more of the show's limited resources, whether they be time, money, or both.

It was apparent that Acomba didn't seem to understand how the television business worked. Television shows don't generally run on the same kind of budgets that films do, as Larry Heider explains. "There were expectations that [the Special] would be something like the film. So, the idea was to try to do this show with our television crew but make it seem like we were doing something that might have come out of the film world. The goal was to make it part of the *Star Wars* culture that was developing. We tried our best to do that but, you know, television's a different world."

Coming from the documentary and film world, Acomba had never directed a multi-camera shoot before. He was used to shooting one camera at a time. "We all liked him a lot, but he had a very unorthodox way of working," Vilanch recalls. "He shot this thing like it was a movie, and it freaked everybody out."

It was a mixture of worlds—film and television—and Heider notes that Acomba's approach was to shoot on videotape but in film style, "and be more thematic about it." Heider did not agree with Acomba's one-camera system, calling it "troublesome. . . . In a movie production, you would do maybe four or five pages in a very long day, whereas in television, if you had multiple cameras, you'd sacrifice a little bit of creative vision for expedience in getting a shot. . . . There are multiple cameras on television shoots for a specific reason." He adds that the show could have gotten more done, and much more quickly, "which would ultimately make the days a little less expensive."

Erwin can't recall how many hours the second day of shooting went, but he says he wouldn't be surprised if he was there for twenty-four hours straight. "It seemed like Groundhog Day," he recalls. "It was just like an endless shoot. It never stopped. It just kept going and going and going for so many hours."

As the second day turned to night, the several dozen union employees were going into their second straight day of overtime. Union rates and penalties were serious business; they couldn't be overlooked, ignored, or negotiated down.

While most television shows were shot in television studios, they needed to rent a film soundstage. "We never could have built that large, two-story treehouse in a TV studio," said Rita Scott. "We needed the height." Thus, they were bound by the strict union rules negotiated by the International Alliance of Theatrical Stage Employees (IATSE), which required producers to hire a minimum of film backlot employees for the show's sound, camera, and lighting needs, as well as dozens of stagehands. These were all union workers—almost one hundred of them for this Special—all with potential overtime and meal penalties accruing while the Smith–Hemion bean-counters were seemingly asleep at the wheel.

With this specific union, the rates in 1978 went as follows: the basic day was eight hours, but once you go past that, now you're in overtime, paying time-and-a-half. After twelve hours, you're into double time, with the pinnacle of penalties—the ever-illustrious "golden time"—just around the corner. If you work past midnight while in double-time, now you are paying five times each union worker's basic rate, with meal penalties being accrued as well.

Using the start and stop times for the Special, it's pretty easy to see how these three shoot days—most of which started at 4 a.m. and ended at 2 a.m.—nearly depleted the show's entire budget.

For example, if a union worker making $40 per hour started at 4 a.m. but only worked eight hours, they would make $320 for that day. However, once that worker goes into overtime at $60 an hour for four hours, that adds $240 to their day's pay. If the worker goes past twelve hours for eight more hours at $80 per hour, that adds another $640 to their pay. Finally, if they go past midnight, they go into golden time, and they are making $160 per hour, adding another $320 to their pay.

So, the $40-per-hour union worker hired for eight hours, totaling $320 per day, *receives an additional $1,200 per day.* Multiply that one worker's overages for a hundred employees and that makes *$120,000 in overages paid in one single day.* That does not take into account their basic pay and meal penalties—or that higher-paid union workers, like directors and others, make significantly more per hour.

The amount of overtime that Smith–Hemion was now obligated to pay out was absurd. "I remember that we shot a considerable amount of the entire show budget the first three days of the production, because we were over into overtime so much," Erwin recalls.

Erwin had spent enough time on television stages to know that you can't just do long days and pay out that kind of money without causing a lot of tension with the show's producers. "For the unions, when you hit certain numbers of hours, you go into golden time and you're paying, like, $1,100 an hour for a guy to hold a hammer," he explains. "It was great for me, because I think I was making, like, $1,500 an hour or something, and I think we may have gone over twenty hours the first couple of days of the show."

However, the problem wasn't just the budget, Heider adds. While he admits that he—like most of the crew—was excited to be getting double-time pay, he notes that working under those conditions "kind of affected people who were getting really, really tired. And it's not easy to keep doing your best work when you're not getting enough rest yourself."

Erwin agrees that there was far more at stake for the cast and crew than budgetary issues. "This has a cumulative effect," he explains. "Let's say you go on Monday and you work twenty hours. Then Tuesday you work twenty hours. By the time you get to Thursday, even if you only work *a few* hours, you're completely hallucinating. So, it's very, very hard on the cast and crew. That leads to all sorts of complications, from exhaustion to people losing their tempers, to actors deciding to just leave and not come back, and stuff like that. It's like you just want to go home." And, he adds, "Forget about the *director*—nobody wants to listen to *him* after that long."

Newt Bellis, who provided extensive technical equipment for the Special, was at the time dating his future wife, Rita Scott. According to Bellis, the producers were all over her to keep a lid on the budget. "I know that [Smith–Hemion finance director] Henry Jaffe was worried," Bellis recalls. "He was worried about the money and what the overtime was going to be. I remember him asking her, 'Are we over?' And Rita turned around and said, 'We're over a hundred grand,' and Henry just fell back in his seat. I thought he was going to faint. It was total chaos while Acomba was there."

Bellis felt that nothing was progressing, adding that there was no way the production could keep going at that pace: "They weren't getting anything on tape . . . [Acomba] was trying to figure out what was going on, and the time kept rolling and rolling. And, of course, [executive producer] Gary [Smith] was there, and Rita was going nuts because people were just waiting around."

Acomba's frustration was no secret. He was becoming more stressed, and Heider sympathized with the difficult situation he was in. "He was under a lot of pressure to get things moving," he recalls. "But, at the same time, he didn't want to lose what he considered to be his vision of what he wanted to do. What we [originally] thought would be a pretty quick day of shooting turned into another really, really long day."

As this hot August day quickly spiraled into a hot August night, Scott went over to stage manager Peter Barth with sheer exhaustion in her eyes from what was likely to be her second twenty-plus-hour day in a row. She was dead serious when she asked Barth, "Do you think we'll ever get out here?"

CHAPTER 8

THE *STARSHIP* CONNECTION

IF YOU DIDN'T know any better, you might assume that the *Star Wars Holiday Special* was the worst gig George Lucas has ever been involved in. It wasn't. Neither was his experience executive-producing *Howard the Duck*. There was another that was far worse.

In 1969, two weeks after the twenty-five-year-old Lucas had finished filming *THX 1138*, he was hired to help shoot a local concert. Although he was about to start editing his movie, the subject matter sounded amazing: a music festival featuring CSNY, Santana, the Flying Burrito Brothers, Jefferson Airplane, and the Rolling Stones.

The gig was Altamont.

Many people call it the day the sixties died. On December 6, 1969, approximately three hundred thousand people attended what was optimistically called the West Coast Woodstock. By the end of the day, four people had died—two in a hit-and-run accident, one in an accidental drowning, and the last, famously, stabbed to death by a member of the Hell's Angels about fifteen feet in front of the stage where the Rolling Stones were performing.

Lucas had been sent with Walter Murch—who co-wrote the screenplay for *THX 1138* and would become one of the most acclaimed sound engineers and editors in the industry—to a hilltop a mile away with a forty-pound lens to capture a wide shot of the entire stage. Unfortunately, his camera jammed on him, and he only managed to shoot about 100 feet of film. In a bizarre coincidence, that one short clip is used to tremendous effect as one of the last images of the 1970 documentary film of the concert, *Gimme Shelter*. Author Joel Selvin describes how effectively Lucas's long shot works to end the film: "The spacey, otherworldly panoramic sweep of concertgoers stumbling out of the concert in the darkness" is placed at the end, just before the film cuts to an "ashen-faced" Mick Jagger, who has just watched the footage of the killing. Lucas's one and only contribution, which would probably have been considered an outtake by many, creates one of the most moving moments of the film.

"The vibes were bad" at Altamont, Jefferson Airplane lead singer Grace Slick later recalled. "Something was very peculiar—not particularly bad, just real peculiar. It was that kind of hazy, abrasive, and unsure day. I had expected the loving vibes of Woodstock but that wasn't coming at me. This was a whole different thing."

After the breakup of the Jefferson Airplane in the early 1970s, Slick and guitarist Paul Kantner retooled the Airplane into the more progressive-sounding Jefferson Starship. Airplane vocalist Marty Balin soon reunited with Slick and Kantner and wrote and sang lead vocals on their 1975 hit "Miracles." In February 1978, with the release of *Earth*, Balin's songs "Runaway" and "Count on Me" became huge US hit singles, catapulting the Jefferson Starship to worldwide success.

A few weeks into *Star Wars'* record-shattering theatrical run, Kermit Eller was making promotional appearances dressed as Darth Vader in the Northern California area and somehow coordinated a visit to Kantner and Slick's home overlooking San Francisco Bay. The band had been rehearsing, and they all stopped to pose with Elder, who at one point feigned holding Slick and Balin up by their necks.

Around this time, Slick's onstage antics were getting incrementally more violent. Sometime in 1978, she was reportedly dragged off of a local San Francisco game show for abusing the contestants. That June, matters got worse. While the band was touring Europe, Slick fell ill and could not perform at the Lorelei Festival in Germany. The promotors were nervous; the crowd was already upset that the Atlanta Rhythm Section had just canceled their appearance. After guitarist David Frieberg bravely went onstage and announced that his band would not be performing either, keyboardist Pete

A year before the Special, Darth Vader (played here by Kermit Eller) crashed a Jefferson Starship rehearsal at Grace Slick and Paul Kantner's Bay Area home. The band's guitarist, Craig Chaquico, can be seen behind them. © *Roger Ressmeyer/CORBIS/VCG via Getty Images*

Sears recalls, "People started throwing rocks and bottles. A couple of our roadies got hit by stuff. Somebody got an axe and started chopping up the drum kit. Somebody got some gasoline and set fire to the stage. People started stealing stuff and started throwing amplifiers over the cliffs into the Rhine River. It was pretty bad."

All of the band's instruments and equipment were either stolen or destroyed, so they had to borrow items for the following night's taping of a television show in Hamburg. By then, Slick's health had improved, but now she was drunk and baiting the audience members, asking them, "Who won the war?" and calling them Nazis before giving the "Heil Hitler" salute. As Sears put it in a *Rolling Stone* interview shortly before the incident, "Grace has a serious problem . . . she's such a beautiful person when she's sober, but it's like an instant change after one drink. Dark forces seem to take over."

At some point afterward, Kantner asked for her resignation and told her to check into rehab. By all accounts, she did exactly that.

Looking back at the incident several years later, Slick was ashamed of her behavior that night. "I'm in Germany and I'm gonna get back at them for Dachau or some dumb, drunken decision?" she asked. "That's what that night was about, dumb, drunken decisions."

The rest of the band members were quite relieved when they returned to the States, Slick-less. Their only upcoming gig was an August televised appearance on the *Star Wars Holiday Special*. But if the band thought *Slick* was challenging, they had yet to spend twenty hours shooting a five-minute music video for David Acomba.

Jefferson Starship had just recorded a new song called "Light the Sky on Fire," written by guitarist Craig Chaquico, which they planned to perform on the show, featuring the lines, "The great god Kopa Khan . . . came from the stars and vanished . . . / He will come back again someday." The song is a bit pretentious but is emblematic of the era. At its best, it's a half-hearted attempt to capture the alleged spirituality and pseudo-mysticism being blasted from several rock bands of the time, specifically Jethro Tull and Led Zeppelin. At its worst, it's not as good as the music Christopher Guest, Michael McKean, and Harry Shearer wrote and performed in *Spinal Tap*. Chaquico's lyrics hearken less Led Zeppelin's "secret elders of the gentle race" and more Spinal Tap's "Rock 'n' Roll Creation": "When there was darkness and the void was king . . . / When there was silence and the hush was almost deafening."

Chris Taylor, the author of *How Star Wars Conquered the Universe*, suggests that the song was not as mind-expanding as Chaquico perhaps thought it was, calling it "standard rock" and adding that they had "put a mystical wrapper on it for the stoner in the record store. It's like that whole *Chariot of the Gods* thing that was popular in the '70s, and *Battlestar Galactica*, which comes out at almost the same time, has that whole thing in [its opening crawl]: 'Maybe among the stars, the ancestors of the Egyptians, or the Toltecs, or the Mayans,' and that whole original intro. Like, we're going to get you interested in this, through *Chariots of the Gods*. ['Light the Sky on Fire'] kind of feels the same as that, but it's in *Star Wars*, where it doesn't belong."

For his part, Chaquico says that his actual lyrics did not refer to "Kopa Khan"—which already might be mistaken for Kubla Kahn, the subject of the famous Samuel Coleridge poem referred to in a newsreel in *Citizen Kane*, which describes a "stately pleasure-dome." Chaquico's actual reference was *Kukulkhan*—a serpent deity worshipped by the Mayans. "The original god from the stars I was referring to is the lizard serpent god," Chaquico explains. "I've heard it pronounced several different ways. It's not Kopa Kahn, though. Marty [Balin] took some creative license."

Confused? You should be.

"*Kopa* Kahn, *Kubla*-kan, *Chaka* Kahn, Count Chocula . . . I mean, they could have been talking about Kukla, Fran, and Ollie for that matter and it still wouldn't have made a difference," says comedian Tony Douglas. "The song still sucks."

With Slick away at rehab, Balin sang lead vocals on the recording, and the band prepared to fly down to Los Angeles to lip-synch the track for the Special. Meanwhile, at the Smith–Hemion offices, there was a discussion about whether or not to cancel their booking because of Slick's absence. As Vilanch puts it, "Why would we bring in Jefferson Starship without Grace Slick? *She's* the show." Booking the band without Slick was akin to booking Dawn without Tony Orlando. In the end, however, the producers had no time to look for a replacement act as popular as Jefferson Starship (or with such a fitting name).

When the band arrived at Warner Bros Studios, the set was in chaos. "It just seemed the most clueless operation I can remember," recalls saxophonist Steve Schuster, "and I've been around a lot of clueless operations."

One of the many issues that the crew was dealing with that day was Slick, who—according to several wire stories at the time—was desperately trying to reach the band, wondering why they were taping the song without her. An unnamed CBS spokesperson was quoted as saying that the stage was "closed on orders from nearly everybody, because of Grace Slick . . . you know, her not being there and all," and that "aides to the Starship were warned to tell no one that Grace had started calling frantically at the start of taping, to find out why the group was filming without her and where they could be reached."

It is unclear whether Slick was in rehab at that exact moment or if she was at home, but the concept of her feeling slighted by not being invited to participate in the Special is one of the biggest ironies of the entire event. As *Fanboys* director Kyle Newman notes, "She's gotten unceremoniously removed from the band, and here she's trying to illegally get onto the studio lot to become a part of this thing, which becomes one of the biggest failures in the history of popular culture."

Now in her mid-eighties, and having admittedly consumed insanely voluminous amounts of drugs and alcohol throughout her lifetime, it's not surprising that Slick "doesn't remember any of it." Jeff Jampol, the current manager of the Jefferson Starship adds, "It was a strange time. She doesn't remember if she was actually in rehab at the time…there were many trips to different facilities back then."

When Slick watches the band's Holiday Special performance at the author's request, she is extremely relieved to have not been part of it. "Indeed, I am very happy to have missed it," she says.

Although the previous days' shoots had been difficult, there seemed to have been *some* pre-production planning for the scenes that had already been shot: the cantina, the holographic acrobats, and Harvey Korman's Julia Child parody. By comparison, the Jefferson Starship scene was apparently thrown together pretty quickly.

At the time, twenty-three-year-old Chaquico was by far the youngest member of the band, and while they all seemed excited to be there, the guitarist was particularly, out-of-his-head jazzed to be part of the production. Like everyone else, he was completely unaware of what he was going to be doing, but he seemed to be the most excited about the *Star Wars* TV project. He guessed they would "be in this science-fiction scene, and I'm thinking of a rock 'n' roll version of the [cantina] bar scene."

The band members had been told that costumes would be provided for them, which would normally mean individually custom-made outfits put together by a wardrobe designer. When Chaquico learned that that person was Bob Mackie, he had even wilder expectations.

"When they said 'wardrobe' and then you recognize this name of the guy that's been nominated for Oscars and things, you're going, 'Wow, what'd they dig up for us? *Star Wars* came up with those cool stormtrooper outfits, what are *we* gonna be? Are we gonna be like Jedi Knights, or what are we gonna look like?'"

Reality must have hit hard when the band members were led into a small room full of unrelated articles of clothing and accessories hanging on racks, resembling less Mackie's dressing room and more a thrift shop. Sears says, "They let us loose in a room full of props, like a costume room kind of thing. They said, 'Just try and make up an outfit.' No direction, really. 'Just individually make up anything you want. Just as long as it looks like it's from another galaxy or something, or from the future.'"

Chaquico says the costumes were more like the assorted pieces of traditional Halloween getups you would purchase in a drugstore. "It wasn't like there were seven or eight outfits laid out," he recalls. "It was just a mishmash of costumes from different TV shows and movies, from all sorts of period pieces. I definitely recognized Westerns; there were gladiator things and a [costume from a] Viking movie."

The six of them proceeded to fish through the unorganized garb, much like four-year-olds looking through a costume bin in a playroom. "We just found a little bit of this and that," Sears recalls. "I had a scarf and wrapped it around my arm. I don't remember what anybody else was wearing."

Ultimately, Chaquico ended up not even wearing a shirt. "I kind of went for the Indian part of it because I thought there probably were Native Americans on other planets that they evolved on G-type stars or atmospheres. And so I picked a pair of leggings and some boots."

The props weren't organized any better either. According to Steve Schuster, although he played saxophone in the band, the prop instrument he was given was made from a bass clarinet. He is still heartbroken that someone had taken this "ancient and wonderful instrument" and spray-painted it silver, rendering it useless for any future use. "There's some poor kid in an orchestra living in Watts that will never play bass clarinet as a consequence."

David Frieberg was given by far the most ridiculous prop instrument to use—a keytar. "They handed him one of those things that were brand new at the time," Sears recalls, "those keyboards that you wear around your neck." It was the sort of instrument that looks like it belongs in a Devo video, not one produced by Jefferson Starship. In musician Jeff Babko's view, "It's a desperate attempt at trying to force this band into a futuristic box . . . it looks utterly ridiculous, because you know David Frieberg didn't play a keyboard like that on the record."

Sears, who had recently lost his bass guitar at the Lorelei riot, usually played a "beat-up" bass, "but I chose the white one just because I thought, 'Maybe our people in the future would play a white bass.'" Overall, Sears tried to keep a positive attitude. "We just kind of went for it. You've been hired to do this thing and you go along with it. Just to be a part of the *Star Wars* thing was cool. We all loved the movie, and we were just happy to be a part of that. . . . I didn't really know what to expect. I mean, I figured that they had their stuff together, you know?"

Heider, who had previously done camerawork for *Don Kirshner's Rock Concert*, was excited about shooting the band. "When I found out that Jefferson Starship was going to be part of the shoot, that we were actually going to shoot a number with them, I thought, 'Wow, now I know how to do rock 'n' roll' . . . I thought this was going to be really cool." Unfortunately for him, the day would become another nightmare shoot.

As for Acomba's directing style, nothing much had changed. Sure, none of the band members fainted that day, but he seemed even more lost than he had the previous days. "He would look at some shots and then even go outside the truck and walk around and think about what he was going to do," Newt Bellis recalls. "It was a very strange situation. And all the time, there were a hundred people there standing there doing whatever."

By now, the job was weighing on Acomba even further. With Lucas now gone, he later admitted, "There was no center. I couldn't seem to grasp it. I'm the director. I'm supposed to know. I'm supposed to draw on something that makes it all work. And so, in those first days of shooting, everything came home to roost. And it was hell."

Sears recalls the shoot seeming to last forever: "I remember the long hours. It seemed like hours because we'd shoot a bit and then stop and start again. It was quite fatiguing."

In Heider's memory, the shooting was delayed by one of the band members arriving late, though he doesn't remember which one. Once that person arrived, things got started, but "we kind of like weren't directed. This was one thing we were just told, 'Let's just shoot this as a rock 'n' roll video and let that play out that way,' and that's what we did."

Someone had convinced Acomba to finally use all of his available cameras for this music shoot, so, with this segment, they had the use of five in total: three studio-based, one Steadicam, and one on a crane.

"We did it several times with different angles," Heider says. "I had the camera with the lens to do more of [the close-up work]. I was doing tight shots of the guitar strings and moving from hand to head—things you would do in a music video. The Steadicam was doing some weird-angled rock 'n' roll thing, and the crane was going up and down, zooming in and out. I shot some guitar shots, low and high, and tried to throw in everything I could into the mix and give something to use in editing." As Heider recalls, the finished product was supposed to look like a music video, but it didn't really come off as such. "It was just kind of a one-off, kind of weird part of the show."

The cameramen weren't the only people on the set without direction. Sears says the band was given little information, and definitely no context at all as to how this segment would be incorporated into the Special. "We didn't really know how they were going to use it," he recalls. "I'm not even certain *they* knew how they were gonna use it."

In the Special that aired, the setup of the scene would be fairly basic: Trader Dann (played by Art Carney) presents a video player to an Imperial officer that will project a miniaturized hologram of Jefferson Starship in order to distract him. Before Carney starts the video, he channels Ed Norton, the character he played on *The Honeymooners*, spending way too much time trying to swat an imaginary fly. (The script included the specific direction, "Trader Dann does Norton schtick." There are similar directions elsewhere that require R2-D2 to give a "[Jack] Benny stare," as well as ending a scene "as Oliver Hardy would as he looked into the camera and gave us, 'Oh.'") Irritated at all the nonsense, the officer—channeling Ralph Kramden— abruptly stands up and bellows, "Will you get on with it?"

Meanwhile, Acomba was getting increasingly frustrated with the scene. The track was being played repeatedly, dozens of times, and he still wasn't getting what he had envisioned. "It wasn't really what I wanted," Acomba recalled. "I was trying to take the music someplace else and [do] something different." At one point, the visual effects on the stage were not working according to plan. Acomba threw down his headset and stormed off the set, according to assistant to the producers Elle Puritz.

According to Mitzie Welch, Acomba's original plans for shooting the band had been rejected as being too convoluted for just one song in a two-hour special. "He called us all to his room and he showed us this incredible set. I mean, *quite elaborate.* There was no way to afford that kind of dream that he had. There was no way to make it happen in the amount of time or with the budget that was given."

Ken Welch agreed that the time that would have been required to actually produce Acomba's idea made it impossible to attempt. "He had laid out in such a way that, had we continued to shoot it in the way he had it laid out, we'd still be shooting. Every shot, I think, would've taken a day to set up, had we done it David's way."

At one point, Hemion saw that Acomba was having a sort of "director's block" and asked if he could "take a shot at it."

"Go ahead, be my guest," Acomba responded.

"He's about the only person I would step out of the chair for, because he was a great television director," Acomba recalled.

The third day of shooting couldn't have ended a minute too soon. "We were pretty exhausted at the end," Sears says. "We just put everything we had into it and probably overdid it a bit. We all looked pretty silly, really."

In the end, Chaquico saw it as two worlds colliding, and he was in the middle of it. "It was a strange iteration of the original big-screen movie concept and your regular variety-show, Carol Burnett vibe. I was, like, tripping on it myself, man."

* * *

By this point, Smith and Hemion had an even bigger issue on their plate beyond the budget and the schedule. The division between Acomba and several of the producers needed to be addressed and resolved immediately. Many of the crew were now aware of the growing tension on the set. "It got to the point where no one was understanding Acomba's approach to the project," Heider recalls.

On the other hand, Acomba was also tremendously frustrated that he was not given the amount of control that he was used to having as a director. In this era, a television director was less of a visionary and more someone who worked with the cameramen to get the most ideal coverage of what was being produced.

At the time, Heider was one of the top cameramen in the genre. The only attribute that outweighed his technical skills was his tremendous patience. "We, as camera operators, tried our best to do what he wanted to get done, and to help him anyway we could," he says. "But he wasn't too interested in getting outside help."

During the Starship shoot, Heider says, "I would see Dwight [Hemion] and Gary [Smith] go off somewhere and have some conversations by themselves, which is kind of unusual." In his experience of past shoots, he says, "it would be pretty much a family thing, where if somebody had a problem with something, you'd just speak it out loud, and everybody might be able to come up with an idea to help fix it."

Acomba would later recall that when he was initially hired, his intention was to "first see what George [Lucas] wanted and to see what Gary [Smith] wanted, and to be given those jumping off points. But quickly Ken and Mitzie were assigned to the show, whom I didn't know." The idea that producers could be assigned to the show without his consultation caught Acomba off guard. "Then, when I found out what they did—that they wrote the music for the singing numbers [on *The Carol Burnett Show*]—I just thought that was one of the worst parts of the show, singing all those kinds of sort of fake Broadway forgettable show tunes."

Although Acomba did not get along with the Welches, he developed a great working relationship and friendship with the writers, and he hung out with Ripps often. "David was the voice of George, and we really liked David," Ripps recalls. "If David had an idea or we wanted to run something by him, or there were questions, our assumption was that it was also what George wanted."

Rita Scott thought very highly of Acomba creatively, but she was frustrated that he didn't value the experience of or input from the show's producers. "David was one of the most imaginative, creative young guys I had worked with, but, like so many people who are creative, they didn't really share their thoughts, their ideas," she recalled. "So, what happened was that the producers and David were working in different directions, because they weren't talking to one another, particularly on the musical numbers."

Scott explained that Acomba would change major portions of the Welches' segments without telling them, which worsened their already strained relationship. "You have to remember that Ken and Mitzie were very, very successful special-music writers, and they would write something and David would change it without any discussion. And that became problematic. You had four extremely talented people [Acomba, Joe Layton, and the Welches], and they weren't able to talk. And it became problematic because, even when we had a discussion about how important communication was, David agreed, and then something would happen. And we would be back in the same predicament that we were in. It didn't hurt the show, but it was problematic for [Smith and Hemion] and for Ken, Mitzie, and Joe."

But by this time, Joe Layton had had enough and left for another show. Although this may have been the result of the growing in-fighting between Acomba and the Welches (who were Layton's partners at the time), it is more likely he just got offered a better gig—possibly one that involved less stress and was more within his wheelhouse than the *Star Wars Holiday Special.*

Although Vilanch was aware of much of what was going on at the show, he didn't know about the ongoing rift between Acomba and the Welches. "I know that Ken and Mitzie were old-school, and they were used to doing it a certain way, and David wasn't crazy about that. They just weren't on the same wavelength, and David felt that he was on George [Lucas]'s wavelength."

Acomba's over-shooting, the schedule and budget problems, and his conflict with the producers were all starting to worry CBS. "Everything was taking forever, and there were lots of stops and starts," Vilanch says. "And the network freaked out." CBS was concerned that Acomba was going to continue to go over budget, the show was going to get farther behind schedule, and they wouldn't have enough material shot to edit and deliver the two-hour special. According to Vilanch, Smith and Hemion finally said, "We have to get rid of him. We have to lose him."

Acomba left town before Smith's lightsaber could be drawn, however. There was no time for goodbyes. "I sent a telegram—how romantic," he recalled. "I didn't even tell my agent."

According to the Welches, Acomba sent a telegram to them and a few other staffers, advising them of his resignation and his impending return to Toronto, where he would resume his film career. Ripps and Proft were particularly disappointed, as they had nothing but high marks for Acomba as a collaborator, although Ripps acknowledges they were likely in the minority.

"When David left, there were problems, because directors don't leave when things are going well."

Twenty years later, it was still upsetting for Acomba to revisit that time period. "It was traumatic for me," he reflected. "One of the reasons why I left was that it just was not working, and it was very confusing because so many people had their fingers in the pie ... I thought I would have more control than I ended up having." He recalled calling Lucas a few times to say he was having a hard time, "but I couldn't keep calling him, nor did I want to."

Vilanch feels sorry for Acomba for having to leave such a high-stakes production under these circumstances. "He kind of went back partially with his tail tucked between his legs, but partially with the time-honored, 'Christ, Hollywood, they don't know what the fuck they're doing, no wonder everything is such crap that comes outta Hollywood. I'm going back to Toronto ...' and he went back and did some beautiful stuff."

In addition to removing Acomba as director, Smith–Hemion had another important decision to make. "Given the amount of overtime that they were creating, and how expensive that was all becoming for the production company, something very unusual happened," Heider recalls. "We just hit the brakes, and we came to a complete stop. Everybody was told we were going to be down for a while until they figured out the direction that they wanted to go next. ... So we had some time off, which was good for some of us to sleep and relax, and that's what we did."

There was also a practical reason to halt shooting: there was a big set change to deal with. They had to strike the huge cantina set and build an even larger Wookiee treehouse. That process would take a while anyway, even if they found another director to help them out of this mess. But Miki Herman recalls a feeling of panic at that point among the producers: "They were scrambling. ... They didn't know anything about science fiction."

CBS would soon be making a decision about the future of the Special, and Smith–Hemion would need to find a new director—or just give up, admit defeat, and recycle the tapes. Most of those involved were hoping for the latter, as Smith–Hemion always had lots of shows in production that needed staffing. No need to get back on the Lucas-less Holiday Special train if there were other options available.

What would the network executives decide? If they quit now, they would

After only three days of shooting, Acomba's overtime shoots had exhausted nearly the entire budget for the Special. Cameraman Larry Heider caught executive producers Gary Smith (*left*) and Dwight Hemion contemplating their next steps. After the decision was made to fire Acomba, he wound up quitting anyway and headed back to Toronto. *Photo by Larry Heider*

lose all the money they'd advanced Smith–Hemion that had already been spent. And they would only have three months to replace a two-hour prime-time slot in the middle of a sweeps period.

At that point, Vilanch says, "It was clear that it had to be salvaged by somebody else."

Gary Smith says his choices were limited. Some just assumed that Dwight Hemion, one of the most critically acclaimed TV directors in the industry, would take over for Acomba. However, Smith says that wasn't an option. "I know Dwight didn't want to do it, as I recall."

To channel Dr. Phil, "It's like you've got a five-alarm fire and you ain't got no hose."

But they didn't need a hose. They needed a fireman.

CHAPTER 9

THE FIREMAN

STEVE BINDER WAS in between gigs, relaxing at home for a few weeks until his next show, *Christmas at Walt Disney World*, started production. One of the top producer-directors in the business, he had just won an Emmy for producing *The Barry Manilow Show* and had spent most of 1978 producing and directing the second season of the series *Shields and Yarnell*, as well as finishing an Olivia Newton-John special.

Breaks like these were hard to find for busy directors like Binder. Then the phone rang. It was Gary Smith, whom Binder had known since the mid-'60s, when they both worked on the rock music TV series *Hullabaloo*.

Smith making his first call to Binder was an obvious move: "I always liked working with him, we enjoyed each other's company," Smith recalls. However, over the years, Smith says, Binder probably always considered himself a second banana to Hemion. "I think that he always felt that he was filling in for Dwight a little bit."

When Smith asked what Binder was doing, Binder said he was down for two weeks until his next project started. So Smith made the pitch.

"He asked me, 'How would you like to do me a favor and go back to work during those two weeks?'" Binder recalls.

To say that at this point Binder was arguably the top director in the industry is no reach. At the time, he'd been nominated for six Emmys, but just like the Grammys and the Oscars, the academy's members always seemed to omit the best work. One of the first films he ever directed was 1964's *T.A.M.I. Show*, which featured the Rolling Stones, Chuck Berry, Marvin Gaye, the Beach Boys, Jan and Dean, James Brown, the Supremes, and the

Miracles with Smokey Robinson—and, to this day, it is considered by many critics to be the greatest rock film ever produced. More importantly, it was one of the first times that white and Black acts performed on a stage together on film. Binder broke that barrier.

Binder's résumé also included a 1968 television showcase for Petula Clark, which likewise became a game-changer in TV race relations. While taping a duet between Clark and Harry Belafonte of the civil rights song "On the Paths of Glory," Binder was having issues getting a good take; they had done three, but he was unhappy with all of them. The original staging of the song called for Belafonte to be upstage; after he sang his verse, Clark was to walk downstage and stand just behind him. On the next take, Binder told Clark to continue walking and stand right beside him. She did, and at one point, caught up in the emotion of the song, Clark reached out and put her hand on Belafonte's forearm.

"There was the sound of elephants storming into the control room as the ad-agency reps ran to go alert their bosses," Binder recalls. After an NBC executive phoned the control room to tell Binder he had their support regarding the controversial shot, Binder—along with Clark's husband—went down to the editor and directed him to erase the other three takes. "The Touch" would eventually be remembered as one of TV's most controversial moments.

Most famously, Binder had rehabilitated Elvis Presley's career by directing and producing the infamous *'68 Comeback Special*. Binder fought Colonel Tom Parker throughout the production, encouraging Elvis to reunite with his original bandmates, Scotty Moore and D. J. Fontana, and play acoustic versions of his hit songs. Binder unknowingly created *Unplugged* decades before it would become just another predictable twist in a recording artist's music career. (In Baz Luhrmann's 2022 biopic *Elvis*, Binder is played by *Stranger Things'* Dacre Montgomery and is undisputedly the hero of the story.)

As the director of the *Comeback Special*, Binder fulfilled an amazing challenge: he made Elvis look undirected and spontaneous, uniting him with the raw soul that had initially propelled him to want to perform in front of audiences in the first place. "For me, the '68 special is seeing a man rediscover himself. I saw it on his face and in his body language as we progressed."

During production of the special, Bobby Kennedy was assassinated, which left the entire crew devastated. Elvis—still mourning the assassination of Martin Luther King Jr. just two months earlier—was told by Binder that he needed to make a statement. Binder had music director Earl Brown write a civil rights piece for the end of the show, and Brown penned arguably the greatest song Elvis ever recorded for the special's climax, "If I Can Dream." (In an amazing coincidence, Brown was a staff songwriter for dozens of variety shows, including *Donny and Marie*—where, ten years later, he would write the lyrics to all the songs in their *Star Wars*–themed episode.)

"I wanted to let the world know that here was a guy who was not prejudiced—who was raised in the heart of prejudice, but who was really above all that," Binder recalls. "Part of the strength that I wanted to bring to the show was [that sense of] compassion, that this was somebody to look up to and admire."

Elvis's return to basics blew critics and audiences away. It was one of the most amazing rehabilitations that entertainment audiences had ever witnessed. It revitalized a career gone stagnant, reminding everyone that Elvis was still very much in the building. So, if Binder could go up against the likes of Colonel Tom Parker and help build back Elvis's post-Army, B-movie career with the *'68 Comeback Special*, he could certainly get this *Star Wars Holiday Special* for Smith–Hemion out of the supply closet and back on track—right?

* * *

On the phone, Smith explained his predicament: that he had started a two-hour *Star Wars* special with George Lucas for CBS, they had just shut down production, and they were way over budget. "There's a decision being made right now on whether to continue making the special or shutting it down permanently." Smith was basically asking him to come into the office, evaluate the situation, and help convince CBS to keep the production going. Binder was curious enough. He said he'd come and meet them at Warner Bros Studios.

In the meantime, Smith sent Binder something that he considered "invaluable" to the project: Lucas's twenty-five-page backstory about Chewbacca's family and the planet Kashyyyk. "It was brilliantly put together by George," Binder recalls, referring to it as a "bible." It included backstories of several of the main characters, as well as outlines of a dozen or so *Star Wars* stories. "I read it the night before I went out to Warner Bros so I would know the backstory." Binder knew that if the show resumed production, Smith would want him to start shooting immediately.

When he arrived to meet Smith and Hemion at the soundstage, Binder learned that Lucas had been "heavily involved in making this." Smith explained Lucas's reasons for wanting to do a special—that Lucas had a huge financial interest in the sale of Kenner Toys' *Star Wars* merchandise, which the company had drastically ramped up production of for the upcoming holiday season. Then, during the Special's November 17th broadcast, Kenner would inundate CBS's airwaves with *Star Wars* toy commercials.

Smith told Binder that Lucas conceived this two-hour variety special "to sell toys, which is totally logical." Binder understood the dynamic instantly: "George found himself sitting with what could be a bigger moneymaker than the film was with all the toys."

As the three continued to discuss the Special, they walked onto the soundstage where the carpenters were putting the finishing touches to a massive treehouse built from a design by Ralph McQuarrie, the conceptual artist who had designed Chewbacca, R2-D2, C-3PO, and Darth Vader for *A New Hope*. Unfortunately, the builders had followed McQuarrie's design a bit too closely, creating a four-walled interior set. This was something that a film director would choose to do, not a television director equipped with almost a half-dozen cameras that need to go in and out of the set.

"The first thing I noticed was that this incredible set that they built was totally realistic, but not practical," Binder explains. As exquisite as it was, the treehouse had no openings to allow them to bring equipment in and out of the set: "This was a four-camera shoot, and they would only be able to get one camera in there at a time." (Typically, television sets have only three walls—the "fourth wall" is the one facing the eventual audience, which also allows the cameras and other equipment to occupy that space to get the best possible coverage.)

Lucas had told McQuarrie exactly how he envisioned the treehouse, "and he did a beautiful job," explains Miki Herman. The massive treehouse was to be the home of Chewbacca's family on the forest planet of Kashyyyk.

McQuarrie, however, has said in interviews that his treehouse design was not designed specifically for the Special but for *The Empire Strikes Back*. "I was drawing this forest with the mile-high trees and was deciding what the Wookiees' treehouses should be. We then segued into the Christmas special through that."

In fact, according to the Special's assistant art director, Leslie Parsons, there were originally plans to create a forest on the Burbank soundstage, similar to what Endor looks like in *Return of the Jedi*. However, due to the massive amount of overtime spent on the first week of shooting, this idea had to be scrapped.

Binder delivered the bad news about the treehouse to Smith. "The first thing that you've gotta do is, you've gotta [create] a fourth wall." He explained that he needed to have the art director cut out one of the walls so that the cameras could move in and out of the area. "When [the wall is] out, you can bring all your equipment in—multiple cameras, sound equipment, and obviously a lot of humans. You'll be able to shoot the show in a practical way."

Always one for a challenge, Binder agreed to help out Smith and Hemion, while clearly emphasizing that he only had two weeks to give them and would not have time to oversee the show's editing. That responsibility is almost always given to television directors and hardly ever transferred to anyone else. But editing was far off in the future for these two desperate producers. The most important thing for them at the moment was putting the fire out.

CBS gave Smith–Hemion the go-ahead to resume production, so Smith called Binder to tell him they would have the fourth wall removed from the treehouse set by the time he arrived on Monday. Smith added that they would start shooting from "the actual script, just as it was originally written and approved by George." It was almost as if Smith had predicted that Binder might have issues with some parts of the script and that their timetable wouldn't allow for any changes. But Binder wouldn't have a second to mess with it anyway: he had to start getting some tape in the can before they shut the whole production down again.

When the staff came back from the break, most of them welcomed Binder's arrival. "As soon as we knew Steve was going to be there, I think people breathed easy, because Steve is a very, very good man to be in control," Heider recalls. "He brought a sense of control that was missing from the production, which helped get things back on track."

When Erwin learned of the switch, he was grateful as well: "I thought, 'At least stuff's going to start working relatively normal from now on, now that Steve Binder's here.'" He called Binder a "top-notch guy" who spent the first few days "gathering the troops, making sure he could make an assault on the show." However, by the third day, "the look on his face . . . he had started losing blood in his face." It was evident to Erwin that Binder could indeed put out the fire and give the producers something substantial to edit with, but it would be no walk in the park.

One of the restrictions Binder was given was that none of the actors in Wookiee costumes could use human voices. "When they dubbed *Star Wars*, they inserted authentic audio of bears grunting and communicating," Binder says. These specific Wookiee costumes were designed so that "one can manipulate the mouth and the eyes and the expression of the Chewbaccas," as Binder so fondly referred to the Wookiee family. "The actors weren't allowed to say anything behind those masks, and they could only move their mouths."

On the first morning of the treehouse shoot, production assistant Peter Kimmel was told to drop everything he was doing and go pick up Peter Mayhew at his hotel. Smith–Hemion had flown Mayhew in from London and put him up at the exceedingly luxurious Westwood Marquis hotel on the Westside, but someone had apparently forgotten to order a limousine to transport him to the studio, which was located in the San Fernando Valley. Kimmel jumped in his car, hopped on the Ventura Freeway, and headed toward Westwood—a drive that, with traffic, could take anywhere from sixty to ninety minutes.

When he arrived in front of the hotel, he realized someone had forgotten to fill him in on Mayhew's specifications. "It was kind of a chore because the man is fifteen inches taller than I am," Kimmel recalls. "I had a '75 Camaro at the time. Good thing I didn't have my '63 Porsche that I had sold a couple years before, because there was no way he could have gotten in that car."

Most Camaros from that time period came with lots of legroom, but they rode very low to the ground and had low ceilings. "I pull up in front of the hotel and he comes out, and then we have to figure out how to get him in the car." Kimmel says he pushed the seat all the way back and Mayhew climbed in, bending his knees so severely that they were up against the dashboard and pushing up against his chin. His head was bent to the side with his cheek pressed up against the ceiling of the car as they took the hour ride back to the set. "We chatted, but it was hard, as his head was numb" from the way he was positioned in the car. "He couldn't have been very comfortable, but he didn't complain, because that's who he was," Kimmel says. "He was a really wonderful, gentle soul, and he just was happy to be where he was."

On the ride home, Mayhew said he particularly enjoyed his job because he got to be "a different being," telling Kimmel that his character "was not a man and not an animal but some sort of new and different creature. I remember reading something that Spielberg said that no matter how hard Peter tried to be fierce, he just never was able to pull it off. He had a particular characteristic when he roared or when he got angry, but that was Peter Mayhew bringing that to the character, and it became a Chewbacca trait."

When Heider arrived to begin shooting the first scene in Chewbacca's living room, he noticed that the set looked "sitcom-ish," so he shot it like it was one. At the same time, "I thought this was just a really interesting set that we'd never seen before on television. Usually, it's somebody's apartment or house, and it's very obvious what it is, and this was a little more exotic." He had worked for the producers many times and thought "it was something that I wouldn't expect from Smith–Hemion. It was like a movie."

Brian Ward remarks that the living room is quite jarring at first. The story starts out with Han Solo and Chewbacca trying to outrun a Star Destroyer, then all of a sudden they're on "what looks like the set of a sitcom . . . essentially a sci-fi version of *The Brady Bunch* household, with the weird carpet and furniture that you just don't expect Wookiees to have."

Frankly, the "sitcom" reference is not too far out there. Back before *Star Wars* was even released, Fox's Pevers had dangled the idea of a possible television show to Kenner Toys CEO Bernie Loomis. Several crew members were aware of the interest in potentially launching a television series about the Wookiees, recalled set designer Garrett Lewis, who thought the Special might have been a precursor to a possible show. "So that's why we developed that Wookiee world, which you never got to see in the movie," he said.

According to Mitzie Welch, "We didn't know it then, but I think what [Lucas] was actually interested in was the possibility of a sitcom." She adds, "He had plans for perhaps a series based on the animated series," likely referring to the Boba Fett cartoon. Rita Scott confirmed that "there was talk about it, but it was very minor," while Patty Maloney, who played Chewbacca's son Lumpy, counters that "there was definitely talk about it," adding that Peter Mayhew "would have just made guest appearances, because he lived in England. Unless they would have made it worth his while to move here for a time." Mayhew added that "there may have been some concepts under development, but that's another story."

Nelvana's Michael Hirsh hadn't heard anything about Lucas wanting to do a sitcom about *Star Wars*, but he thought that the cartoon they were working on together was more along the lines of what he wanted to do in the first place. "If he did the Special, there was a possibility Fox and CBS would fund *Star Wars* cartoons. The variety show itself wasn't something he was particularly interested in."

Although Mayhew is one of the few cast members who didn't regret appearing in the Special, he did find it humorous how his family was cast and portrayed. "I learned a lot about my family—a family I knew nothing about," Mayhew recalled at a convention in 2011. "It was just nice to know that I have a wife, I think . . . a transsexual wife, because my wife was played by a [male] actor who was six-foot-four and about three hundred pounds," he added, referring to Mickey Morton, who played Malla (short for "Mallatobuck"). "My son was played by a little female"—Patty Maloney— "and my father-in-law was played by a nineteen-year-old student." Paul Gale, who played Itchy, was actually twenty-nine at the time and is otherwise best known as the green-faced, red-haired Horatio J. Hoodoo from *The World of Sid and Marty Krofft*. (Mayhew mistakenly refers to Itchy as his father-in-law, when during the opening of the Special he is specifically identified as Chewbacca's father.)

Itchy, short for Attichicuk, was a silver-backed four-hundred-year-old cuss. In the living room scene, he is carving an X-Wing fighter the size of a model airplane, while Lumpy (short for "Lumpawarrump") is playing with a completed model of one. So, in the first minutes of the Special, the toys—which would finally become available during the weekend after the show

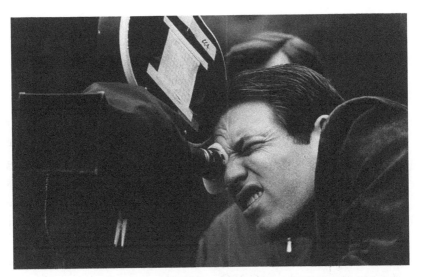

After David Acomba quit, executive producer Gary Smith called in critically acclaimed director Steve Binder to resume shooting. Binder, who had produced and directed Elvis's massively successful '68 Comeback Special ten years earlier, brought what cameraman Larry Heider calls "a calmness" to the production. *Photograph by Bob Willoughby*

aired—were fully on display, not limited to commercials but strategically and organically inserted into the show's storyline. Years later, this sort of "screenwriting" would simply be called product placement.

* * *

Steve Binder sought to create a much different working environment than the one Acomba had overseen. First, it was a tradition on all of his shows to gather the crew around and have everybody introduce themselves. "I find a lot of times, when people go to work, they have no clue who they're standing next to, even though they're doing the same show and working together," he says. "So it's really important to me that we bond as a family."

According to assistant art director Leslie Parsons, "There was a redrawing of the parameters and the re-establishing of priorities: 'This is a *television* special, this is a *television* budget, this is a *television* time frame. And we can only afford two hours of overtime a day.'"

There was now a more stringent policy on hours worked—especially for those in heavy costumes. A mandatory break system had been established for all of the scenes involving costumed actors.

Binder learned quickly. "They had to breathe, and those costumes were totally suffocating." He recalls that his actors and extras could only wear these costumes for about forty minutes of every hour, to allow them a twenty-minute break. "They had to get out of their costumes in order to breathe again, recuperate, and be ready for the next hour of shooting."

Indeed, the Wookiee costumes that they were planning to use were far bulkier and heavier than the aliens' costumes in the cantina scene. And the Wookiees weren't the only ones suffering: Anthony Daniels was struggling with his C-3PO outfit, which wasn't porous either. Jay Osmond says Daniels's costume was "so thin it looks liked like it was heavy metal. It's a very fine material. But it really was weird, because when it's right in front of you, it doesn't even look like metal."

When Donny Osmond was performing with Daniels on *Donny and Marie*, he too noticed that C-3PO's outfit was extremely cheap-looking. It did not seem metallic at all, but plastic—and the production team would have to foley over the tremendous noise it made when Daniels sauntered around the stage.

The stormtrooper costumes weren't very comfortable either. When Jay wore one to dance on the show, he noticed the costume was not a hard-shelled outfit. Likewise, on the set of the Special, the stormtroopers' costumes "weren't porous or allowing air in," recalls Mike Erwin. Actor Jack Rader, who played the Imperial Guard officer stationed at Chewbacca's home, saw one actor in a stormtrooper costume completely lose it. "There were a lot of extras running around in these white plastic costumes with the headpiece on and all, and they were sweating. One of them actually threw his headpiece on the floor. I think he was having trouble breathing. I felt really sorry for those folks. That's a tough job, walking around in a costume that you can't move in and you can't breathe in. . . . They were just extras. I felt kind of sorry for them. I guess they'll do anything for money."

Erwin also saw the "endless discomfort" the actors were in that had to wear the stormtrooper outfits. "I remember one actor . . . I don't remember his name, but he was one of the lead stormtrooper guys, and he just lost it by the end of the day. He just started screaming, pounding, stomping around and just kinda lost his mind a little bit. He had a little nervous breakdown, which by that time was not uncommon. Then he got it together and came back."

A record heatwave in the summer of 1978 was just one of the factors that made for a stressful shoot. Mandatory breaks were enacted for the characters to take off their masks, resulting in additional overtime bonuses for the union workers, which placed more stress on the already precarious budget. *CBS via Getty Images*

The Wookiee costumes were designed by Stan Winston, who didn't have a studio. Makeup artist Tom Burman offered to share his and also offered the use of his crew to help deliver costumes back and forth to the soundstage. Burman says Winston referred to his first day on the set as "a tough shoot" and added, "They put this show together very quickly, and it wasn't with a lot of preparation."

Winston had definitely bitten off more than he could chew. He was given the monumental task of delivering all of these costumes within the producers' absolutely unrealistic turnaround time.

"Stan was a very powerful, alpha-male type guy, and under a lot of stress," says Erwin. However, he notes, line producer Monroe Carol was under equally tremendous pressure as he attempted to hold to the budget while "money's going through a sieve. Every fifteen minutes they're spending thirty, fifty, sixty thousand dollars . . .

"Between Monroe Carol and Stan Winston, there was quite a bit of acrimony and ongoing argumentative interactions," said Erwin. "It made quite a stir. It was really chaotic and quite upsetting for everybody in the whole cast and crew. I kinda felt [Winston] was mean to Monroe Carol, and it didn't need to go that far. They could have come to many different levels of understanding other than creating the chaos that they did in their arguments." He adds, "He was a bully. That's my opinion."

While Erwin recalls that the two clashed mainly over the budget, one argument became violent, and for a fairly ridiculous reason. According to Burman, Winston was hauling costumes and other props and equipment back and forth between his truck and the stage, and they got into a fight over his temporarily parking in Carol's space, which was located right next to the stage entrance. Carol was livid and told him to move his truck or he would be fired, to which Erwin says Winston "blasted him like crazy," daring Carol to fire him. "I heard it even came to blows," he adds.

Winston "could be explosive that way," says Burman. "He was a very forceful guy." He says the feud ended with Carol unsuccessfully attempting to fire Winston. In a sad, ironic twist in this battle, Winston went unreprimanded, and Carol was forced to give up his parking space to Winston.

Just after the design phase for the Wookiees started, Stuart Freeborn paid Burman and Winston a visit. Freeborn, who had been a makeup supervisor for *A New Hope* and designed the film's original Chewbacca costume for *Star Wars*, brought the original bodysuit from London to Burman's studio. The ride from London had been a little bumpy, so Burman had to perform a couple of small repairs on the costume. "I got to see it up close," he recalls, "and see how it was made. It was very contrived, and all of the hair on the Wookiee that he had made was all hand tied, one hair at a time."

Once Burman saw the quality of the Chewbacca costume up close, he immediately realized they weren't going to be able to just clone it with the Special's encroaching deadline. Not only was Winston tasked with taking special care of Chewbacca's family costumes, but he also needed to add mechanics to animate the Wookiees' faces, so Burman's older brother Ellis—who, like him, had also worked on *Planet of the Apes*—gave Winston a quick tutorial on Wookiee building.

Lots of time and energy was spent creating Lumpy's mask, with Winston taking advantage of state-of-the-art animatronics technology, similar to how the characters at Disneyland were given detailed facial expressions. Electrical wires were fed from the mask down to the arms, which allowed Maloney to pull rings that subsequently moved Lumpy's nose and mouth. At times, Winston sat behind Maloney and assisted her through certain scenes.

Winston also needed to build a few dozen more Wookiee costumes for the show's finale. Burman suggested that they buy a bunch of cheap wigs, take them all apart, and attach long strips of the hair to pairs of long johns. "That's how we were able to make those things in about two weeks," he says, adding that it was the magic of film and television that hid all of the costumes' imperfections from the viewer. The key to making them work was shooting from a distance. "I don't want to put [Winston] down . . . up close, they were pretty funky, but in a distance they were beautiful," Burman says. "They knew how to shoot them and make them look good."

Freeborn's original Chewbacca costume was by far the nicest—and, at eighty pounds, probably the heaviest. During shooting, Mayhew was taking many more breaks than the others, not because he was a sort of celebrity now but because he was carrying a much heavier load. Binder recalls that Patty Maloney came into the studio weighing about sixty-five pounds and insists she lost ten pounds from the heat.

Maloney was one of the busiest little people in the industry. She had started out as a performer with Sid and Marty Krofft's traveling show, starring as Piglet in *House on Pooh Corner*. After moving into television, she soon appeared on such shows as *Charlie's Angels*, *The Love Boat*, and *The Addams Family*, where she played the nonverbal clump of hair Cousin Itt. However, her big break had been playing the costumed character Honk on the Saturday morning children's series *Far Out Space Nuts*. It co-starred Chuck McCann and Bob Denver, the latter fresh off his three-season stint as Gilligan on *Gilligan's Island*. According to author Ted Nichelson, Maloney and Denver struck up a romantic relationship during production.

* * *

The treehouse sequence also includes one of the Special's most bizarre and ill-conceived ideas. "If I ever tell anybody about the *Star Wars Holiday Special*, the first thing I do is to tell them that there is a scene involving a Wookiee watching pornography on prime-time television," says *Fanboys* director Kyle Newman. "I just take people right to that sequence and say,

'Watch this . . . it's the worst five minutes of television you will ever see in your life.' It's uncomfortable. It's inappropriate. It's mindbogglingly awful. And it exists."

To this day, it is baffling that this segment was included in a special targeted at kids. It is by far the most bizarre, out-of-place, and talked-about part of the entire two-hour show. It's not funny or dramatic, nor is it the least bit entertaining. It is inappropriate, tasteless, and about as cringeworthy as anything ever seen on a prime-time network show.

In the Special, Art Carney's Saul Dann comes over with a contraption called a "mind evaporator" and places it on Itchy's head, confiding in him, "I thought you might like this. One of those, well, it's kinda hard to explain. It's a . . . wow, you know what I mean? Happy Life Day," he says, adding, under his breath, "*and I do mean Happy Life Day . . .*"

According to Vilanch, Lucas had very specific directions about the "mind evaporator," as Lucas referred to it. "[George told us] when you put this helmet on, it attached to a port that had been put in under your skin in your brain, and it would realize your fantasies. So you could sit at home in your chair and your fantasies would play out in front of you. . . . So Itchy, the Silverback, had a fantasy. It was supposed to be about Cher, but Cher suddenly couldn't do it. And so Diahann Carroll stepped in."

In the filmed Special, Carroll—playing the holographic character Mermeia—speaks seductively to Itchy before performing an unmistakably erotic dance for him. It is quite hard to believe that no one who read dialogue like "I am your fantasy . . . I am your pleasure, so enjoy me" thought it would be inappropriate for a show targeted at children. "Oh, yesssss," she moans to Itchy. "I can feel my creation. I'm getting your message, are you getting *mine?* . . . Oh, we are excited, aren't we?"

Mo'Kelly learned a lot about Wookiees watching this scene. "I learned that even though they lived in treehouses, they had virtual reality and they were attracted to Diahann Carroll, which was kind of weird in retrospect, [because] *I'm* attracted to Diahann Carroll. So, it's not weird to me, I just didn't know that Wookiees had a thing for Diahann Carroll. So that jumped out at me."

Brian Ward thinks the most disturbing part of the sequence is how Itchy wants to replay her comments to him. "He sits there and rewinds and replays and rewinds and replays," he notes, calling the entire bizarre episode "cringeworthy."

While many on the crew claim they were not aware of the sexual references in Itchy and Carroll's dialogue, it was clearly included in one of the script's final revisions. Film archivist Marcus Herring says the sexually suggestive language is clearly documented on page 62 of the September 17 revision:

> Itchy applauds and stamps his feet with great gusto; Art enjoys Itchy's reaction; Malla comes toward them to see what the commotion is about; Art nudges Itchy to control himself; Itchy abruptly comes to his senses and stops applauding and stamping; Malla shakes her head, turns away, Trader Dann winks at her, *Itchy's groggy with satisfaction.*

"And all of this aired at about 8:30 on CBS," Herring adds.

A network broadcast-standards veteran who asked that their name be withheld is baffled at how CBS could have aired something so grossly inappropriate. "It is wild that the network's creative executives allowed this special to be so acid-trippy and sexually suggestive. The notion that Diahann Carroll is virtual-reality fantasy fodder for an alien species . . . is almost bestiality. I am very surprised this two-minute scene was allowed to be included."

Former *SNL* writer and comedian Taran Killam speaks to the confusion many have after watching this bizarre scene: "In what world, planet, galaxy, in *any* time, has anybody ever wanted their grandpa to enjoy porn in the middle of the room?"

Bruce Vilanch proudly adds, "It was probably the first interracial, *interspecies* romance on network television. So where's *my* NAACP Image Award?"

It should be no surprise to those who have followed Lucas's career over the years that he has inserted sex in the strangest places in his films. According to Carrie Fisher, on the first shooting day for *Star Wars*, Lucas had an issue after seeing her wearing her iconic white dress. "He takes one look at the dress and says, 'You can't wear a bra underneath that dress.' So, I say, 'Okay, I'll bite. Why?' And he says, 'Because . . . there's no underwear in space.'

"And he says it with such conviction, too. Like he had been to space and looked around and he didn't see any bras or panties or briefs anywhere." Fisher ultimately elected to tape down her breasts during filming, using—yes—Gaffer tape.

Fisher included this anecdote in her live shows, and later, when she appeared near Lucas's home turf in Berkeley, he showed up and came backstage afterward to explain his "no underwear in space" mantra. He elaborated that when you go to space, you become weightless, "but then your body expands, but your bra doesn't—so you get strangled by your own bra."

Unlike Hamill, who wore excessive makeup during the Special, Fisher appears nearly exactly as she did in *A New Hope*. "Once again [as in *Star Wars*], George Lucas did not want her to wear a bra," notes Mo'Kelly, apparently because Lucas told Fisher bras didn't exist in space. "But aprons for Wookiees did?" he challenges.

Fisher also wasn't exactly in love with the infamous gold metal bikini she was required to wear in *Return of the Jedi*, when Princess Leia was a slave to Jabba the Hut: "When [Lucas] showed me the outfit, I thought he was kidding and it made me very nervous," Fisher said. "I have to stay with the slug with the big tongue! Nearly naked, which is not a style choice for me."

Jonathan Rinzler recalled that Lucas had been incorporating sex into his films way before *Star Wars*: "Remember, George is the one who made the masturbation scene [in *THX 1138*], and he made it much more obviously a masturbation scene in the director's cut, because it wasn't obvious enough in the original."

Even though audiences felt the "mind evaporator" scene was extremely creepy and way out of left field, comedy writer Anthony Caleca acknowledges it predicted the future in a disturbing way. "Oftentimes, when you look at science fiction and go, 'We're never gonna do that,' you then end up doing it in real life. . . . We said, 'There's no way we're gonna be able to just talk to people on our watches or do this and that with our little gizmos,' and then it happens. Well, [the Special's writers] predicted that people [would] be strapping things on their heads and watching all sorts of stuff to entertain themselves. So they kind of nailed that. They really did."

Heider says that since the scene was filmed in two separate shoots, it's possible that Carroll had no idea who she was entertaining in the scene, if anyone at all. Caleca surmises that she was not given the context for her dialogue or told how it would be used: "I'm sure that when she looked at it afterward, she was like, 'Oh, wait a minute . . . is he doing what I think he's doing while he's watching me?' And the guy is making some weird grunt sounds—granted, he's a Wookiee, but still a little bit over the line."

Nearly all of the crew members interviewed about the scene do not recall shooting the "Wookiee porn" scene, as it's known to Special aficionados. Heider reiterates that the Special was shot similarly to how a documentary is: short segments were sometimes accumulated without a clear idea of how they would subsequently be incorporated into the project. Also, hardly any of the crew received a script for this project, as it was constantly being updated. Heider says that Hemion would often tell the crew not to worry about the meaning of it all. "We're just doing a lot of different things," he'd say. "We'll do the magic when we get into editing."

Heider doesn't recall the order in which these shots were taped. "I know we had a couple stops where we had to pick up and do it again for camera angles. But I'm not sure exactly if her dialogue happened for that whole scene, if we did that before or after we did the song, but she was only there for that one day. So everything had to happen in that one time frame, but it didn't necessarily have to happen in order."

As Kyle Newman points out, in the process of filming, "You're just seeing Diahann Carroll talking alluringly to somebody. It's a close-up; it's a wide shot. You don't really know what's going on . . . but when you intercut that with a Wookiee moaning and groaning—that's where that becomes something completely different. That could be Diahann Carroll talking to a child, and then suddenly it has a totally different context. But once you cut to a perverted old Wookiee, it has a whole different meaning."

Several crew members feel that, if they'd had the power to, they would have cut this entire scene out of the Special. *Star Wars* Fan Club head Craig Miller regrets that he couldn't have done anything. "The way they set it up as being a sexy thing for Chewbacca's father to watch and get turned on by just seemed really kind of weird and out of place. I didn't have approval of anything, but that just seemed wrong."

Producer Ken Welch said at the time that—just as Acomba had wanted to do—they wanted to do a little experimenting with the Special. "We wanted to do things you've never seen before." He was proud of the visual effects that they had created for the controversial segment, saying, "We got the camera in a lighted mirror box and it endlessly repeats the image to infinity."

Produced by ILM, it wasn't.

In Kyle Newman's opinion, there were many people—like Welch, actually—who should have spoken up about the scene's inappropriateness for prime-time viewing: "I don't think people making it totally realized, but people in editing should have realized. People in post should have been like, 'What are we doing?' George Lucas, when he watched this, should have said, 'Maybe that's a bit too far.'"

Mitzie Welch, who was Ken's co-producer on set as well as during the editing, told *Vanity Fair* that the scene was intended to be a "softcore porno that would pass the censors"—a way of testing the waters to see how much they could get away with at the network.

Newman's take? "They got away with *a lot*."

* * *

Even with Acomba's departure, the production team had only resolved a small portion of the show's issues. Binder's arrival arguably gave a false sense of security to many of the crew. Sure, things were a lot calmer with a seasoned director steering the ship—he was likable, calm by nature, and not a screamer—but there were still problems that Binder had no power to change or improve upon.

For example, the script. When Binder first read it, he was concerned that the first ten minutes or so had no human words spoken: "I'm saying to myself, 'I'm not sure this is going to work.'" Although he's proud of the fireman role he played in getting the show completed, he regrets to this day that he had no time at all to discuss the concept and go over scenes with Smith, Hemion, and the writers: "There was none of that, unfortunately; there wasn't time. I think it was important for everybody to just get it done and make it airable, so they wouldn't have to shut down again and cancel the show."

Ideas in the script were getting killed on a regular basis. The budget, or lack of one, was affecting everything. Because the original prototype Millennium Falcon was built and filmed at London's Elstree Studios,

Lucasfilm was housing it overseas, requiring Smith–Hemion to construct a much smaller version of it in Los Angeles for the Special.

Prop builder Ted Baumgart is proud of most of the work he has done in his career, particularly at the Glendale prop house Serrurier and Associates. The owner, Steven Serrurier, was the grandson of Iwan Serrurier, who invented the Moviola in 1924; twenty years later, his son Mark redesigned it and expanded its use all over the industry.

Baumgart recalls that at one point in the project, there was a change to the Millennium Falcon's budget, and Steven Serrurier cautioned Baumgart and his crew to "not get too involved here." Serrurier told him that Smith–Hemion was crying poor about their budget, and "he knew that me and others could really take it over the top and make it nice, but we didn't have the budget and we didn't have the time."

Steven Serrurier wasn't intimidated by Smith–Hemion or other high-roller production companies. Heck, the following year his father Mark would be given a special Academy Award for "Technical Achievement," and five years later he would be given a star on the Hollywood Walk of Fame.

Serrurier only did what he was budgeted to do. At one point, the ship's control-panel lights were eliminated; Baumgart was told to mark their positions with tape so that the lights could be added during post-production. Eventually, Serrurier told the crew to "just go get some little buttons and knobs and gizmos at an electrical supply shop" and attach them to the side panels.

As a result of Smith–Hemion's limited funds, Baumgart says the completed Millennium Falcon they built was "shoddy work": "It was basically just some plywood and set lumber. This almost looked homemade."

Baumgart is most embarrassed about the two "hokey levers" poking up out of the board acting as individual throttles. He doesn't recall levers like these in the original Millennium Falcon. TV historian Rogers Johnson says, "On a good day the levers more closely resemble the steering apparatus of a farm tractor than the Millennium Falcon that can allegedly outrun Correllian ships. On a bad day, those levers could double as joysticks on an arcade claw machine."

Baumgart agrees. "It looked really bad. I mean, we're professionals."

In a behind-the-scenes photo of the opening Millennium Falcon scene from the aired Special, Ford and Mayhew are seated in the pilots' seats, but Chewbacca's furry feet are exposed in the bottom portion of the shot. An often-mocked part of the scene is where Ford and Mayhew are being pursued by the Empire and the ship is rocking back and forth like they're in a shopping cart and some mad uncle is whipping them from side to side. The visual of the Falcon being jostled around resembles what has been referred to as looking like the work of "a tired, off-screen Teamster."

That brief scene was stressful, too, for Ford, who was dealing with the heat and the constant stops and starts of television. He had acted on TV dramas before, but those productions were often sleek and efficient, and by the time Ford showed up to work on them, the wrinkles had more or less all been ironed out.

The Special was far from that. Heider was setting up to shoot Ford and Chewbacca from outside the front of the cockpit, looking in. Stage manager Peter Barth was standing outside of the Falcon, getting Binder's directions through his headset and passing them on to Ford and Mayhew. Heider says Ford was growing increasingly impatient with the constant delays: "He just wanted to get his lines done, and he made that very clear. Finally, he just yelled out, 'Can we just do this? How long is this going to take?'"

Although many of the crew members had worked together on other productions, Smith–Hemion was used to working on half-empty stages and focusing the attention on the main celebrity, whether it was Barbra Streisand or Mikhail Baryshnikov. This production was story-driven and unlike anything this Emmy-touting company had ever done. As experienced as the crew was, Vilanch was right about this not being in their wheelhouse.

Vilanch was also right about the Wookiees not speaking, and—more broadly—about focusing the entire plot on Chewbacca's family. "It was cute for a minute, but after a while it kind of became ridiculous. You were looking at the 'sensitive homelife' of the Wookiees. It only happens on this TV show. I mean, we only get to see Chewbacca's conflicted internal life in this particular television show."

It's a reasonable criticism that the Special didn't do a great job in casting the Imperial guards and commanders. In *Star Wars*, all of the Imperial leaders had British accents, but for some reason, on the Special, these same leaders speak with American accents. But it was more than just the voices. Cushing and the British actors back at Elstree Studios in London could destroy their enemies with a mere look; a furrowed brow became a silent weapon. These actors were tremendously controlled and restrained, yet with the ability to create stunning fear in others without uttering a breath.

For the most part, the officers in the Special are simply silly. Veteran TV actor Jack Rader plays the Imperial Guard officer who comes to search Chewbacca's home for Chewy and Han Solo. Not only are Rader and his colleagues' American accents weak but the seemingly endless snapping he does to "intimidate" others is comical.

It turns out, though, that this was Binder's intention. Rader recalls the director giving him specific directions on his movement and approach. "From that, I took that he wanted it just a little bigger than reality. Reality can be quite boring and quite inconsequential, and an audience doesn't want to watch that. It gets boring unless there's some intensity involved. When one is pursuing that kind of approach as I thought the director wanted, it can be right on the verge of being over the top and over theatrical. So I approached it from that direction."

As Binder spoke with Rader, he decided to roughen him up a bit. "He looked at my face and he [tells] the makeup girl to put a scar on my face," Rader recalls. "I thought, 'Oh my goodness, here we are in a great advanced civilization, why would anybody have a scar?' Then I thought, '*Saber* scar, how romantic. That's quite wonderful. That director's a genius.'"

There were also additional changes to the post-Acomba shooting schedule. In an early version of the script, exotic birds were to fly intermittently throughout the interior of the treehouse. Rita Scott confirmed that this had been the original concept, but they subsequently decided it would be more cost-efficient to animate the birds and lay them into the shot in post. In the end, though, they weren't even able to do that: "The budget got a little out of kilter."

The seemingly never-ending stream of script revisions was one of the crew's biggest frustrations. Sometimes a half-dozen per day were distributed, often with an additional one to follow in the evening. This was specifically annoying to the writers who had to write new material, the script supervisor who had to revise them, the production assistant who had to duplicate them, and the actors who now had to learn them.

When a show is as troubled and behind schedule as this one was, the general rule of thumb is, "shit rolls downhill." And, when it does, it winds up being the underpaid, underappreciated, and overworked production assistants who became knee-deep in it.

P.A. Peter Kimmel was often asked to deliver new pages of rewrites up to the homes of the cast members. He would also do beer runs for Harrison Ford during production. "I was enamored by his position in life," Kimmel recalls. "I wanted to be his friend, but I was the least important guy on the show." At one point, Kimmel showed up at Ford's door with his dry cleaning and some new rewrites. The actor simply grabbed the laundry and the script, "rolled his eyes, and then slammed the door in my face."

Nearly half a century later, Kimmel still remembers the incident—and laughs it off. But, as he laughs, one can denote a bit of embarrassment. "You know, I felt privileged to have a door slammed in my face by Harrison Ford," he says, almost rationalizing Ford's behavior. "I mean, it was frantic at times. The unfriendliness or just the stoicism on that set was not necessarily because no one liked each other but because there was so much going on. You had to be up on what's happening *this* hour, as opposed to *last* hour, and [things] could change like that. They might throw a scene out and bring a new scene in, and again, those rewrites, they just kept coming out of that room."

Mike Erwin recalls a family friend who had a crush on Ford and desperately wanted to meet him. After Erwin set up the meet-and-greet outside Ford's trailer, she asked Erwin if she could also kiss Ford. Erwin stepped into Ford's trailer and clarified that "she doesn't want to just meet you, she wants to kiss you." Ford shrugged and came out of his trailer.

"He was kind of shy," Erwin recalls, "and then it was almost like he was doing a take or something. They kind of looked at each other, and then all of a sudden they started making out, and then—*Boom!*—it was over. It was like, 'Cut!' And then they just left. There was no ceremonial 'thank you' or anything. He just left and went back into the trailer, and she gleefully marched off in her glory of getting her wish."

Erwin says that a couple making out outside of a trailer didn't particularly stand out at the time, considering the era they were in. "So this was the time in the United States when cocaine was a big deal, it was all over the place.

Working on all these high-end shows, there were always high-end people, and the high-end people have people, and they come with an entourage. I just started to notice more and more little vials with spoons on them. This particular *Star Wars* show, because of the hours and the tension and stuff, I saw quite a bit of drug use amongst a lot of people—around the crew, the crew trailers, and the cast trailers. I don't wanna mention any specific actors or actresses, but there was quite a bit of powder flying around that set."

The party atmosphere that was present on the set didn't stop at drugs. Erwin says he saw something quite unusual in Art Carney's trailer. "He had filled the shower with ice and [and put] bottles of different kinds of alcohol in the bottom of the shower. He had vodka and gin and those big half-gallon [jugs] ... I figured, he's gotta be dipping into that stuff, but despite that, he was a real pro. He hit his mark and delivered his lines every time."

Binder, who was starstruck by Carney, saw the same problem. "When I met Art, he was pleasant enough," Binder recalls. "But I learned soon that I had to shoot all of his scenes early in the day because—it was my impression anyway that wherever he went to eat lunch, he'd had a little bit too much to drink at the time."

Coincidentally, many have joked that the Special *must* have been written by someone on drugs: "I'm not convinced the Special wasn't ultimately written and directed by a sentient bag of cocaine," says AV Club contributor Nathan Rabin. "If it has a single virtue, it's that it does eventually end."

Vilanch reminds us that the Special was produced in a completely different era, with different rules and expectations, and that what seems today like an insane and chaotic workplace was back then almost normal working protocol. At the time, drug use was rampant in the industry, and the filming of the Special was no exception. "We were all chemically altered," he says. "It was 1978. In those days, we had something called 'fruit salad,' where you would put a whole bunch of pills in a bowl, and you would just pick up one. Everybody knew what every drug looked like, so you would know not to kill yourself. ... People would just say, 'I think I'll go up today.' It was a strange and wonderful era."

Strange, yes. Wonderful? Very few of the show's crew members thought these few weeks of production were "wonderful." But Erwin did. Racing from one end of the soundstage to the other, escorting guest stars as well as Wookiees and other costumed aliens to their places; nothing seemed to wear on him. Fellow crew members found him to be a particularly steady presence—always with a smile on his face and a hop in his step—despite the twenty-plus-hour days he was putting in.

One reason might have been that he had been through more in his twenty-nine years of life than anyone else on staff. He grew up in the Topanga Canyon area of Los Angeles in the late 1960s. Just under ten years earlier, he got a call from his best friend's mother, who had not been able to reach her son, Gary. Erwin went to his home to check on him, only to discover him lying on his back, dead. He had multiple stab wounds, and "Political Piggy" was written on the wall in his blood. The L.A. County Sheriff's Department eventually ascertained he had been dead for about a week.

Erwin hadn't just stumbled across the dead body of a close friend. This gruesome crime scene would precede the infamous Tate–LaBianca murders in Benedict Canyon by a week, and Gary Hinman had become the first murder victim of the Manson Family. Further, Erwin had become the first person ever to experience the horror of a Manson Family crime scene.

Since it was Hinman's murder that connected the Manson Family to the Tate–LaBianca homicides, Erwin would subsequently have to testify—*in person*—against Charles Manson at his trial.

As difficult as working on the Special was, he had been through far worse.

CHAPTER 10

FINAL-LY

THE LAST DAY of shooting was just days away. The crew members—who to some extent had appreciated all of the overtime—were getting anxious to move on. Binder had read in the script that the final scene called for the main cast from the film—Hamill, Ford, Fisher, Daniels, and a Kenny Baker–less R2-D2—to gather with Chewbacca's family at a Life Day ceremony, along with several dozen extras in Wookiee costumes.

This scene needed to be larger than life, and Binder had been curious ever since he took over what kind of set the art department was planning for it. He called the art director, Brian Bartholomew, for an update, and got the bad news: "He looked at me straight in the eye and said, 'Steve, I hate to break it to you, but we're out of money. We have no set for the finale.'"

No set for the finale? Binder was frustrated, but he sent Bartholomew on a mission: "I told him to go into Hollywood and go to every candle store you can find and buy every candle they have in their shop." The night before the finale, Binder says, he and the art department "placed fat candles, thin candles, tall candles, short candles, all over the floor of the stage, and spent the morning of the actual shoot" lighting them.

The overall effect worked, and it was affordable, but it still wasn't exactly up to the standards of a set for a Smith–Hemion production. "The set itself looked so fake," remarks Mick Garris, who operated R2-D2 for the scene. "Film is very forgiving, especially if it's lit properly, but this just looked so cheesy."

The scene begins with a few dozen Wookiees assembled near a stage that our main characters are standing on. C-3PO addresses the audience, each

Makeup artist Verne Langdon puts the finishing touches to the Wookiees for the finale, which director Steve Binder shot with no set-design budget. He told his art director, "Go buy every candle in town, and we'll just use that." *AP Photo/George Brich*

of whom is carrying a glass globe. "I've spoken some rubbish in my years," Daniels recalls, "but this topped everything as I addressed the furry throng: 'It is indeed true that at times like this, Artoo and I wish we were more than just mechanical beings and were really alive so that we could share your feelings with you.'"

Four decades later, Daniels challenged the writers' notion that C-3PO is a "mechanical being" and not "really alive." "Threepio has always had feelings. Would he rather be a Wookiee? Doubtful."

* * *

Whether or not Carrie Fisher actually lobbied to sing in the Special or not, she was scheduled to perform in the show's final scene. The only question in the weeks leading up to the start of production was *what* she'd be singing.

"I had been singing in my mother's act since I was about thirteen," said Fisher, who would alternate between singing backup vocals and performing solos like "Bridge Over Troubled Water" for Debbie Reynolds's vaudeville show. (It was quite a foreshadowing of her eventual marriage to and subsequent divorce from the song's composer, Paul Simon.)

Vilanch, who had befriended Fisher a year before the Special, says that Reynolds was relentless in promoting a singing career for her daughter, constantly pitching her to every music producer and record-company executive she came across, "but she had no interest in becoming a performer like her mother." Fisher embraced singer/songwriters like Joni Mitchell, while her mother was more of a variety performer at heart: her nightclub act included singing, dancing, and, most importantly, lots of comedy.

Todd Fisher, Carrie's brother, says their mother took her performances very seriously. "It *is* important," he says, defending the need for entertainment. "It's important for a variety of reasons ... not the least of which is 'make 'em laugh,' because that's a healing thing. My mother lived by that mantra—that it was important to make people laugh. She always had a clown act in her show. 'I love it,' she would say. 'It makes people laugh, and that's what this is all about.'"

According to Todd, during the time the Special was in production, Carrie and her mother were not on speaking terms. Previously, he and Carrie had been performing in Reynolds's nightclub act at the Desert Inn in Las Vegas, but soon the Frontier casino—which stood directly across the Strip—offered Todd and Carrie an opening-act spot.

"My mother didn't want us to go out on our own," Todd says, "and Carrie was furious that she wouldn't let us do it. She then refused to sing after that. That's how Carrie operated to punish my mother: 'If you tell me what to do, I'm gonna punish you and not do it at all ...' She was that way in 1976 on the [*Star Wars*] set when she stood up to Darth Vader. I mean, she was always that way. That was her. My mother had groomed a Beverly Hills princess, and George Lucas simply converted her into a space princess."

Decades later, Carrie would reveal in the documentary *Bright Lights: Starring Carrie Fisher and Debbie Reynolds* that "the biggest thing I ever did that broke my mother's heart was not do a nightclub act. My mother would say, 'Do drugs, do whatever you want to do, but why don't you sing?' That was *my* big rebellion."

It mystified Reynolds that Carrie—who had a very strong voice—would walk away from a potential singing career that was literally being handed to her. "Carrie's dad, Eddie, had a great voice, a really beautiful voice," Reynolds says in the film. "I guess she doesn't want to be Eddie and she doesn't want to be Debbie. So she'll do it her way." After listening to an old recording of Carrie singing, she becomes emotional and breaks down: "I love that voice. Isn't that a great voice? Wish *I* had it."

Although Carrie did rebel against her mother, Todd explains that they were taught to be respectful in professional situations. She treated the *Star Wars Holiday Special* with that same respect. Carrie did think the script was "corny," but no one asked her opinion about it. "She was not super famous at that moment," Todd explains. "You do what you're asked to do. You'd have to make the best of it."

For the show, she had expressed interest in singing Joni Mitchell's melancholy ballad "River"—definitely a holiday song, but hardly joyful or uplifting. The song has been recorded by more than five hundred musicians, all of whom have embraced it for its sweet and light holiday introduction coupled with its evocation of the desperation and hopelessness that often comes during the holidays: "I wish I had a river I could skate away on."

One day during pre-production, Vilanch recalls, Fisher came into the office, sat at a piano, and performed "River" as well as a few other "very lachrymose ballads. She was singing about heartbreak and all the Joni Mitchell things. She very much wanted to show this side of her talent. And there was general dismay because this was not what we wanted Princess Leia to be doing."

Nonetheless, Vilanch thought Fisher did a pretty nice job with the song, so the two of them decided to reach out to Mitchell personally to ask for permission to cover it. After using some back channels to get a hold of the singer's phone number, they got on a phone and called Mitchell personally. "But when we called Joni to ask her permission," Vilanch says, "Joni gave us, in her laughing, silvery voice, a big 'nooooo!!!'

"She possibly thought the whole thing was a joke," Vilanch surmises. "Who on earth would think that was a real request?"

In the end, the decision was made for the Welches to just go ahead and write a new song, basically just adding lyrics to the *Star Wars* theme. It had a "why can't we all just get along?" feeling to it, and Carrie was set to sing it at the end of the Wookiee Life Day ceremony. According to the Welches, Fisher did not seem happy with the song.

According to Anthony Daniels, although it was "clearly intended to be emotionally moving," the song "was just maudlin and depressing . . . more like excerpts from *Preludes in a Sanatorium.*"

Binder recalls Fisher being more low-key than he was expecting. "I felt she was low energy. Now, whether she didn't want to do it, or didn't like the song, or whatever, I never had any knowledge of, but I felt had I really been involved in it and participated in it, to make creative decisions, it could be a fault in my direction. I would've liked to see more energy coming from her when she's [speaking]. I just thought that was part of her personality, truthfully."

Fisher offers a sort of toast meant to inspire the Wookiee herd, channeling less from the wisdom of Obi-Wan Kenobi and more from Martin Luther King Jr.: "This holiday is yours, but we all share with you the hope that this day brings us closer to freedom, and to harmony, and to peace. No matter how different we appear, we're all the same in our struggle against the powers of evil and darkness."

Gottfried chimed in: "The minute she saw herself and heard herself singing, that's when she said, 'Nothing left to do now but heroin.' I think there was never a drug strong enough that she could use to block that special out."

Some disagree about Fisher's vocals. Sue Raney, who recorded dozens of pop-jazz albums in her sixty-year career, praises Fisher's performance in the Special: "She has a warm sound, and you can't teach sound. You're born with the sound of your voice . . . she owns her notes. She has a wonderful vibrato. She has good range, good pitch, and good phrasing. And she told the story. She's got all that stuff. I loved it."

Todd Fisher thought his sister did a great job, but perhaps he would have thought that—even if her performance was atrocious. He points out that, back in the 1970s, the variety shows had a low bar. "You'll hear some people say that the world doesn't need another mediocre singer," he says. "You know, it's not important that you be the best thing in the world. There are singers that are exceptional. My dad was an exceptional singer, and then there are people that are just pretty good. They can do a nice job with it, and what's wrong with that? Not everybody has to be Nat King Cole, you know?"

* * *

Viewers of the Special have often contended that Hamill, Fisher, and Ford look unhappy to be there, but not Jason Lenzi. "I don't know what show these people are watching. Whatever alleged issues the three of them had about being there, it sure doesn't come off in their performances. They all do an amazing job of continuing to suspend disbelief portraying these beloved characters in a completely surreal adventure. They totally deliver."

Daniels agreed, writing, "'The Best Actor in a Turd' award must go to Mark and Carrie and Harrison. They managed to mouth their saccharine lines without once showing their gritted teeth, though they did seem to cling rather closely to each other on stage, for support."

Daniels was not very forgiving of the physical set. "Every religion has its festival days, and Life Day is for the Wookiees," he said at a press conference for his book, *I Am C-3PO*. "And there we were meant to be celebrating this event, and there's Mark and Carrie and Harrison and me in this very dark, basically black drapes. It was like a funeral. It was dreadful. And then you watched it and you thought, 'I didn't realize it was as dreadful as that' ... well, it was."

Although the outfits for Malla, Lumpy, and Itchy were handmade, almost all of the extras were wearing inexpensive Don Post costumes. Verne Langdon, who had worked with Winston on the *Planet of the Apes* films, was part of his makeup crew and went from Wookiee to Wookiee, trying to make sure the several dozen costumes looked halfway presentable.

If indeed Hamill, Fisher, and Ford were even remotely thinking of complaining about anything, all they had to do was look at the hot, uncomfortable Wookiee suits. At least they had their own private, air-conditioned trailers to relax in.

Todd Fisher, who had traveled to London several times to visit Carrie on the set of *Star Wars*, wasn't going to miss this shoot. Asked if the scene was chaotic, he responds, "Well, they all are, aren't they? I've yet to be at a show like that where there *isn't* chaos." Based on his extensive experience seeing the behind-the-scenes action on TV specials, his view is that every one of them is reeling with last-minute changes and general mayhem. "There's no way you can put together something like that and expect it to run like a series. It's always chaos because it's a one-off."

In Todd's recollection, Ford was "not really thrilled about the whole

The chemistry between Harrison Ford and Carrie Fisher—shown here on the set of the Special—has always been a key to the *Star Wars* story. According to Fisher's final memoir, *The Princess Diarist*, there was more going on behind the scenes, and they were romantically involved during the filming of *A New Hope. AP Photo/George Brich*

concept, but Harrison's a very different bird, you know? He's not really an entertainment guy in many senses of the word. I don't think he really wanted much to do with Hollywood."

Despite the more generous break schedule for those wearing the costumes, Mick Garris recalls that the shoot was still difficult, and the conditions inside the suits hadn't changed a bit. "This was not the safest shoot," he says. "These actors, many of them, had never acted in suits before. They're covered in fur suits; they have latex masks over their faces. It's like they're acting one hundred percent covered in a mink coat. So, breathing is an issue. Sweating is an issue. They were under the unbelievably hot lights of a video shoot in a sound stage that doesn't have any ventilation in between takes. They couldn't run air conditioning because the sound was an issue. So here are a lot of inexperienced actors in suits for the first time, and they're on the verge of heat prostration. There had to be breaks in the shoot constantly, far more than anybody had anticipated, just for the safety of the actors in these suits. So this was a long shoot, much longer than anybody had planned on."

But now it was over. For Smith–Hemion's cast and crew, Warner Bros Studios was history, as were all of its nightmarish memories.

* * *

Binder finished up the last day of shooting and said goodbye to all, offering the best of luck to the Welches in delivering the two-hour special to CBS on time. Ken and Mitzie were the highest-ranking full-time producers still on staff, so the responsibility of supervising the final edit and delivering the completed show to CBS went to them. They seemed concerned.

"They came to me and said, 'We've never produced anything like this,'" says Binder. "They admitted to me that this was the biggest assignment of their life. They had basically no idea or control over really being on the set, producing what was going on."

It turns out that Smith and Hemion had not made any arrangements for another director to replace Binder to supervise the edit, or even found another *senior* producer—either on staff or as a hired gun—to help with post-production.

When he was hired, Binder had made it very clear to Smith that, because of a previously booked job, he regretfully "would not be able to participate in one day or one second of editing." It bothered Binder to not be able to oversee the process—he considers post-production to be "where shows are really put together"—and it is a decision he still regrets. "I knew it would fall on Ken and Mitzie, and I knew they had zero experience. Shows are made and broken in post-production editing, and to this day—in fact because of that—I swore I would never not do my own post-production after a show that I had shot, and I've lived up to that."

Binder thinks that the Welches deserve much of the credit for keeping the show on schedule, and he feels it was unfair for them to be left holding the bag on the editing. It is unclear whether or not Smith and Hemion were aware that the Welches had never edited before. "They were there to get the show done," Binder says. "It would never have gotten done otherwise."

The show's lead editor, Vince Humphrey, was sitting in his edit bay at Complete Post in Hollywood on the first day of post-production when the Welches arrived. There were dozens of ISO reels—individual camera-recorded loads—piled high on his edit console, the sheer magnitude of which horrified Mitzie. "I saw all of those tapes and I thought, 'What am I gonna do?' And I do remember I burst into tears. I started crying. I was so overwhelmed."

Finally, Mitzie confessed to Humphrey. "I never edited anything in my life," she told him. "I write, and Kenny had never done special-effects editing before." Humphrey handled her with an amazing bedside manner, Mitzie recalled. "He asked, 'Do you know what you want to see?' I said, 'Absolutely,' and he said, 'Let's start with that.'"

The Welches—being specialists in music—started with what they knew, and with Humphrey's help they began editing the specific scenes that featured music: the cantina bar, Jefferson Starship, and the Diahann Carroll trip scene.

After those initial scenes were edited at Complete Post, the team moved to Newt Bellis's brand new, state-of-the-art facility, Mobile Video Systems in Hollywood. Humphrey would still be taking the lead, but he'd now be assisted by Jerry Bixman, an all-around utility man at MVS who worked cameras, lighting, and audio equipment and was now being trained as an editor. He would focus on compiling all of the elements together, working on transitions, and adding special effects. "I was excited," he recalls. "This was the biggest thing I'd ever been involved with." After all, one of the Special's draws would be its special effects. What would *Star Wars* be without dramatic laser fights and digital creations? Even though it was television, viewers expected that the Special would have its share of innovative effects.

Once at MVS, Ken decided to split into two groups. Mitzie stayed with

Humphrey, overseeing the editing of the story segments, and Ken worked with Bixman on the sections that required special effects. "There was just a vast amount of work to be done," Ken recalled. "Actually, the show was longer than it was supposed to be. Too much had been shot. . . . Whatever the word for David [Acomba] is, *practical* is not the word."

One thing that would have helped the editing process was having access to more stock footage from Lucas. Ken Welch recalled the first meeting with George, when this subject was brought up. "When we talked about shots available from him—like star fields, et cetera—I said, 'Well you must have just reels and reels of extra star fields and whatnot.'" Lucas responded, "As a matter of fact, we don't even have ten feet." Lucas told Welch they had used every foot of the film. According to Welch, "The budget was so tight on the first *Star Wars* that there's no extra footage of a star field—or apparently anything else."

But that wasn't entirely true. While Lucas told Welch that every graphic effect wound up in *Star Wars*, there were several shots from the film on the cutting room floor that made their way into the Special. For example, in the "Life on Tatooine" segment—played on the wall screen at the cantina— there are several shots of various characters wandering around Mos Eisley that had been shot for the movie. Marcus Powell, who appeared uncredited as the character Rycar Ryjerd in the film's cantina scene, had been filmed in a separate, unused scene just outside the spaceport that docked the Millennium Falcon. Powell, a little person, is being chased by stormtroopers and sees an alien with outrageously tall legs, which he uses to evade capture. That moment found its way into the Special, as well as a short clip of Darth Vader speaking with one of his henchmen.

It's a shame that there weren't more *Star Wars* clips available for use in the Special. One of the biggest complaints about it is that it moves at a sloth's pace—almost as if the editor is trying to stretch the footage due to lack of available content. After all, the Special had gone from running to one hour to ninety minutes to two hours, all in a fairly short period of time, and without significantly expanding it with additional guest stars, scenes, or production numbers. Sound editor Ben Burtt said in a 2000 interview that the Special needed "re-editing . . . if you tightened up the story, I think you could have another little episode."

With nearly all of the staff now gone, associate producer Rita Scott was left alone to keep everything on schedule, moving toward their impending delivery date. In addition to Scott, Smith and Hemion would pop into the edit sessions from time to time, but they weren't a constant fixture at MVS.

The biggest delay Scott was dealing with was with the sound effects. Burtt had quite a lot to record and not a lot of time allotted to do it. He was near the beginning of what would become an illustrious career in sound editing, having already been recognized by the Motion Picture Academy with an award for "Special Achievement in Sound Effects Editing" for *Star Wars*, for which he designed the sounds for R2-D2, lightsabers, blasters, and Darth Vader's heavy breathing. He would receive another one for *Raiders of the Lost Ark* in 1981. The following year, the Oscars would finally create a category for "Sound Effects Editing," which he would win in 1982 for *E. T.* and in 1989 for *Indiana Jones and the Last Crusade*. He would eventually work on all of the films from both the *Star Wars* and *Indiana Jones* franchises, as well as on such Pixar films as *WALL-E* and *Up*.

However, what Burtt is most known for in post-production circles is naming and popularizing the infamous "Wilhelm scream." The stock sound effect was first used in the 1951 film *Distant Drums*, and then again in 1953 in *The Charge at Feather River*. It is typically used when someone falls from a great height and their terrified scream fades away as they descend farther and farther away.

Since the release of those two Westerns in the early 1950s, this specific sound effect has been used in hundreds of films, including *Star Wars*. Burtt had found it in the Warner Bros film library while looking for sound effects for *Star Wars*, and, after its years of theatrical cameos, named it after the character Private Wilhelm, who gets shot in the leg by an arrow in *The Charge at Feather River*.

Burtt wound up including the scream in *A New Hope*—less out of editorial necessity and more as an homage to his friends from USC film school, where they had begun to notice the same scream in several different films. During the shootout between Luke and Leia and the stormtroopers in *A New Hope*, Luke launches a grappling hook high above a bridge port on the Death Star and swings with Princess Leia to freedom. Just before their escape, he shoots a stormtrooper who falls to his most certain death, and Burtt inserts the Wilhelm scream. In the Special, Burtt would also use it when Han Solo tricks a stormtrooper into crashing through a fence on Chewbacca's treehouse and falling to his death.

Because Binder had not been allowed to have the Wookiee performers make their own noises during filming, the editors were now waiting on Burtt, whom Miki Herman says was "proprietary on the effects that he created, and he didn't want them to get out there for other people to be able to use." To create the original voice of Chewbacca in *Star Wars*, Burtt had gone to Happy Hollow Zoo in San Jose, California, and recorded the cries of walruses, lions, tigers, bears, camels, rabbits, and badgers. However, it was the voice of a black bear named Tarik that would wind up becoming one of the main elements in creating Chewbacca's original voice.

For the Special, Burtt was now charged with creating voices for three additional Wookiee characters, Malla, Lumpy, and Itchy. Even more challenging was the fact that, in *A New Hope*, Chewbacca's dialogue was limited to just quick roars and grunts; the Special included many sitcom-style scenarios where actual Wookiee dialogue needed to be created and inserted.

"I was faced with creating and sustaining a whole hour of Wookiee conversation," Burtt says. He went to the Olympic Game Farm in Sequim, Washington, where he spent two days collecting the sounds of various bear species. He used grizzly bears as the basis for Itchy, and some black bears for Malla. For Lumpy, he needed a less ferocious sound, which he obtained from a cub at the San Jose Baby Zoo.

Scott would eventually receive the sound effects from Burtt, just in the nick of time. The editors inserted the last-minute elements into the nearly two-hour master they had assembled, and Scott then sent the final deliverables to CBS for the following week's broadcast.

CHAPTER 11

THE BROADCAST

ON NOVEMBER 17, 1978, approximately thirteen million households tuned in to the *Star Wars Holiday Special*, whose ratings came in just behind *The Love Boat* and the second of three segments of a Pearl Harbor mini-series, *Pearl*. Most of the cast and crew were not particularly happy with the finished product, and the actual reviews were all over the map.

While the Associated Press called the special effects dazzling, it slammed the "tenuous plot," calling it "bubble gum for the brain" and adding that it was an "exploitation of the biggest-grossing movie of all time." *TV Guide* called the special "unintentionally hilarious."

Former *Hollywood Reporter* business editor Paul Bond, who refers to the Special as "the definition of cringeworthy," recently discovered a surprisingly glowing review of the much-maligned show. "I looked into our own *Hollywood Reporter* archives from November 20, 1978, and I was dumbfounded to find out that our reviewer actually liked this thing." Reviewer Gail Williams praised everyone involved in the technical accomplishments of the Special, singling out its art direction, sets, costumes, and lighting and effects, while describing elements of the show as "touching," "sensuous," and "spectacular." According to Williams, "The plot smacks of sentiments typical of *The Waltons* and is filled with cleverly integrated musical numbers and amusing special effects [that] were the real stars of the show."

One common critique of the Special concerns the quality of the footage. Those fans who had seen *Star Wars* in a theater had seen something shot on film, while the Special was shot on video. Today, shooting on film is becoming increasingly rare, due to the extra time needed to develop the

The two-hour *Star Wars Holiday Special* aired on CBS at 8 p.m. on Friday, November 17, 1978—a week before Thanksgiving and a day before the Jonestown Massacre. The ratings were mediocre, with the Special coming in second after two ABC programs: *The Love Boat* and *Pearl*, a TV movie about Pearl Harbor. *CBS*

film, the significant costs involved, and the current availability of cheaper alternatives that, for some viewers, might be indistinguishable from film. At the time, however, the visual difference between film and video was staggering.

Video was chosen simply because it was an inexpensive medium—and you got what you paid for. Mick Garris was shocked to see a Lucas project "shot on video with television lighting, where everything is just bright, just blown out. So you see everything, no sense of cinematic lighting technique or anything. . . . It seemed so weird, even at the time. And when it came out, it was like, 'Oh my God, *this* is what they did for the Holiday Special?' It was a travesty."

It would take nearly two decades for Julie Welch, who was a teenager at the time of the Special, to realize how negatively her parents' project had been received. However, she knew there was something different about it. She says it was fairly routine for Ken and Mitzie to hold viewing parties for the shows they had produced for talent such as Barbra Streisand, Julie Andrews, and the Carpenters. "This one we didn't, really."

Jeb Layton grew up attending those viewing parties regularly, but, like Julie, he also doesn't remember one being thrown for the broadcast of the Special. Jeb was the son of Joe Layton, the Welches' producing partner. The kinds of specials Joe usually produced wouldn't really impress his son's tween friends: Diana Ross, Bette Midler, Raquel Welch, Dolly Parton . . . Jeb might as well have told them his father worked for the IRS. But when the younger Layton first heard about his father's *Star Wars* gig, he was extremely proud and excited.

Jeb moved around quite a lot as a child, and it was hard for him to make friends, so he couldn't wait to drop his *Star Wars* bombshell on his classmates. Everyone was impressed when he belted out the news, but Jeb got a tad nervous after his father brought home some of the dailies for him to watch. They were a red flag that perhaps this special wasn't going to be the coolest thing he'd ever seen, so he stopped bragging about it. His friends *hadn't* forgotten, however, and so, when it aired, Jeb got the attention he had initially been seeking. The comments ranged from "That was awful" to "I hated it" to the truly biting "Why did your dad *do* that?"

It's important to remember that, at the time, these variety shows weren't tailor-made for specific demographics. "The idea was to try to have a program that would ideally appeal to everybody in the family, or offer *a little something for everybody in* the family," says TV archivist Dan Schaarschmidt. "Variety was that vehicle. That was the way you had something for the grandmothers and the grandfathers and the parents and the kids, music for the kids, comedy for the kids, romance for the mothers, and variety was the way they figured they could do that."

Consequently, no one person in the family got an entire viewing experience targeted at them. "Ed Sullivan was always trying to satisfy everybody," recalls Garris. "He had the rock bands for the kids, and then he would have Topo Gigio, and he would have the plate spinners and Mamie Van Doren. In those days, you consumed entertainment like that. You'd wait for the Beatles to come on *Ed Sullivan*, and then you'd leave when Trini Lopez came on."

The quality of the programming suffered, however, because of the way these producers tried to reach bigger audiences. As Brian Ward notes, "It became a way to bring the family together in front of the television set without fully satisfying any one member of that family."

Youngsters knew that only a portion of a variety show was produced for their specific entertainment. So, if they only got a taste of what they had tuned in for, they weren't disappointed. They had low expectations watching shows like these because they knew the show wasn't produced specifically for them.

The Special was booked with that mindset. While the main cast—Hamill, Fisher, Ford, Daniels, and Mayhew—was selected to appeal to the kids, Carney, Korman, and Arthur were booked to appeal to the adults. Carroll was obviously brought in to attract the male demographic, leaving Jefferson Starship to reel in the teenagers.

However, this compartmentalization would result in low expectations from viewers. Because producers were trying to attract demographics from all over the spectrum, adults knew they weren't going to get an hour-long Barbra Streisand special without some comedy sprinkled in for the rest of the family. Likewise, David Bowie wasn't going to sing more than one or two songs before they focused back on Bing and his other older guest stars.

There would wind up being a huge difference between kids who saw the

Special on its original 1978 air date and those who saw it in later years on an unauthorized DVD or YouTube. The kids who watched the Holiday Special in 1978 *knew* they weren't going to get much of Han Solo, so they didn't complain when the show spent three times as many minutes on Bea Arthur. It was almost as if children of that time period were prisoners: they were given their allotted portions and told to be happy about it.

And, to a certain extent, they were. Anthony Caleca was one of those children. "From what I remember as a kid, the *Star Wars Holiday Special* was tremendous. I was super excited. I was overanxious simply because something from the *Star Wars* world was gonna be on television, and I was like, 'I don't care if they're gonna juggle, sing, dance—I'll take anything.' I was overjoyed to see the characters that I loved so much. To revisit them again, to see Han Solo, to see Luke Skywalker, to see Princess Leia, to see Chewbacca..."

On Scott Kirkwood's fan site, the feedback section features fans' personal memories of watching the special when it aired. "I still have a soft spot for the damn thing," writes Kevin K. "Unless you were a kid at the time, you have absolutely no idea how momentous this occasion was."

Caleca doesn't remember anyone criticizing the show, at least in the schoolyard. "Sitting there and watching that special, it was a hit for me. Nobody would have to wait for a sequel to see these characters that I fell in love with. Who cared if it came off as goofy? For us, it was a chance to see all of our friends again."

* * *

According to Gary Kurtz, before the Special aired, he watched one of the final cuts with Lucas. He doesn't remember Lucas's specific reaction to it, but he knows he didn't like it. "The determination was that it was a bit too late then to do much about it," Kurtz recalls. Biographer Dale Pollock also says Lucas was very unhappy about it. "We just didn't talk about it that much. It was kind of a one-liner: 'Oh, that's an embarrassment,' or I think he said, 'I'm sorry I ever agreed to do that.'" Pollock mostly remembers Lucas's disapproval. "I think he had been talked into it and regretted it. It didn't take a lot of our time in my interviews, because he dismissed it fairly quickly."

To this day, Steve Binder has never met Lucas. "All I heard was, he tried to buy the negatives and never ever show this again." He thought that, after the Special aired, Lucas would have at least contacted him. "Never got a phone call or anything. Which was disappointing to me. It was his show, he developed it. To totally walk away from it and critique it negatively was, I felt, not cool."

Pat Proft was surprised Lucas had wandered from the project in the first place. "I know he probably was off on other projects, but holy shit, this was his brand, and I don't know either why he didn't have somebody ride herd on it and report to him. I sure as fuck would've done that."

After Proft wrapped the Special, he wound up writing some the most successful comedies of the 1980s and 1990s—*Police Academy, Naked Gun, Hot Shots*—and watched them become first huge hits, then multifilm franchises. As those films turned into franchises, to save money, their producers hired less expensive writers and subsequently churned out increasingly inferior sequels. So, Proft can relate to the feeling that Lucas must have had, watching his original idea become twisted and morphed to the point it is nearly unrecognizable. Yet he wonders how Lucas—who had a plethora of top-notch talent at Lucasfilm—could have been so busy as to have left the project in mid-production to be carried out by people in a genre he didn't really know.

However, in addition to David Acomba—who served as Lucas's eyes and ears for the brief period he was working on the show—Lucas *did* have someone in that position: Miki Herman, Lucasfilm's liaison for the Special.

Two years before the airing of the Holiday Special, the thirty-one-year-old Herman had been volunteering at the American Film Institute. She had also worked as a production manager on a short film called *Minestrone*, starring Danny DeVito and Rhea Perlman. When the head secretary at the AFI left for a gig at the *Star Wars* offices, Herman tailed her and lobbied for a job. She started out filling in during the holiday break but was soon offered a full-time job.

By this time, *Star Wars* had concluded principal photography, and Lucas and the crew had just returned from London to begin editing. Herman was hired to help get pickup shots of landscapes in Death Valley and of some new aliens Rick Baker had created for the cantina scene.

Throughout her time at Lucasfilm, Herman bounced back and forth between various duties in post-production, sound, editing, and working with the newly launched Industrial Light and Magic. After the unexpectedly colossal release of *Star Wars*, she worked under Charles Lippincott as the "robot wrangler," delivering and preparing the film's costumes for various promotional events. "Miki Herman was basically the keeper of the characters," says Garris. "She was in control of how the characters were handled and taking care of the actors who were in the suits."

With Lippincott now gone and Lucas and Kurtz up to their knees in pre-production for *The Empire Strikes Back*, the job of liaison for the Holiday Special set went to Herman. Today, she offers some defenses of Lucas and Kurtz. "They were busy," she says. "They just went moving on to *The Empire Strikes Back* and moving ILM up north. They just left it up to the variety-show producers, and they regretted it."

"It would've been nice if George could have been involved more because a lot of the stuff just could have been a lot better if he would've been, but that's just the way it was. [Lucas] created it and it took on a life of its own. My job was to try to keep it as authentic as possible, and just to make sure that everything was complete."

According to Mitzie Welch, Herman was at most of the tapings and attended nearly every edit session. She also remembered Herman being very green at the time and carrying a lot on her shoulders: "She started out as just a production assistant, and she hadn't been out that long when this special was done. She already had a lot of responsibilities . . . I liked her."

The feeling apparently wasn't mutual. Although the Welches recalled having a good working relationship with her, today, several years after they had both passed away, Herman is direct in her opinions about their being hired and their subsequent creative decisions.

"The Welches were in over their heads," Herman recalls. "They didn't know how to edit. They would look to myself and Ben Burtt—they would go, 'Help us . . . what are we doing?' It was just like a runaway production for Ken and Mitzie. They just didn't know how to do it. And it's unfortunate that they were assigned to be the producers on this, because Smith–Hemion had some top-notch producers. [But] Ken and Mitzie were variety-show producers [who] didn't know anything about science fiction."

Herman has criticized several of the Special's elements, particularly the often-disparaged opening minutes, where the Wookiees communicate in no discernable language for several minutes. Audiences, she says, "were very disappointed and lost interest very quickly in the first seven minutes of the Wookiee family grunting and groaning." (Again, the choice to focus the story on the Wookiees had been Lucas's, against the advice of a barrage of Smith–Hemion's producers and writers.)

She has also referred to the Special's guest stars as "mediocre" performers who were relegated to doing "corny" bits "that I guess in the '70s were popular for variety shows, but kids didn't follow." She also calls the script "weak" and the circus performers' scene "too long," and trashes the late associate producer, Rita Scott, who "didn't really add anything or subtract anything. She just was there, smoking cigarettes."

The "mind evaporator" scene gets the biggest thumbs-down from Herman. "When I saw the Diahann Carroll thing—she's a beautiful woman," Herman recalls. "The whole thing was so—in my opinion—was really poor taste for a family show. The whole idea of the grandfather being seduced . . . it was, like, really poor taste."

With all that being said, the question seems fairly obvious: why, as Lucas's direct liaison—and someone who had been present throughout all of the tapings and edit sessions "to keep [things] as authentic as possible"—didn't Herman voice any of her many disapprovals during *the actual production*? Why was the Diahann Carroll segment (or others she disapproved of) allowed to be written in the first place, much less recorded, edited into the show, and broadcast?

Herman defends her decision to not interfere with the production: she was just there to observe. "Well, we couldn't, you know, tell them what to do. I mean, that was *their* project, *their* show. It was, like, *out of control.*"

She says she did go toe-to-toe with the Nelvana producer Michael Hirsch, who was working on the Boba Fett cartoon, and that Hirsch got very upset with her after she looked at the models Nelvana had drawn for each character and insisted Princess Leia should be wearing a belt. "To me, that was really part of her costume," Herman recalls. "I was there to make sure their costumes were complete." Hirsch told her it would be tremendously expensive to start over and add the belt, but Herman insisted. "I mean, that

Despite Lucas's later criticism of the Special, a little more than a year later he allowed *The Muppet Show* to use Mark Hamill, as well as Chewbacca and C-3PO, on an episode that aired on February 23, 1980. Was this an example of a lesson that Lucas hadn't learned, or was he fine at the time with how the Special turned out? © CBS

was kind of my job—to be there just to make sure everything was complete. And so he went back and they added a belt to her costume."

Herman's reasoning on when to intercede and when not to is a tad inconsistent. Why she felt the need to admonish Nelvana over a belt but neglected to speak out about such glaring issues as the fantasizing Wookiee is confusing.

After the Special aired, Herman says Lucas "was very disappointed [with] the way it turned out, and embarrassed, really. And so I think that Gary [Kurtz] learned you can't just leave it to chance. You have to be more heavily involved, and because Gary was busy promoting *Star Wars* internationally, and George was busy writing *The Empire Strikes Back*, that was it. It was just a lesson learned not to do something that they didn't really know about: variety shows."

It is also confusing, given how upset Lucas allegedly was about the Special, that there were no repercussions for Herman, being as she was his eyes and ears on the show. She was the one who could have "phoned home" to report what she was seeing.

"It sounds like the approval systems and what needed to be approved, all that just wasn't ironed out," Jonathan Rinzler suggested, "because Lucasfilm had never done this kind of stuff before. . . . That Miki Herman kept her job is a testament to the fact that it probably wasn't such a big deal. Otherwise, if it's as bad as everybody says, Miki Herman should have lost her job. And she didn't."

Of course, it's also possible that, contrary to popular belief, Lucas did *not* initially hate the Special as much as he later said he did—that, like most of the viewers who saw the show in 1978, he was satisfied enough with it at the time, only realizing how awful it was decades later, when it became available on YouTube along with all the other TV variety schlock of that era. If he thought it was so bad, why would he then greenlight Hamill and C-3PO appearing on *The Muppet Show* a little more than a year later? On that show, unlike his appearance on the Special, *Hamill actually sings*.

"I think at the time when the Holiday Special was broadcast, it was not considered to be the big failure or giant anomaly that it is considered to be today," said Rinzler. "I don't know for sure, but I certainly didn't hear from anybody that there was any fallout from the show, [or] that anybody was fired. I think life just went on at Lucasfilm." The Special, he added, is a kind of anomaly for fans, "because it was kind of the one big thing that Lucasfilm did before it got its act together and got a system together to make sure that things like this never happened again."

One popular rumor about the Special—an unsourced and unconfirmed rumor, mind you—is that Lucas hated the final cut so much that he demanded his name be taken off the credits. But this is dubious, at best. Who is to say that Smith–Hemion planned on including him on the credit roll at all? He would have probably only qualified as a producer in name only, as he never accepted a credit as a writer—even though he wrote the original treatment, wrote most of the cartoon, and helped the writers formulate a way to tell his story on the show. Officially, it remains unclear whether the omission was Lucas's decision or not. Nearly all of the producers who would have negotiated an "exit strategy" for Lucas are no longer with us—or, like Gary Smith, they simply can't remember.

It's possible that Lucas saw some of the dailies or an actual rough cut of the show, then demanded his name be taken off early on in the production. Some have speculated that his name might never have been intended for inclusion, just the Lucasfilm logo, to ensure he remained in control of all the merchandising for the Special as well. But the logo didn't make the cut either.

Alternatively, though, as Rinzler suggested, "George didn't fully understand the changes that were happening, or maybe just figured, 'This is a variety show—who cares?' This is not *Star Wars: The Movie*, this is *Star Wars: The Variety Show*, and maybe he underestimated how big of an effect this was going to have."

Whatever the truth is, Lucas has spent decades downplaying his involvement. But for those who are aware of his obsession with revising his previously released films—particularly *A New Hope*'s "Greedo Shot First" controversy—it's obvious that he has a penchant for rewriting history.

It's far too convenient for Lucas to say he was *barely* involved in the Special. Besides pushing the Wookiee storyline, there were several other ways in which he controlled the creative direction of the show:

- One of the first things he did was give a copy of the treatment to Ralph McQuarrie, who immediately started drawing Chewbacca's family, the treehouse, and various pieces of furniture and domestic appliances.
- It's pretty much universally agreed that he wrote the treatment, which includes special guest Raquel Welch as a sultry Imperial spy who uses her body to distract the rebels.
- He brought a makeshift version of the "mind evaporator" to Smith–Hemion's offices. For the Special, it was used for Itchy to visualize his fantasies.
- He pressured Dwight Hemion to step aside and have the Special be directed by his friend David Acomba, who created overtime/budget issues with his documentary-style shooting and perfectionism.
- He spent more than an entire workday going over the story with two of the writers, Lenny Ripps and Pat Proft.
- He prepared a forty-page "bible" with a "treasure trove" of background info on Kashyyyk and the Wookiees for director Steve Binder.
- He had the Nelvana representative fly out to Northern California to pitch his animation company for the cartoon.
- He wrote the treatment and the script for the cartoon, then met with the animators to approve drawings and conceptual artwork.
- He begged Hamill, Fisher, and Ford to appear in the Special, which they did, despite their reservations.

Taking all of these factors into account, it seems clear that Lucas has a selective memory of his involvement. In a recent interview for a Boba Fett documentary on Disney+, he continued to claim limited involvement with the Special: "*They* were doing this holiday special, and there wasn't much of our involvement . . . but I came up with the idea of, why don't we take the Boba Fett character and put him in that . . . make a little movie out of it." (As the *Hollywood Reporter*'s Paul Bond notes, "Lucas *has* taken credit for . . . coincidentally the segment most say was brilliant entertainment.")

Years later, Lucas couldn't seem to recall even the most basic information about it. "The special from 1978 really didn't have much to do with us, you know," he told Staticmultimedia.com in 2005. "I can't remember what network it was on, but it was a thing that they did. We kind of let them do it. It was done by . . . I can't even remember who the group was, but they were variety TV guys. We let them use the characters and stuff, and that probably wasn't the smartest thing to do, but you learn from those experiences."

Kyle Newman doesn't accept Lucas's contention that he wasn't very involved in the Special, asserting that this entire "bonkers chapter in *Star Wars* history" would never have happened without him spearheading it. "He got his friends from college and galvanized the original *Star Wars* lead actors," Newman continues. "He gave them the narrative footprint to go marching ahead on this crazy adventure. And they did it. But it would never have happened unless George Lucas envisioned it."

Lucas regrets not exercising a tighter grip over the Special's production. Kurtz added that his and Lucas's experience with it "certainly added to the idea that the only way to make sure it turns out the way you wanted is to be in control."

However, the idea that Lucas doesn't bear any responsibility because he left the production before shooting began doesn't hold water. There is tremendous damage one can do to a production—which Lucas arguably did with this Special—by ignoring the advice of experts, leading your followers into the dark, and then leaving them to navigate on their own after you pull out. It's similar to driving a car and then jumping out before it goes off a cliff.

Ripps adds that the production could have really benefitted from Lucas's insight, particularly when things were starting to go south. "I did not know the extent of his involvement and how much involvement he intended to have," Ripps recalls. "But I think if he was more involved, it probably would've stayed closer to his vision. . . . When Lucas walked away, he said, 'You do whatever you want.' And then he got upset because we did whatever we wanted. If he didn't like the way his *movie* was going, he would've worked eighteen hours a day or thirty hours a day and made the movie better. Instead of walking away, why didn't he jump into [this] and say, 'I want this and I wanted to do this . . .'? He didn't do any of that."

Newman agrees, pointing out that it would have been out of character for Lucas to surrender all creative control to someone else. "This wasn't something that he totally pawned off to someone else and said, 'Go do whatever you want.' He actually set the train in motion. And while he may not have had the time and manned resources to fully stay focused on it, it did pervert into something else. There's a difference between ownership and responsibility, and I would say George is culpable in the fact that he set it all in motion. He's also probably culpable because he then didn't police it. He had the opportunity to probably review it and edit it before it came out. But he either felt it was too far gone or he thought it was fine, and that's something he can only answer."

Fans have been pressuring Lucas for decades to embrace the Special—and, more importantly, to stop insisting he was not involved or didn't participate in the editorial process. It might be time for him to take responsibility for whatever mistakes he made, and stop blaming others—particularly those who have yet to achieve even a *smidgen* of the professional success that he has.

"Pass on what you have learned," Yoda advises in *The Last Jedi*, as Luke struggles with the results of the mistakes he made with Kylo Ren. "Strength, mastery, but weakness, folly, failure also. Yes: failure, most of all. The greatest teacher, failure is."

CHAPTER 12
THE GREATEST DISCOVERY

EVEN IF LUCAS genuinely hated the Special when it first aired, one reason why there was no bloodshed as a result may have been that his galactic-size ship had finally come in. Something big had come his way that Thanksgiving weekend in 1978, and it wasn't the Special.

During the prior holiday season, Kenner's "Early Bird" offer had proved tremendously effective in quenching the thirst of holiday shoppers looking for *Star Wars* toys to put under the Christmas tree. Kenner held to its "empty box promise" to customers and was able to deliver action figures to those fans by March of 1978.

However, this holiday season was going to be much different. In the fall of 1978, Kenner released the X-Wing Fighter, which was sure to be a hit. It didn't hurt that in the first few minutes of the Special, Lumpy is seen playing with one—and Itchy is building one. There was no need for Kenner to buy a commercial, since the X-Wing Fighter—the *Star Wars* toy they had the most hope for—had been organically placed in the script. It was practically an infomercial.

By this point, Kenner had also had more than a year to develop and manufacture several other toys, which would be on the shelves the day after the Holiday Special aired. As of this writing, more than $20 billion in licensed *Star Wars* merchandise has been sold. A significant portion of those profits was made within the first two years after Lucas first negotiated a split of the merchandising with Fox and then, when negotiating for distribution for *The Empire Strikes Back*, made a successful attempt to grab Fox's half as well.

Most of the young fans who saw the Special soon forgot about it. Scott Kirkwood says that his friends talked about it at school the next day but, after that, it was never brought up again. Lenny Ripps says he experienced the same response: everyone had an opinion, and then every shred of evidence that the Special ever existed disappeared. "I think it's probably like the plague in the Middle Ages," he says. "After everybody died, they decided to change the subject."

The Special only ever aired once. It was not scheduled to repeat on CBS or any other network. Thus, those who happened to record its one and only broadcast were the only ones who could rewatch it. This was decades before anyone could see it on YouTube.

Before the internet era, unauthorized copies of the Special were traded between collectors in various analog formats. In 1975, Sony had launched the Betamax machine in the United States, which allowed consumers to record television broadcasts. With the purchase of a second recorder, they could also duplicate that home-recorded content, as well as make copies of commercially released Betamax videotapes of theatrical films. At that time, Betamax versions of everyday, run-of-the-mill films retailed for $50 to $100, creating unheard-of profit margins. To ensure that their videotapes couldn't be duplicated, the studios soon developed a "copyguard," so that anything copied from commercially produced Betamax tapes would become garbled and unwatchable.

Even though Betamax recorders were available to purchase legally, the studios considered the actual recording of copyrighted content illegal. In 1976, Universal and Walt Disney sued Sony in federal court, claiming that the product's users were infringing upon the studios' copyrights, and therefore that its manufacturer was liable for the law being broken. Two years later, the district court for the Central District of California sided with Sony, deciding that noncommercial home recording was considered fair use, as supported by the First Amendment. Then, in 1981, the Ninth Circuit Court of Appeals reversed that decision, ruling that Sony was indeed liable for copyright infringement. "The Ninth Circuit is one of the most liberal courts, yet also one of the most inconsistent courts," according to Hector

Del Cid, an ABC production attorney. "They ruled that Universal had a legitimate claim, but they couldn't figure out how to assess damages."

The case ultimately went to the Supreme Court, which reversed the circuit court's decision three years later by a ruling of five to four. "That's why they call it 'the slow hand of justice,'" says Del Cid. Whether or not the eight-year legal battle directly affected Sony's sales, it is definitely the case that, by 1984, its Betamax one-hour recording tape was losing to JVC's newly released VHS format, which allowed up to two hours of recording time (extended to six hours in a lower-quality recording mode). Betamax was aced out of the market and replaced by the new VHS standard.

Between the late 1970s and the mid-1990s, a growing volume of unauthorized programming was recorded on audio cassettes and VHS—and eventually DVDs—to be shared and traded.

One of the first genres of unauthorized content to become popular was audio collections of bloopers and outtakes: tantrums by Casey Kasem doing *American Top 40*, Orson Welles debating English grammar for a frozen peas commercial, Beach Boys stage father Murry Wilson micro-managing his kids in the studio, and Buddy Rich surreptitiously recorded tormenting one of his musicians.

Bootleg videos—like William Shatner's bizarre reading of "Rocket Man," as well as the unreleased Jerry Lewis–directed *The Day the Clown Cried*, a terribly maligned film about a clown imprisoned in a Nazi concentration camp—were also collected and traded. News bloopers were another popular genre. In the mid-1980s, a network blooper reel was assembled for the Washington Press Correspondents' Association Dinner honoring President Reagan. CBS, NBC, ABC, and Fox each assembled bloopers and sent them to the event's editor, who created a lengthy reel for the event. It featured top anchors and reporters like ABC News' Sam Donaldson losing their tempers on air. These reporters likely never thought that something presented at a non-broadcast event could wind up duplicated in enormous amounts and distributed among the masses, but that is exactly what happened.

This era was sort of a golden age for collectors of this material. Of course, it was all still analog, so tapes had to be traded or sold in person at science-fiction conventions and comic book stores, or sent through the mail. Advertisements in the back of niche magazines also offered copies of extremely rare videos for sale—forbidden fruit that wasn't on the shelves at the local Blockbuster.

"At a certain point, if you were somebody who collected weird footage, you'd seen it all," says Nick Prueher, who curates the Found Footage Festival with his partner, Joe Pickett. (Prueher insists he still hasn't seen it all; he continues to seek out video chestnuts, which he presents at live events all over the country.) Prueher and Pickett were part of a larger but deeply entrenched tape-trading circuit in the 1990s and early 2000s, when—to make their rent—many in their niche, like Prueher and the late Rick Scheckman, doubled as footage researchers at "caught-on-tape" clip shows, or for David Letterman and Jay Leno's late-night shows. However, for the rest of us, this content was just pure entertainment, to be enjoyed at parties that didn't stop until the last video was played.

"Part of the charm of these mixtapes is you would see all the crude editing that non-professionals were doing at the time," adds Prueher, who in the days of analog would also connect two VCRs to each other with RCA cables to duplicate tapes. "You'd lose a lot of quality. Imagine somebody takes that tape that has all the tracking problems, and then makes their own dub of that . . ."

One of the most famous of the kind of tapes they traded was one they stumbled onto themselves. Several years ago, the two heard about an RV commercial shoot hosted by a former news anchor with an extremely short fuse. They tracked down the raw footage and assembled a hilarious out-take reel that had more F-bombs than a fistful of Tarantino films. It became a favorite among traders, earning the anchor, Jack Rebney, the title of "The Angriest Man in the World."

But the really coveted tape was the *Star Wars Holiday Special.* "It became a currency of sorts in geek culture," says Kevin Smith. "Talking about it, dropping references to it. Producing a copy to watch . . ."

The lengths some people had to go to watch the Special were ridiculous—and then, once it was in hand, the quality of the tape was nearly unwatchable.

"I had to get a tape of a tape of a tape," recalls comedian and filmmaker Bobcat Goldthwait. "The Zapruder film was easier to watch than the copy of the Holiday Special that I got."

Prueher agrees. "We had a really bad recording—I believe some

Philadelphia TV station that still had the commercials in it. The quality was extremely washed out. It was probably an eleventh-, twelfth-generation dub. You had to squint to see it, but it was worth it because you just couldn't believe what you were seeing."

The Special tape became a part of Prueher and Pickett's live show, a kind of "video show-and-tell" where they alternated showing their favorite clips to the audience. They screened the Special in private theaters or smaller classrooms—careful not to promote the event too loudly and prompt Lucasfilm attorneys to knock on their door with an injunction forbidding the unauthorized screening.

Over time, tape trading broadened awareness of the Special, even among those who hadn't been alive to see it broadcast. It also played an important role in the video for "Weird Al" Yankovic's 2006 song "White and Nerdy," a parody of "Ridin'" by Chamillionaire featuring Krayzie Bone. In one scene, Yankovic—playing against type, of course—portrays a rabid *Star Wars* fan who goes to a back alley to purchase some sort of illegal product. He slips the dealer a few large bills in exchange for a wrinkled paper bag. Inside, to Yankovic's delight, he finds a VHS copy of the Special.

"The *Star Wars Holiday Special* is sort of like the holy grail among *Star Wars* fans," Yankovic says. "If you tell somebody you can't have something, they want it even more. So I thought that the *Star Wars Holiday Special* on a VHS tape, sixth-generation copy—that would've been valuable currency to a prototypical nerd *Star Wars* fan. So I thought it was appropriate for that back-alley barter deal."

These bootleg tapes started becoming more readily available to the public; copies could now be rented under the table at some video rental stores. Lucas cursed the Special when asked about it in an interview. "He said, 'Oh, *that* damn thing,'" recalls Steve Sansweet, the curator of Rancho Obi-Wan, the Northern California museum that houses the world's largest *Star Wars* memorabilia collection. "[Lucas] said, 'If I could personally go out and find all of the VHS bootleg tapes, I would smash them all.'" Sansweet adds that after he told that anecdote at an Australian convention, it "sort of went around the world. So I take some pride in having started that anecdote. And I got it right from the horse's mouth."

In the mid-'90s, Julie Welch was teaching improvisation at the infamous

Groundlings Theater and School in Hollywood. Once every few weeks, the directors would take a break from performing and hold a screening—usually some off-the-wall film or TV show that was unintentionally funny or "so bad it's good." One day, written on a large whiteboard near the entrance of the theater, that week's entertainment was listed: *The Star Wars Holiday Special.*

Welch recalls, "This can't be good, because I don't think I realized—and nor did my parents—until [many years] after the Special aired that it had this kind of history of going down as something that was made fun of."

In these pre-YouTube days, Welch tracked down a copy of it, only to realize that the Special was "notorious for the wrong reasons. I started googling and realized, whoa, lots of people are talking about this, and not, for the most part, in a positive way."

As more bootleg copies of the Special became available, Julie's parents began getting interview requests to talk about it. She says her parents had always thought that the Special was a bit before its time, so the new attention they were getting must have felt like sweet revenge to all the naysayers who had criticized them back in 1978. At one point, Julie had to explain the "so bad it's good" angle to the show and advise them not to do any interviews about it.

"I feel like it made my mom a little wary of doing interviews," Julie said of Mitzie. "I hated to see her hurt," she recalls. She says that it broke her heart to have to explain to her that they were being used or possibly manipulated into doing something for the wrong reasons: "I think they were a little surprised. They just really didn't know. They really poured their heart into things. I'm protective, especially [now] since they're gone and they can't speak for themselves."

Welch is in a tough position, being in the comedy business. She doesn't necessarily resent the relentless criticism of the Special, but even if she did, it's pretty much dictated that she teach her students how to take such criticism. She adds that her parents grew to understand that the Special was "kind of a mishmash": "There were certain elements that they probably remained proud of, but I don't think they were to put it on their list of ten most significant accomplishments."

* * *

Even with the Special being traded among collectors, for many years there was not much written about it all—only faint whispers by those who had allegedly watched its one and only showing on that Friday night in November 1978, or who had subsequently watched a video copy of it. To everyone else, it was just hearsay.

However, by the late '90s, two important changes had taken place. First, a new generation of *Star Wars* fans had been born—the children of the parents who were kids when the original trilogy was in theaters. Now, twenty years later, these parents were returning to the theaters, this time with their children, to see Lucas's "Special Edition" re-releases.

Secondly, more and more households now had internet access—many upgrading from dial-up service to high-speed, uninterrupted access—which helped this new generation of new fans catch up on the twenty years of *Star Wars* culture they had missed. As Lenny Ripps points out, the internet was a great resource for things that weren't meant to be seen. "In a way, the fact that Lucas has spent so much time denying [the Special's existence] makes it more popular for some people, because it seems like it's something they shouldn't see or can't see. So they flock to it."

The Special has what Kyle Newman calls "an inescapable stigma" to it. "And it has it because everyone's been so cagey about it. It actually worked against what they wanted. By Lucasfilm being so weird about it, they made it so it lives on forever—as opposed to just being, 'Yeah, it happened,' and not making a big deal about it, [then] it probably would have disappeared."

Brian Ward agrees, saying the Special had a mysterious vibe to it, since most fans didn't believe it actually existed. "It became a little bit of a mission for fans to find the Special. They were saying, 'If this thing does exist, we're gonna find it.'"

By the time the "Special Editions" were released, *Star Wars* had become practically a religion to many people. "There were people combing the internet for anything *Star Wars*," Vilanch explains. "And they came upon [a reference to] this special which they'd never heard of, and they said, 'What is this?'"

It wasn't available at Best Buy or on Amazon, so it mystified them. And as more people became aware of the Special, under-the-table sales of pirated copies rose significantly in the unofficial used-video market.

The idea that you could easily upload actual video content to a website, view it, and share it with others was hard to imagine in the late 1990s. But by 2005, with the launch of YouTube, the moon shot was now a reality. Now, the combination of widespread broadband adoption and new file-sharing sites—with enough bandwidth to successfully stream decent-quality video content—meant the Special would be available to all. The World Wide Web had become the Wild Wild West.

At this point, for Lucas, the toothpaste was already out of the tube. Owners of copyrighted content like the Special were essentially helpless in preventing it from being shared online. In an attempt to protect content owners, President Clinton signed the Digital Millennium Copyright Act into law in 1998, prohibiting copyrighted content from being uploaded online without permission. A copyright takedown—the digital version of a cease-and-desist order—could be filed against the unauthorized uploader, which would theoretically result not only in the content being deleted online but in the user having their future ability to upload content curtailed or revoked entirely.

However, these uploaders of unauthorized content soon found loopholes in the new law, and dozens of recordings of the Special and other unauthorized recordings continued to be uploaded to YouTube and similar sites. Even today, if a copyright owner submits a takedown request to YouTube, and even if they are successful in getting the content taken down, it's quite a waste of time. Often, once one is deleted from a file-sharing site, another copy from another uploader instantly resurfaces to take its place, leaving the owner stuck in a never-ending video version of Whack-a-Mole.

At this point, anyone could view the Special. No duplication costs. No shipping fees. It was now just a Google search away.

The two off-air recordings of it that are currently online can be sourced back to two CBS affiliates that broadcast the show in 1978, WCBS (New York) and WMAR (Baltimore), complete with local news promos and commercials. A third copy seems to have been copied from some sort of master, without commercials.

Over the years, these unedited off-air recordings have helped to serve many purposes. The most obvious one is that they have preserved the Holiday Special, offering proof to non-believers who wouldn't accept the rumors that this actually happened. If not for these recordings, one has to wonder if Lucas would have ever admitted to the fiasco. He could have just played stupid about the whole thing while the two-inch master sat in Lucasfilm's cold storage.

However, the recordings have also served to preserve other content. In fact, these specific recordings were so popular that some of the commercials and promos included in them have become infamous as well. One example of this is from the WCBS broadcast of the Special.

Rolland Smith has over sixty years of broadcast and television news experience in New York City, first at the independently owned WWOR-TV, then at the CBS affiliate WCBS-TV, where he was the news anchor at the time of the Special. In his illustrious career, he has won eleven Emmy awards, two Telly Awards, and numerous other awards and accolades. He has interviewed presidents and the pope. He has traveled into war zones and natural disaster areas. Yet despite his dedication to the craft he loves and respects, his reporting would not become the most famous aspect of his career.

There are four months during the year that are considered "sweeps" periods: February, May, July, and November. Networks place their best shows, specials, and specific episodes during these months, especially May and November. This is the time when one might see such visually stimulating shows as *The Victoria's Secret Valentine Special* or *World's Scariest Police Chases*, or when special guest stars make appearances on your favorite sitcoms. Advertisers pay closer attention to ratings during these specific times, and thus networks will regularly program highly rated season finales in May and special holiday events and specials in November—hence the Special's broadcast date in November 1978.

The news business works the same way. News directors will routinely program multipart investigative reports, salacious stories, and pieces specifically designed to help consumers—both physically and financially— to increase their ratings during these months. The promotion of these types of stories during these time periods was vital to the station. "We had to do these things called 'teases,'" Smith explains. "So, for an example, I might say, 'Car crash on the George Washington Bridge at eleven.' The local stations would run these teases in between the commercials during prime-time network programming to promote stories coming up later in their news broadcasts.

"One of the teases that I think one of the writers wrote was, 'A case of the frizzies … at eleven.'" It was this short tease that Smith read during one of the Special's several commercial breaks, and for which he has become famous. He read a few variations of the line throughout the two-hour broadcast, but one specific line caught on: "Fighting the Frizzies … tonight at eleven."

"The anchor is the funniest part," says Dani Tenerelli, a commercial artist and huge fan of the Special. "It's hilarious." In fact, Tenerelli loves the part so much, she included Smith in a cast illustration she did of the Special. "[He's] become part of the charm. [He and other commercial actors] have become part of this."

For several years, Smith was completely unaware that one of the most duplicated and uploaded copies of the Special was his own station's broadcast, or that his teases were all through it. Over the years, people have since created memes and parodies of the promo, giving viral celebrity status to the legendary newscaster.

By December 1999, Smith's tease had made it into the *South Park Christmas Special*, marking an amazing high point in the anchor's unique fame. However, more significant was that the *South Park* special aired six years before the launch of YouTube, meaning that the show's creators, Trey Parker and Matt Stone, had not seen the promos online and could have only been aware of this obscure reference because of an unauthorized VHS or DVD they had seen or obtained.

"When I saw that on *South Park*, I was like, *I don't believe it*," recalls Tenerelli. "You know they have the bootleg. That's amazing."

The popularity of this tease has now dwarfed Smith's successes in the news business. On his Wikipedia page, nearly half of the section devoted to his news career details the popularity of the infamous tease. "You've got four paragraphs of my career, which spanned close to fifty, sixty years," he laments. "Then all of a sudden you got two paragraphs on just 'fighting the frizzies.' I mean, that's the American media. Nobody remembers the serious things and the profound things that I did in my career, but they all remember 'fighting the frizzies at eleven.'"

Over the years, off-air recordings like the Special have helped in many other ways, mostly in repairing a "hole in the archive." For a few decades now, it has been the standard protocol for libraries that archive news articles to remove the advertising from newspapers and magazines to save badly needed space.

"Who needs the ads?" archivists most likely say. "I saved the most important part—the news."

In their article "The Rise of Periodical Studies," media scholars Sean Latham and Robert Scholes implore archival institutions to include advertisements when curating newspapers and periodicals for their libraries. They explain that there is far more to learn from a society's commercial propaganda than from its news stories, but that these insights are being lost as advertisements are systematically deleted in order to save space.

Andrew Ferguson, an assistant professor at the University of Maryland, learned of Latham and Scholes's "hole in the archive" and made a bizarre but amazing connection. He realized that the two recordings of the *Star Wars Holiday Special* had unintentionally taken the first, badly needed step in repairing that hole. Ferguson says these recordings give us far more than just a copy of the Special. The commercials reveal less of what the networks want us to see and more about how the advertising world sees us.

For starters, out of the thirty commercials and network promos that ran during the two-hour special, a surprisingly low fifteen percent of them were for toys. Yet more revealing is comparing the commercials slated for the New York and Baltimore affiliates, which are mostly the same but significantly different in a few areas. For example, in New York, Universal Pictures booked a movie trailer for *Animal House* at the end of the fifth commercial break. However, at the same moment in Baltimore, the same studio booked an ad for *The Wiz*.

A stranger example can be found at the end of the second commercial break, where an A&W Root Beer commercial was booked for the New York market, while a commercial for a Reggie! Bar was shown in the same slot in Baltimore. At the time, Reggie Jackson was a New York Yankee who just a year earlier had led his team to win the World Series over the Dodgers, memorably hitting three home runs off of three separate pitches from three separate pitchers. Most people in their lifetimes will never witness such a display of physical strength as fans at Yankee Stadium saw that night. So why would the folks at Standard Brands choose to advertise the Reggie bar in Baltimore but not New York? Again, the commercials sold during this two-hour special say much about how advertisers—and specifically network programmers—see us.

"I think it's fascinating to see what gets advertised and when, and to speculate as to why," says Ferguson, who thinks CBS had no clue who its audience was. "It's kind of interesting capturing this moment where . . . they don't know who's going to be tuning in and how to try to sell them things. So they're just kind of throwing a little bit of everything at the wall just to see what sticks."

On one hand, Binder contends that the Special was designed to sell toys to kids. However, CBS had sold only five toy commercials in the two-hour show; Kenner had purchased only two commercials, and only *one* was *Star Wars*–related. Yet the network sold two commercials to movie distributors for R-rated films, *Animal House* and *The Wild Geese*. The latter, which starred Richard Burton and Roger Moore, had received criticism for filming in South Africa in cooperation with the apartheid government. Anti-apartheid protestors demonstrated at its European premiere in London over what they considered to be a negative portrayal of Black Africans.

Latham and Scholes's 2006 call to action needs to be restated to each new generation of potential purchasers. The advertising industry is an international multibillion-dollar business that isn't clueless, though it can feign stupid if it is pressured to act as such.

After reviewing these commercials, Ferguson is certain that, back in 1978, CBS could not identify its audience, so just acted blindly and cast a huge net, sending leads everywhere. If, as Ferguson believes, these marketing experts were innocently asleep at the wheel, this clearly proves one thing: knowing what our advertisers are trying to sell us should be of great importance to us, dwarfed only by our pressing desire to know exactly who they think we are.

* * *

As more people were finally able to view the Special online, many were greatly offended that such unauthorized non-canon elements made their way into an official *Star Wars* program, much less aired on a prime-time network special. Many fans charged Lucas and the others who made the

Special with violating the original vision of *Star Wars*, thus beginning the never-ending debate between fans over which films, television shows, and literary works should be allowed to remain within the *Star Wars* Universe as official "canon"—the official continuity of Lucas's saga—and which elements would be relegated to the Outer Rim territories of the disregarded expanded universe.

"Once again, the Royal Order of *Star Wars* Devotees were mortified by it," says Vilanch. "And that was when [Lucas] tried to really bury it, because it was, you know, getting dangerous. And George got death threats from these crazy people."

Part of the problem is that the story of *Star Wars* is pretty simple but near perfect. While Lucas's script (bolstered by Willard Huyck and Gloria Katz) is a simple tale of good versus evil, it is filled with engrossing complexities in its background stories that give the whole film a huge sense of reality. Consequently, many avid fans feel that it's *their* world as much as it's Lucas's. This seems to be why the Special gets such a visceral reaction from *Star Wars* fans: they're questioning their own reality, asking themselves, "How does this fit into my worldview of what *Star Wars* is?"

"George created a universe that was so complete that the fans immediately lived there," said Jonathan Rinzler. "They immediately moved into this place that George had developed, and it was so real. George had lived there in his mind, and they came in and they saw little things that George had missed." So, when the fans noticed things like Chewbacca not getting a medal, they took these slights strangely personally.

"When you have a bunch of people that love something and take it into their hearts, they claim it," says Kevin Smith. "And when these things don't behave the way we want them to, well—it seems like we've become a culture that doesn't know how to handle that."

For Vilanch, this wasn't the first time a show he worked on in the 1970s disappeared, only to suddenly reappear decades later. He also wrote eight episodes of *The Brady Bunch Variety Hour* in 1976, before the series was abruptly canceled, seemingly never to be heard from again. "We thought it was dead and buried after it went off the air," he says. "The [*Star Wars*] Special isn't the only television phenomenon that has come back to bite everybody back in our big fat ass."

Because *The Brady Bunch* reruns kept running, a whole new generation was exposed to the show by their parents, and as a result there now have been many iterations, including *The Brady Kids*, *The Brady Brides*, and two *Brady Bunch* movies that are parodies of the original show. And, in the middle of all that, *The Brady Bunch Variety Hour* resurfaced on Nickelodeon.

"There were people calling me saying, 'Dude, I watched this show, and you got a writing credit out of it. And the dad from *The Brady Bunch* was dancing like Carmen Miranda. How'd that happen?'" Vilanch recalls. He would always respond the same way: "You've obviously taken the proper chemical additives to watch that show, which is what we were doing when we did that show."

* * *

Scott Kirkwood was just five years old when his family went to a showing of *Bambi* at the local drive-in theater in Portland, Oregon. His parents were both members of a conservative church that normally stayed away from such dangerous influences as movies and television. But it was *Bambi*, they thought. How could they go wrong?

However, during the coming attractions, the theater showed a trailer for the upcoming R-rated *Texas Chainsaw Massacre*. Kirkwood's parents were devastated that their young children were exposed to such violent subject matter. From that day on, they vowed to never go to see a film in a theater again. Eventually, they even got rid of their television set.

When *Star Wars* conquered the world in the summer of 1977, Kirkwood's parents were still holding firm, leaving Scott with the distinction of being one of the only children in the Pacific Northwest who had *not* yet seen the film. So he did everything *but* see the film. He read the novel, he read the comic books. He collected bubblegum cards and had whatever limited toys were available at the time. He wore *Star Wars* shirts by day and *Star Wars* pajamas by night. At school, he started a *Star Wars* club, and everyone knew him as "The *Star Wars* Kid."

A little over a year later, Kirkwood got the best news of his life. He had learned that there was going to be a *Star Wars Holiday Special* in a few weeks, and, most importantly, it was going to be airing on television. Since his family was still TV-less, Kirkwood's father took him to his grandparent's house to watch the Special. He loved it.

In 1980, *The Empire Strikes Back* was released in theaters, but Scott's parents still wouldn't let their ten-year-old attend movie theaters. As part of the hoopla, *Star Wars* was also being re-released in theaters, prompting a sympathetic teacher of Kirkwood's to figure out a way to get the biggest *Star Wars* fan in the school to see the film for his first time. She organized a field trip for the entire sixth grade to go see it. Kirkwood was ecstatic, but his parents would not sign the permission slip, so while his entire class went to see *Star Wars*, "The *Star Wars* Kid" himself had to remain at school, stuck in a classroom, doing busy work all day.

In 1983, Kirkwood turned thirteen and officially became a teenager. It was also the year that *Return of the Jedi* was released in theaters. Not surprisingly, he was still prohibited from seeing it. However, when *Star Wars* was finally released on video the following year, Kirkwood watched it at a friend's birthday party, and he loved it. All good things come to those who wait.

But was it worth the *seven-year* wait? He thinks so. It would take three additional years for 1980's *The Empire Strikes Back* to make it to television. When the "Special Editions" were finally released theatrically, Kirkwood, now an adult, finally got to see all three films from the original trilogy in theaters. Better late than never.

Kirkwood soon began attending science-fiction and comic-book conventions, scouring tables and various collections for any kind of memorabilia from *Star Wars*, but specifically the Special, as that meant something more to him, since he'd seen it before all of the other films. Over the years, he has acquired early drafts of the Special's script as well as preliminary designs and sketches of various props and sets. He has even gotten his hands on some of the actual costumes before they made their way to eBay.

Being *prohibited* from watching *Star Wars* in 1977 is akin to not being able to google today. For kids like Kirkwood who couldn't embrace the films of the *Star Wars* trilogy, the Special offered the next best thing. Though he couldn't experience Luke Skywalker, Han, and Leia, he could still embrace Ackmena, Saul Dann, and Mermeia. As flawed, misguided, and embarrassing as the Special was to many people, it was still *Star Wars*—and, for people like Kirkwood, it was still something wonderful.

If Kirkwood teaches us anything, it is to be grateful for what we have. For him, it's a two-hour special shot right in the midst of the Lucasfilm chaos, offering fans a glimpse into the lives of Hamill, Fisher, and Ford just before superstardom would totally overwhelm them.

"The Special is the only other time where the three lead characters are together on screen," explains Jason Lenzi. "They're together for a bit in *A New Hope*. You start with Luke and Ben, then they get to the cantina and it's Luke, Ben, and Han. Then they get to the Death Star and Ben takes off. Then they get the Princess, and then it's Han, Luke, and the Princess."

This infamous trio of characters continues the same pattern of leaving and reuniting through the entire original trilogy, as well as the next. Lenzi points out that in the six hours of screen time in the original trilogy, the three of them are hardly together that much, and in the subsequent trilogy, everybody expected older Luke, Han, and Leia to be hanging out with younger characters. But we never see the three of them together again.

CHAPTER 13

THE FOURTH LIFE

ONE OF THE most fascinating aspects of the Special is the many lives it has taken on in its forty-five years of existence. Jason Lenzi counts four—each of them legitimate and well-lived.

"There is its first life, with very little fanfare before it premiered," Lenzi explains. "Maybe a commercial or two, and whatever awareness it had from the people that heard about it before it aired. Those who loved *Star Wars* watched it and either enjoyed it, or it left their heads as soon as the credits rolled."

Lenzi says the second life began around the late '80s and early '90s, when VHS copies changed hands at science fiction conventions. By then, the Special was almost mythical to many, "and soon it becomes something that completists want to get a hold of," he adds. "To the *Star Wars* fans, it is met with both curiosity and confusion, but not derision."

The Special's third life begins once it "becomes available on the internet, and then YouTube changes everything," Lenzi explains. "When it becomes more widely available, that immediately puts a target on its back—to take a piss on it, to make fun of it." Thousands of armchair quarterbacks started producing their own videos of analysis and criticism with a skewed present-day perspective. "There is no looking at this as a product of its time," Lenzi says. The "wave of negativity" and mockery goes on for the next ten to fifteen years.

Not all of the attention is completely hostile, however. Around this time, comedian Seth Green co-created the wildly successful stop-motion sketch-comedy series *Robot Chicken*. "We had done a couple of *Star Wars* sketches and got the attention of George Lucas," Green noted. "The people at Lucasfilm realized you could do a comedic take on *Star Wars* without compromising the integrity of any dramatic take."

Not only did Lucas meet with Green and agree to produce some one-off *Star Wars* specials, he even agreed to contribute his voice to a segment portraying himself. In the sketch, Lucas is speaking with a therapist, regretfully commiserating over the Holiday Special, claiming, "I hate it! I hate it! I hate it!"

Lucas's willingness to somewhat acknowledge the Special but to poke fun at it points toward its fourth life. Lenzi notes that, in 2018, Japan's Hot Toys begin producing twelve-inch versions of the animated Boba Fett, creating both excitement and curiosity about his origins. Then, in November 2019, Disney launched its streaming service Disney+, and among its original programming was the first season of *The Mandalorian*, a space Western that follows the adventures of a Boba Fett–like bounty hunter.

The launch of Disney+ marked the end of seven years of major changes at the company. On October 30, 2012, Disney announced its acquisition of Lucasfilm for $4.05 billion, transferring ownership of nearly all *Star Wars* intellectual property—its films, television shows, books, music, and other produced media. At that time, Disney also announced that not only was *Star Wars: Episode VII* in pre-production but that it would be part of a trilogy of new sequels that would be released over the next several years.

Since *A New Hope* was owned by Fox, it was not part of the Disney acquisition. Disney would have to wait until it acquired Fox in March 2019 to finally have its hands on the original *Star Wars*, and from that point on it would control the entire library. Until then, the ownership of the copyright in the Special had been a bit muddy. It was not entirely clear whether Lucasfilm had originally owned it, or if Fox's TV production arm, Twentieth Television, did. However, the question became irrelevant in 2019, when it all came together under the same Disney flag. To quote Darth Vader, "The circle is now complete."

The Mandalorian was a huge hit for *Star Wars* fans, and it became a critically acclaimed feather in the cap for its creator and writer, Jon Favreau. Many called it the best addition to the franchise since *The Empire Strikes Back*. But what viewers of the series were probably not expecting was the homage it paid to the Holiday Special.

Favreau is not shy in admitting his sentiments for the Special, for he and *Mandalorian* partner Dave Filoni are self-proclaimed fanboys. So it should be no surprise that they didn't simply hide references to the Special in easter eggs but instead wove them into their stories organically.

The Mandalorian rides a "blurrg," clearly referencing Boba Fett's appearance in the Special, riding a creature instead of flying a ship or other aircraft. And when a water beast comes up to attack the Mandalorian's ship in Episode One of the series, he uses a fork-like rifle to defend himself, much like Boba Fett used when a dragon attacked him in the Special. In addition, the prisoner the Mandalorian has captured complains that he had plans for Life Day. Lastly, the creature that uses a flute to call a landspeeder for *The Mandalorian* looks similar to an anteater creature in the Special.

These similarities are no accident. At a *Mandalorian* fan event, Favreau said the Special was "definitely a point of inspiration for what we did in the show." One of his favorite elements of the Special is clearly Boba Fett's weapon, which he made sure was featured prominently in the series.

"The forked rifle that the Mandalorian carries is a direct reference to the Holiday Special, because Boba does not have that weapon when he appears in *The Empire Strikes Back*," Scott Kirkwood notes. "It's not in any of the movies; it's only in the *Star Wars Holiday Special*."

The weapon looks like a cross between a rifle, a branding iron, and a bug zapper, its end shaped like a tuning fork. "Let's talk about that gun for a second," Favreau says to Filoni in the behind-the-scenes footage of the series. "That was one of the deep cuts we had, the zapper that he uses to corral whatever that dinosaur he's riding."

Favreau seems to enjoy bringing up the taboo subject to Lucas. "Did you see the gun we had?" Favreau asked Lucas on a visit to the set. "Did you know that was an homage to [the cartoon portion of the Special]? That's canon, right? Because you wrote it."

"Not really," Lucas quickly responds, offering another instance of him denying his involvement, particularly with the cartoon—even though his name is on the script and he has admitted that the cartoon was his idea.

While Favreau acknowledges the Special's flaws, he loves the cartoon and its introduction of Boba Fett. "That animated piece still holds up," he said in a 2019 interview. "It's pretty cool." He has even floated the idea of doing a

Mandalorian version of the Holiday Special. "I've been thinking about it," he said. "It's ready, the ideas are ready. I think it could be really fun." However, he recoiled when asked about any *Mandalorian* cast members making guest appearances. "I'm not going to say who I would be interested in. But one is a member of the cast in an upcoming episode of the show. So we'll leave it at that for now."

This was not the first time elements from the Special made their way into officially licensed *Star Wars* content. In the 2001 LucasArts game *Galactic Battlegrounds*, Chewbacca's father Itchy is revealed to have been a great warrior in his younger days. "Chieftain Attichitcuk"—a contemporary of Qui-Gon Jinn's—successfully led a group of Wookiees in a fight for colonization rights and helped force the Trade Federation off their moon.

However, it's awfully hard to discuss Chewbacca's family in any half-serious manner with the ridiculous names they have been given. Adam Goldberg, who created the hit TV series *The Goldbergs* about his own family, agrees. "I think the characters are named in such a silly manner, it lessens the impact. It makes the whole thing feel a little cheap and childish." This frustrates Goldberg so much that he includes it in a scene from his show, where young Adam watches the Special for the first time with his father, played by Jeff Garlin. "Chewy's family had to be named something," young Adam says defensively. Garlin lashes out in confusion: "Lumpy and Itchy? Couldn't they have spent fifteen more minutes on the names?"

Another television show that referenced the Special is *The Big Bang Theory*. In one episode, Sheldon tells the gang that *Star Wars* Day is rapidly approaching and they should finalize their plans.

"That's a real thing?" Penny asks. "What is it, *Star Wars* Christmas?"

"No, don't be ridiculous," Howard answers. "That's Wookiee Life Day."

Another episode features Mark Hamill taking questions from fans. Raj asks Hamill whether he understood the language being spoken when he was on the Wookiee home planet. Hamill responds that he doesn't remember ever *being* on a Wookiee home planet.

Stuart clarifies: "Actually, Luke was on the Wookiee home planet, Kashyyyk, in the Holiday Special, when he helped Chewy get back to his wife."

Hamill is even more confused. "Chewy had a wife?"

"Her name's Malla," Stuart responds affirmatively.

References to the Holiday Special can even be found on the stage. In December 2019, it went *Off*-Broadway after film fan and writer Andrew Osborne penned a play called *Special* (as well as an accompanying comic book) documenting all of its behind-the-scenes drama. The play had a month-long run at Hollywood's Theater of NOTE, and among the actors was Lance Guest, star of *The Last Starfighter*.

Guest played Lippincott, whom he calls "the brainchild of the whole thing," and about a dozen other roles. "It highlights how tone deaf some producers or whoever [was] responsible [were], how they don't really get what this is, how the world of *Star Wars* and the world of the Holiday Special have so little in common."

Special features six actors playing over three dozen characters, including not just Hamill, Fisher, and Ford but the behind-the-scenes creatives: Binder, Acomba, Vilanch, Ripps, Proft, and the Welches. Vilanch and Ripps attended the play and met their respective alter egos; Vilanch's double dressed in a T-shirt, with curly blonde hair and trademark red glasses.

Osborne is currently working on adapting his play into a screenplay.

References to the Special in *Star Wars* novels are even more common. There are several allusions to it in the many non-canon books that were once part of the "Expanded Universe," which have since been rebranded "Legends" after Lucasfilm's infamous canon vs non-canon reclassification. For example, in 1996's *Tyrant's Test*, the third book in Michael P. Kube McDowell's *Black Fleet Trilogy*, Lumpy is shown being trained by Chewbacca to be a warrior. When Han Solo is captured, Lumpy joins Chewbacca aboard the Millennium Falcon to rescue him.

Rebel Dawn, the third book of A. C. Crispin's Han Solo Trilogy, takes place after *Solo: A Star Wars Story* and *A New Hope*. Crispin's trilogy is best known for chronicling the continuing back-and-forth gambling drama between Han and Lando Calrissian for the coveted prize of the Millennium Falcon. It also features a brief Holiday Special reference when Han and Chewbacca stop off at Kashyyyk and Chewbacca marries Malla.

Ackmena appears in *Fate of the Jedi: Allies*; the short story "We Don't Serve Your Kind Here," from the anthology *From a Certain Point of View*, which refers to her life on Tatooine with her wife Sorschi; and *Inside the Worlds of Star Wars Trilogy: The Ultimate Guide to the Incredible Locations of*

Episodes IV, V, and VI by James Luceno, which includes an illustration of the "nightshift bartender requesting better hours" from the Wookiee owner of Chalmun's Cantina.

The most infamous of the characters that were newly created for the Special, Mermeia, has also been introduced into the Expanded Universe. Although he is not a fan of the Special ("It kind of dragged quite a lot"), science-fiction author Kevin J. Anderson was intrigued by Mermeia's bird-like feathery design. So, for his "Jedi Academy" series, he designed not only one of his main characters, Qwi Xux, to look like Mermeia, but an entire race as well.

"I was thinking of the Diana Ross glittery-feathery alien when I designed my lovely female alien scientist, Qwi Xux," he says. According to the series art, Qwi Xux sports a similar purplish-white feathery hairdo, but hers is closely cropped. In the book, she is revealed to have originally conceived the Death Star. (Of course, according to *Rogue One*, the Death Star was further conceived by Galen Erso, who also supervised the creation of the space station. Like Qwi Xux, he soon learned of the Empire's desire to make the space station a first-strike weapon, then went AWOL. He was eventually recaptured and forced to build the Death Star, which he did, leaving in a hidden weakness that the rebels would use to destroy it in *A New Hope*.) *Entertainment Weekly* recently listed Qwi Xux seventh in its list of "The Best *Star Wars* Characters Disney Left Behind."

A notable attempt was also made to reference the Special in the 2018 film *Solo: A Star Wars Story*. The film was co-written by Lawrence Kasdan— also the co-writer of *The Empire Strikes Back*, *Return of the Jedi*, and *The Force Awakens*, as well as *Raiders of the Lost Ark* and countless other critically acclaimed movies—and his son Jonathan, an accomplished actor and writer in his own right. Jonathan was also such a huge fan of the Special that, in writing *Solo* with his father, he attempted to sneak in references to it several times, mostly without success. He was only able to get one past his father and the other executives: at one point in the script, Chewbacca introduces himself as the son of Attichitcuk. This passing reference to Itchy would have made him officially part of *Star Wars* canon, not simply the "Legends" or "Expanded Universe" stories that are considered separate from the core narrative. Alas, the scene did not make the final cut of the movie.

Apparently, Itchy had almost become canon more than a decade earlier, when Lucas was considering "reinventing" his character for 2005's *Revenge of the Sith*, in which he would be killed, according to conceptual artist Sang Jun Lee, who adds that this plot point from the prequel would have prompted Chewbacca to run away and eventually meet Han Solo. Lucas later told his *Revenge of the Sith* editorial team that a young Han Solo would be included in the film, at a time when he was being raised on Kashyyyk by Wookiees. He would eventually scrap all of these ideas, however.

The success of *The Mandalorian* has marked a major turning point for the future of the *Star Wars* franchise as a huge step toward Lucasfilm formally recognizing the Holiday Special. The series—with its references to the Special—premiered in conjunction with the launch of Disney+ in November 2019, one month before the theatrical release of the final chapter of the third *Star Wars* trilogy, *The Rise of Skywalker*. Unlike *The Rise of Skywalker*, which received disastrous reviews and a 52 percent rating on Rotten Tomatoes, *The Mandalorian* was a huge hit with critics and fans.

In April 2021 Disney+ took another step closer to (indirectly) formally recognizing the Holiday Special. The Boba Fett cartoon within the Special had always been revered by fans, so Disney decided to formally release the nine-minute animated adventure "The Story of the Faithful Wookiee" on Disney+ on November 17, 2021, or Life Day, for the uninitiated.

The decision to formally embrace a portion of the Special has opened up a Pandora's Box. "Compared to the way things have been previously, this is kind of a sign that maybe Lucasfilm is opening up toward the Holiday Special," says a hopeful Scott Kirkwood. Many feel that without requiring Lucas's formal approval, Disney should just go ahead and stream the entire Special. However, even though Lucas's sale of Lucasfilm to Disney subsequently released all of his rights to *Star Wars*, Lucas is still a valuable asset to the brand. It would be foolish for Disney to do *anything* that would upset him; the company desperately needs him by its side to help promote all of the new *Star Wars* projects in production and under development. You can't put a price tag on the promotional value of having him remain part of the *Star Wars* family, and Disney isn't about to jeopardize that scenario just so it can broadcast a special that few seem to care about, and which even fewer have given their thumbs-up.

Nonetheless, Disney has recently begun selling merchandise at its parks containing references to Life Day, including mugs with Chewbacca dressed in his red holiday robe. Books available for sale under the Disney banner include *Life Day Treasury: Holiday Stories for a Galaxy Far, Far Away*; *The Life Day Pop-up Book and Advent Calendar*; and even *The Life Day Cookbook*, which includes recipes for "Bantha Surprise," "Jelly Life Day Orbs," and "Mudhorn Eggnog." Additional available merchandise includes a $40 Blue Orb that doubles as a light, as well as Life Day–adorned T-shirts, holiday ornaments, and collectible pins. And, just a few days after Life Day 2021, Marvel re-released a comic book called *Life Day*, with Han Solo and Chewbacca on the cover.

"A lot of these new products reference Life Day, which is an exclusive reference to the Holiday Special," Lenzi says. "Now there's the cartoon airing on Disney+. So the Special can't be 'the worst thing ever made.'"

Further confusing things is that Life Day is celebrated on social media every November 17, commemorating the one and only broadcast of the Special. Fans have watched Lucasfilm try to bury the Special for generations, but Disney's recent efforts amount to a ninth-inning attempt to legitimize it—or at least to monetize it. A recording of the song Carrie Fisher sings at the end of the Special was even included on a CD accompanying the 2007 book *Star Wars Vault: Thirty Years of Treasures from Lucasfilm Archives*.

"The Special hasn't been buried," Kyle Newman notes. "It's being merchandised, but under a different moniker. They just don't address where [Life Day] is from, or they do it very loosely."

However, if one thinks that Lucasfilm embracing these minimal Life Day references has somehow magically satisfied the fans pushing for the formal release of the entire Special, that would be incorrect, for it has just lit a fuse under them. Despite the negative criticism, there is still a contingent of fans like Scott Kirkwood who wish that Lucasfilm would do just that.

"Maybe this could mean down the road at some point they might release the entire Holiday Special," says a hopeful Kirkwood. "They say everything gets better with age. It's been forty-five years already. I think that's long enough."

However, others disagree about officially releasing it to the public. "Because it existed, I wouldn't hide it—if it were me," says Mick Garris.

"But I totally understand why anyone would, because it does put a stain on *Star Wars*."

Donny Osmond agrees, adding that fans of this generation should have to find it like we did. "Allow it to have a cult following," he says. "Let the audience discover it, and when they discover it, it means more."

Although "Weird Al" Yankovic would love to have a "nice pristine copy of the *Star Wars Holiday Special*," he's apprehensive about the idea of formally releasing it. "I understand why [Lucas] probably wouldn't want to put that out in the world," he says, doubting that the Special will ever be officially released. "I could be proven wrong," he adds. "[Lucas] could be working on a special edition right now in which *Bea Arthur* actually shoots Greedo first."

Pressure has been mounting more than ever for Lucas to face his demons, stop denying his involvement, and embrace what he considers his most embarrassing work. Lenny Ripps acknowledges that his writing career has had its share of failures along with successes. "When you work on any project, you fall in love with it. You come in sincere and you want it to be the best show possible. I have worked on shows that were really popular and shows that were horrible, and I didn't work any more or less hard on any of them."

When Ripps is asked about Lucas's alleged decision to have his name removed from the credits, he has a moment of clarity. Would Ripps himself also ask to have his name removed from a project with which he was ashamed to be associated? He admits to his own weakness: "I have my name on all the good things I've done and all the bad things I've done . . . but maybe if I could have taken my name off of the bad things, I would have."

He adds that he has been lucky enough in his long writing career to have had more successes than failures, and he knows when to appreciate those successes. "Sometimes the magic happens, and sometimes it's the *Star Wars Holiday Special*."

EPILOGUE

FACED WITH THE choice of another day of shooting more of the *Star Wars Holiday Special* and freedom, director David Acomba chose the latter. After three exhausting days of shooting the cantina scene, the circus performers, and Jefferson Starship—and nearly depleting the show's entire budget on unnecessary overtime rates and penalties—he ducked out the back door of Stage 2, sent a few telegrams to those he thought would miss him, and ran for his life. He would end up back in Ontario and would jump right back into Canadian TV, directing an Andrea Martin special and a *Second City* pilot featuring Mike Myers.

In 1985, Acomba directed and produced a sketch-comedy series called *Four on the Floor* for the CBC. It featured a group called the Frantics, who wound up experiencing many of the same Acomba-isms that the crew of the Special had endured. Founding member Paul Chato recalls, "It was very difficult to be spontaneous when eighty percent of the time was spent on camera moves, and twenty percent was actually spent on the performance."

Acomba, Chato says, "was too fixated on putting his own stamp on the show than making it a true collaboration. My experience was that he just wanted to make sure he had peed on everything. From a business point of view . . . his scent was on everything. . . . We would never work with him again. He just burned us out."

In 1998, the *Star Wars Holiday Special* was still a bit of a secret, only available on VHS at conventions, so Acomba was much more comfortable speaking about it. During a rare interview from that time, he accepted "some responsibility for the show's problems. I'm still sorry that I didn't say, 'Look, you get rid of [the Welches] or I'm going,' but it just got to be too late. I should have done that, and maybe it would have ended up being a together project."

However, this interview took place before the Special was streaming on YouTube for all to see. Nowadays, it has become fodder for endless online criticism and has been parodied far more than it warrants or deserves.

Over forty years later, Acomba has moved on from the Special. Reached at his home just outside of Toronto recently, he was cordial but extremely resistant to talking about it, noting that he was not credited as the show's director. "I don't want my name on it, and it's not on it. And I'd just like to forget about it. So I'm not interested in anything connected with it." When pressed for a response, he becomes frustrated: "I don't want to answer any more questions about the show. Okay? It's just—it's just that simple. You know, you go ahead and do whatever you want. You do whatever you wanna do with all the people you get and all that, but I'm not interested in contributing to the story at all."

Forty-five years later, attitudes toward the Special differ among the other cast and crew members. Mark Hamill seems to be the most visible of all the cast members when it comes to attending Star Wars events, having started as the franchise's poster boy before taking on his current role as more of the elder statesman. During the 2020 presidential debates, he was so embarrassed at the bullying and constant interrupting, he tweeted: "That debate was the worst thing I've ever seen & I was in the Star Wars Holiday Special." But he still seems to have a very healthy attitude about it. "George once asked us, 'Please never mention it again,' and I said, 'George, we should own that because it shows that everybody's fallible. Everybody makes mistakes.'"

Hamill recently told Podcaster Jimmy McInerney from *Rebel Force Radio* that he thought his participation was "fairly minimal," adding, "I don't think I humiliated myself too much, but I haven't seen it. I didn't watch it on TV and I've never seen it. So I should, probably, because—I don't know, I mean—if it's really, really horrible, I mean, because I don't wanna be just mediocre. I want to be horrible. Like, I wanna be in the worst movie ever. I wanna be in *Plan Nine from Outer Space!*"

As for Carrie Fisher, she's an easy target. She sang, and when you put your heart into anything in this industry—when you're *all in*—you become a ripe target not only for critics but for anyone with a Twitter handle. She eventually jumped on the internet bandwagon and made fun of her own singing, in the kind of self-deprecating move that would define her in her later years. She once likened watching the special to waterboarding, adding, "Let's make Cheney watch that thing."

Years after the original airing, when Lucas needed her to record commentary for one of the *Star Wars* DVD re-releases, she said she negotiated for a copy of the Special. "By that time you couldn't get it because it was just so bad [Lucas] had taken it off the market," she told a group of *Star Wars* fans. "I made it a condition that he would give me the ... Special so that I could have something for parties—when I wanted everyone to leave."

Harrison Ford had one of the most memorable reactions to the Special. When he was a guest on *Late Night with Conan O'Brien* in February 2006, the host surprised him by playing a clip from the Special. It would be the highest-profile broadcast of footage from the Special in its cultish history. O'Brien first reminded Ford of the massive success of *Star Wars* in 1977, then said, "Shortly afterwards, a Christmas special came out that was produced by George Lucas in which all of the participants in *Star Wars* came together ... and the tape has been passed around for years, and there's rumors that Lucas is trying to suppress it, because none of you look happy while you're making this thing, and I thought I would just ask you about it. Do you remember making this *Star Wars* Christmas special? I think it was 1978."

Ford shakes his head.

O'Brien asks again, "No, you don't remember it? You have no memory of this incident?"

Ford shakes his head again.

"So it doesn't exist," O'Brien says.

"No, it doesn't exist."

A devilish smile starts to form on O'Brien's face as he asks, "What if I told you I had a little piece of tape right now? What if I were to roll that piece of tape? How would you feel about that?

Busted, Ford gives up. "I don't know, I've never seen it. Maybe it'll be nice." Ford signals to the director, "Go ahead, roll it."

A short clip of Han Solo interacting with the Wookiee family is played to momentous laughter and subsequent applause, to which Ford quietly responds, "Thank you."

Harvey Korman did not look back at the Special fondly, nor did he even recall it well. "I know it's a bit of a thing," he recalled uncomfortably when asked about it in 2004. "I still get letters, and people send me various [items] and strange-looking things, but I don't remember it. I just absolutely eliminated it from my mind—it was too bizarre. It was too otherworldly. I couldn't remember it, I didn't know what it was, I couldn't recognize myself."

However, Korman admitted there was a silver lining in the project: "The only thing I remember out of it was the fun of working with Bea Arthur. I mean, we had fun. But I didn't know what the hell that thing was about."

By contrast, Arthur recalled having "a wonderful time" shooting the Special. She remembered the experience a bit better than Korman, except for one important fact. Apparently, like Perry Como on the Bob Hope special, Arthur was unaware that the sketch she was in was *Star Wars*–related: "I had no idea it was even a part of the whole *Star Wars* thing. I just remember singing to a bunch of people with funny heads."

Like Korman, Arthur would get inundated with unsolicited mail, and she was shocked at the percentage of her fans that reached out to her in conjunction with the Special. "I never gave it much thought once we were finished with it," she said in a 2001 interview. "But even to this day, I get pictures [that] the fans send of me in the costume, asking to please autograph it. I mean, I was never into the whole *Star Wars* thing."

Paul Gale, who played Grandpa Itchy, passed away in 1993, at age sixty-six. Gale's brother Michael says that they never spoke much about the Special, particularly the controversial "mind evaporator" scene. Paul and his siblings were raised by extremely abusive parents, Michael adds, and "since Paul was the oldest, he got the brunt of it." However, he was able to rise above it all by finding happiness as an actor. He took real pride in his work, and to make something [associated with] *Star Wars*—he took much delight in that."

Nearly all of the show's producers have since died. Mitzie Welch passed away in 2014, followed by her husband Ken in 2017. Preceding them both was Layton, who died in 1994. Hemion died in 2008, leaving Smith as the Special's oldest surviving producer. However, at eighty-eight, the Emmy-winning showrunner recalls very little of the hundreds of specials he produced.

No one at the Nelvana production company heard any feedback about the animated cartoon they produced, but considering Lucas asked them to

Left to right: Harrison Ford, Anthony Daniels, Carrie Fisher, and Peter Mayhew celebrate as shooting for the *Star Wars Holiday Special* is completed. Claims that the cast members hated being in the Special contradict Steve Binder's memory that everyone seemed to be having a great time. *AP Photo/George Brich*

produce his subsequent animated series *Droids* and *Ewoks*, he obviously liked the work they did, as did most *Star Wars* fans. "It was a shame. [The Special] was very, very disappointing," says animation director Clive Smith. "We put a lot of effort into that short piece, and I thought we did a pretty good job with it and are pretty proud of it. And it was just a shame that it kind of got buried in the aftermath of the entire two-hour special, or whatever it was."

Before Peter Mayhew's passing in 2019, he was asked how he felt about being part of the Special. Even after it had become such a punch line, he responded quite positively about the experience. "Yeah, that one . . . I'm a little bit proud," he said with a gleaming smile. "I was privileged to be associated with some great actors: Art Carney, Beatrice Arthur, Diahann Carroll . . . it was hard work, but we all had a good time. At least I did."

"It wasn't that bad," he added, separating himself from nearly every cast member who appeared in the Special and putting him in a class all by himself.

Of all the people one might guess would be ashamed of their involvement, Steve Binder is presumably among them. The Special definitely stands out among the library of critically acclaimed shows he's directed, though it hasn't tainted his standing in the industry. However, he holds few regrets about the Special. "I'm gonna shock you and tell you—we had a great time. I loved it. I had a great experience. I couldn't wait to get to work in the morning."

Binder says that of all the *Star Wars* actors he got to work with, he bonded the most with Ford. "He was fun to talk to, to work with. He was always up." However, Binder has seen Ford give interviews where he cringes when asked about the Special, which confuses him. "He gives the implication that he never should have done it. I don't ever remember anybody complaining to me that they objected to the script . . . I mean, Harrison was having the time of his life on the show. I spent a lot of time with him. And now, when they interview him, he [doesn't] want to talk about it because it was so bad and so forth. I mean, it's bullshit."

The multi-Emmy-winning director says he has a pretty good perception of people's comfort levels. "I can feel when there's a mist in the air that's negative, and people are holding back their feelings and not expressing their true feelings. I never felt that [with Ford]. Nothing."

The only negative vibe Binder felt on the set was from some of the main actors who had learned that Lucas had given some people associated with the film extra percentage points of the profits while others had been left out. "There was a sort of a rumbling . . . and they were complaining among themselves. I just kinda overheard this and, evidently, Lucas came through. After we did the Holiday Special, I think I read in the newspaper at the time that he had bonused a lot of the principal actors with percentages of the profits. So it all turned out right. But I never felt anybody was doing it against their will or [hadn't] enjoyed being on the set."

If Binder could change one thing about the Special, it would be the way it was promoted. "I think CBS made a huge mistake and George Lucas made a huge mistake. They didn't tell the people that this was not *Star Wars: The Movie 2*, [with a] multimillion-dollar budget. This was a CBS children's variety special for two hours. I think it was very confusing to the audience that the whole purpose of this show was to sell toys to kids."

Former LucasBooks editor Jonathan Rinzler said that when the Holiday Special was broadcast, it was not considered to be the disaster that it is said to be today. "I don't know for sure, but I certainly didn't hear from anybody that there was any fallout from the show [or] that anybody was fired," he recalled. "I think life just went on at Lucasfilm. The most important thing that they had intended to do was accomplished, which was introduce Boba Fett to the world at large."

Pat Proft thinks that one of the biggest mistakes the producers of the Holiday Special made was not having a lead creative: "Was there anybody ever called the head writer or the story editor or something? I'm surprised that there wasn't some person, you know, [saying,] 'Let me see the first draft. Let me see the second draft. Let me see the third draft.' I don't know who was putting it together."

Proft wishes there would have been one person in charge with a unified vision. But that person didn't exist. "There was no major person saying, 'This is what I want. This is how it's going to be. This is what the look is.' I mean, that's what it missed."

However, what Proft really felt was lacking was that there was no real leader at all among the crew. "There didn't seem to be one person in charge—a captain of the ship, or one person that owned the project. Of the potential candidates, there were some, like the Welches, who *didn't* take control, and others, like Acomba, that were clamoring for control but never got it.

"My thinking was it would be dumb to do things that aren't in *Star Wars*. It would really diminish the *Star Wars Holiday Special* if all of a sudden it turns into something that isn't even *Star Wars*. I mean, *Star Wars* was never a musical. It was an adventure, and it was meeting these characters, and I don't even know the plot of the thing. Now, what was the plot? Was there a plot?"

Yet Proft, who along with Lenny Ripps specifically focused *on* the plot, doesn't look back on the Special with tremendous regret. At the end of the day, it was a television show, and just one of the credits on the massive résumé he has built since then. "Everybody who was involved, you know, no one was evil. Nobody did anything terrible. [Afterward,] the planet still existed."

Ripps tries to keep the entire experience in perspective. "The job was important to me because it was cool to do it with George Lucas, but I don't think any of these things are particularly important," he says. "This isn't the Torah. I don't think it's sacred. I'm sorry, it's a science-fiction movie. It's a good one, it has a lot of impact, but it's not my religion."

He adds that Gary Smith had assembled an amazing all-star team for this project, from the creative writers and producers to the technical talents of the crew. "The people we were working with were all first-rate. I think it's like the people who were welding the Titanic. Everybody made a great weld, but the damn thing still hit an iceberg."

There were those potential interview subjects that either didn't want to be interviewed or whose comments were so brief they were not included. But it seems a shame to not include the efforts made to include them.

For example, early on in this project, film critic Leonard Maltin was contacted for his reaction to the Special. When he said he hadn't heard of it, a YouTube link was sent to him. He soon reached back and said he could not comment on it because it was so awful, adding that Lucas had been so kind to him throughout his career.

Diahann Carroll's agent, Brian Panella, said neither he nor Carroll had heard of the Special. She was forwarded a link to it and subsequently left a voicemail message on the author's cellphone. In an amazingly seductive voice, the eighty-three-year-old Carroll said that she didn't remember doing it, but that she was curious about it and looked forward to talking about it. The number she was calling from did not accept incoming phone calls, and when her agent was notified about the call from Carroll, he didn't see any point in doing an interview, adding that Carroll had nothing to gain from being interviewed.

It was a hard argument to debate. She died a year later, at eighty-four.

* * *

While the cast and crew survived the aftereffects of the Special, there were some casualties. Within ten years, the TV variety genre would be toast.

"What killed variety television was complacency," says George Schlatter, who produced hundreds of hours of TV variety, most notably *Rowan and Martin's Laugh-In*, which he created. "'This works, so let's keep doing it. Here's another thing that works, so let's do more of that.' Actually, nobody killed it—we allowed it to die. Greed, impatience, lack of adventure, lack of variety. The name 'variety' says 'variety.' Variety means something different."

Kim LeMasters, who was president of CBS Entertainment from 1987 to 1989, says the concept of actual variety and the act of presenting something special was no longer built into the genre. "Examine the word 'special' and you'll answer why they're not done anymore. Things aren't special anymore.

"I closed the door on specials," he says, adding that he tried his best to keep the once-dominant genre alive at the network. "The last attempt I remember at variety was *The Mary Tyler Moore Hour*, and that unfortunately did not do well." The half-sitcom, half-variety show was filled with comedy, singing, and dancing, with an ensemble of such unknown hoofers as David Letterman and Michael Keaton.

The fact that tremendously popular stars like Moore couldn't make it hosting a TV variety show was a red flag. Add to that the number of mediocre talents now hosting their own shows, which simply watered down the entire genre. "There was just too much of it," says Schlatter. "I mean, *everybody* had a show." He adds that during one season there were a total of fourteen one-hour variety shows on the air—about two-thirds of the prime-time programming schedule.

By the mid-1980s, the genre was ready to be expunged from the system. "I mean, I brought back the Smothers Brothers as a sort of a desperation move to shore up an evening," LeMasters recalls. "It worked for a little bit, and I think mostly, people tuned in for nostalgia. But the format wasn't riveting. It was not something that people were clamoring for."

LeMasters says that media proliferation changed the public's access to Hollywood entertainers significantly. The 1980s brought about shows like *Entertainment Tonight*, and paparazzi brought the public more celebrity content through tabloid shows like *Hard Copy*. TV specials were no longer the only place the public got to see their favorite stars. "Personal accessibility to stars became easier and easier and easier," LeMasters explains. "Look at the Oscars right now. It used to be you wanted to watch the Oscars because, 'Oh my God, that person's gonna be there, and we'll get to get to see them and the gowns and all that.' Now people see that a hundred times a day through various outlets."

Bob Newhart thinks that, by the 1980s, variety TV shows and specials were pretty much finished. "They had run their course," the Mark Twain Prize recipient explains. He notes that he recently read that even MTV is going off the air. "Television is like a selfish child," he says. "It's just, 'Okay, we had that... now what else do you have? I enjoyed that... now what?'"

Nowadays, Newhart says, young viewers want to choose their own programming, and they don't like being spoon-fed as to what to watch. Back in his heyday on TV, there were just three networks, and as far as performers were concerned, "the viewers got what they were delivered, [but] today's viewers don't want to see what some variety show producer discovered and thought they should see. This generation does not want to inherit their brother's Levi's or their brother's stars. They want to find their own stars."

Variety TV was not only becoming extinct at CBS but at the other two networks as well. In a bit of irony, the late Rick Ludwin, who ran specials at NBC, found a clever way to turn the demise of variety into the biggest hit prime-time television had seen in decades. In 1989, Ludwin commissioned an unusual pilot for one of his favorite stand-up comedians, Jerry Seinfeld. After the pilot left NBC's development executives cold, Ludwin—one of the show's lone champions—pulled from his specials budget to order four additional episodes. Ever so symbolically, he canceled an already-planned Bob Hope special to pay for an entire first season of *Seinfeld*. Nine years later, the show's finale was watched by more than 76 million US viewers. While *Seinfeld* earned impressive broadcast profits of almost $2 billion, as of 2015 it had earned an additional $3.1 billion in syndication revenue.

As for TV variety, Bob Hope's last special aired in 1996. He died seven years later, at the age of one hundred.

* * *

In the Summer of 1976, guitarist Peter Frampton turned the record industry on its head with his double live album, *Frampton Comes Alive*, which yielded three Top 20 hits and was the best-selling album of 1976, selling eight million copies in the US alone.

At the end of that spine-thrashing year, he agreed to the lead role in the film *Sgt. Pepper's Lonely Hearts Club Band*, a musical tribute to the Beatles, with their catalog being performed by Frampton, the Bee Gees, and a rogue's gallery of supporting players, including Alice Cooper, Steve Martin, and George Burns. The film was decimated by critics, leaving Frampton dethroned of his rock 'n' roll standing and his fans running for the nearest bag to put over their heads.

About ten years later, Rob Lowe accepted an invitation to be part of the 1988 Academy Awards, where he was to sing and dance in showman Allan Carr's opening production number. The plot? Snow White (portrayed by a then-unknown and still currently unknown Eileen Bowman) has been stood up on a date, but then, luckily for her, Lowe appears and offers himself as her replacement, belting out reworked lyrics from "Proud Mary" to fit the Hollywood theme of the number:

> *Klieg lights keep on burnin,' cameras keep on turnin,'*
> *Rollin,' rollin,' keep the cameras rollin'*

Bowman had singing and dancing experience, but she didn't realize the entire Hollywood press would be judging this production number and reporting back in their reviews first thing in the morning. "We had the best dancers, the best choreographer on the planet, and Marvin Hamlisch was our musical director," she recalls. "I mean—oh my gosh—how could this go wrong?"

Lowe did a half-decent job, and there were no injuries. No harm, no foul.

The following morning, however, the response was visceral. To this day, the performance is ranked as one of the worst in Oscars history. Every year since, when journalists write up their choice of the worst Oscars moments, Lowe nearly always ranks at the top—higher even than Warren Beatty and Faye Dunaway announcing the wrong movie for "Best Picture."

Further, Carr and company had neglected to request Disney's permission to use the likeness of *Snow White*, so the studio filed a lawsuit against the Academy. However, more devastating for Lowe and Bowman was an open letter from over a dozen Hollywood big shots—among them Gregory Peck, Paul Newman, and Julie Andrews—calling the show "an embarrassment to both the Academy and the entire motion picture industry."

Is there a place in this world where performers like Frampton and Lowe can just choose to switch personas for whatever random project they wish to take on, without having to suffer the slings and arrows of outrageous fortune, also known as the Committee of Self-Appointed Naysayers? Lowe thinks not. "The [Oscars] ceremony is not merely escapist fare for the average American," he writes in his book, *Stories I Only Tell My Friends*. "It is of cancer-curing importance, and an evening of the highest seriousness, to be revered at all costs."

In the mid-to-late 1970s, Dinah Shore had a daytime daily talk show—*Dinah!*—that was ninety minutes long. Producers did whatever they could to fill up nearly eight hours of television per week. It turned out it was the perfect place for the Framptons and Lowes of the world. The show would book film, television, and musical performers, and it cultivated a real sense of community. The half-dozen guests all hung out together, discussed news events and hobbies, and exchanged recipes and parental advice. And then, often, someone like Anson Williams or Donny Most from *Happy Days* would get up and perform a cover of a current hit song; Sherman Hemsley would do an "experimental dance number"; or a shirtless Iggy Pop would dance and twitch for everyone there. It is *this* type of community that has the ability for artists to embrace, support, and subsequently discover their new talents.

Why is it so forbidden for a successful performer—once they have achieved nominal success—to experiment in new pastures, to boldly go where they have never gone before? "It's a very difficult place to be an artist, the public stage, because everybody is watching you and many people are rooting for you to fail," Jonathan Rinzler would note. "And to then be beaten up when in fact it didn't work out as well as it should have, maybe is a hard place to be as an artist. It's easier for painters or writers who suffer failures kind of in relative obscurity, but to suffer a failure at that level takes a certain kind of psyche to survive, I think."

How is it that George Lucas—the man behind such flops as *Howard the Duck*, *More American Graffiti*, and the *Star Wars* prequels, as well as the Holiday Special—is able to suffer those arrows, which are often aimed and heading his way?

"[That's] something every filmmaker has to grapple with, which is: not everything is gonna be a hit," says writer/director Matthew Robbins, a close friend of Lucas's. "With regard to *Howard the Duck* or the [*Star Wars*] Christmas special or all these reverses in the stellar trajectory of George Lucas, I think the key is that, given his makeup and many other moviemakers that I know who have overcome box office flops—I mean, it happens."

Jason Lenzi is frustrated by the quick, knee-jerk negative reaction from fans to the Special. "It's easy to poke fun at stuff after the fact and question how it happened, and sort of make fun of it. It's cliché at this point to crap on the *Star Wars Holiday Special*. It really is."

As far as Rinzler was concerned, whatever these artists will tell you, they care about what people think of their work—particularly Lucas. "These guys are not superhuman. They read the reviews, and it affects them."

Robbins says that the best artists will not allow anything to prevent their artistic progress; that each new project is so demanding of one's time and attention that you are almost required to put the last one behind you. "The storytelling becomes so vivid and important, you're going to just move on because it's exciting. You're going to break new ground, or you're going to work with a new actor, or you're going to tell a story that's fresh and original, or take people in a direction they never expected to go with your story. And if you are psychologically built that way, you can overcome disappointments."

Donny Osmond had a tremendously successful career with his brothers, as well as on his own, before he was offered the job of co-hosting *Donny and Marie.* He was not interested at first, though, as he thought his musical career would suffer. "Time has a real amazing way of allowing you to embrace the past," he reflects. "All my life, since the *Donny and Marie* show was created, I wanted nothing to do with it." He hated the squeaky-clean image, and although he had recorded several legitimate hits, he was embarrassed about being associated with the family show. "Then something happened later on in my life, and I realized, you know, I did the best I could at the time," he adds. "That's what was popular. That's what people were buying and watching, and it was appropriate for the day. I've learned to say, you know, I'm not embarrassed about it ... *as much* ..."

While it's commonplace these days to criticize disastrous artistic performances where an artist is "all in"—completely sincere and dedicated to a new idea—it is a bit unfortunate to attack every new and unusual, out-of-the-box idea that someone tries out on the public. The math is there: the more that these new ideas are mocked and trashed, the less likely it is that artists in the future will have the guts to take chances on innovative and potentially culture-changing endeavors.

Fred Silverman, the ABC programming chief credited with bringing Donny and Marie Osmond together for their variety series in 1975, had moved on by 1978 to NBC, where he tried to create magic again. This time, he brought together a successful Japanese duo, Pink Lady, with one of the top stand-up comedians of the time, Jeff Altman. Unfortunately, due to a language barrier and other factors, their show was canceled after only five episodes.

"Of course it's disappointing," Altman says forty years later. "You get involved, you get excited, you put your all in, you're all into it." But Altman realizes that this kind of national success means "having to appeal to Larry the plumber in Omaha," and that's just not realistic for Altman. "America doesn't want to be jolted," he says. "Unfortunately, the masses kind of make the decision, and they're not always the best ones necessarily to do that."

Since then, *Pink Lady and Jeff* has become code for TV variety-show failure. But Altman takes it in stride, knowing he gave it his all—and that's all that counts.

In 1990, the Prince of Police Procedurals, the late Stephen Bochco, created *Cop Rock*, a one-hour drama where cops—as well as criminals— launch into musical numbers at the drop of a baton. Having created such hit series as *Hill Street Blues*, *L.A. Law*, and *NYPD Blue*, Bochco seemingly felt compelled to test the waters a bit. He received quite the backlash— critically and commercially—and the series was canceled after its first eleven episodes. However, while taking its licks, *Cop Rock* also won an Emmy that year for "Outstanding Achievement in Music and Lyrics" for Randy Newman's contributions to the pilot. In the opinion of Jon O'Brien at the *A.V. Club*, "We should consider *Cop Rock* as more of an admirable failure than an outright embarrassing disaster." Bochco remained very proud of it: "If you have the guarantee of getting that many shows on the air and you don't do something bold and adventurous and experimental, then shame on you."

Comedian Paul Scheer praises Lucas's interest in wanting to test the waters, whether through film, television, or other media. "I believe that George Lucas is, at his heart, an experimental filmmaker, and he wants to make things that are weird and different. And the Holiday Special *is* that."

Musician Neil Young has defined himself as an artist *obsessed* with experimentation. For over six decades, he has gone against the grain, bucked trends, and paved his own way, using trial and error to determine his artistic direction. The results have not always been successful. "You have to trust yourself," he said in 2021, arguing that the recipe for failure is caring too much about what others think. "It's over if you start looking at other people. Your name is on it, it's your life, it's your [work]. Everybody else be damned."

Chevy Chase, Magic Johnson, Dana Carvey, and even *Wheel of Fortune*'s Pat Sajak all tried hosting talk shows without success. After passing the *Tonight Show* torch to Conan O'Brien in 2009, Jay Leno tried a 10 p.m. talk show that was canceled after just a few months. Jerry Seinfeld, whose sitcom aired for two decades on the same network, praised NBC's prime-time experiment, even though it was unsuccessful. "This was the right idea at the wrong time," Seinfeld said. "I'm proud that NBC had the guts to try something."

For trying still matters. Warren Beatty and Dustin Hoffman tried channeling Hope and Crosby with *Ishtar*; while it made for a few laughs, it was no *Road to Morocco*. Michael Jordan tried baseball. Shaq tried acting.

And George Lucas did a TV variety musical version of *Star Wars*.

Donny Osmond has hit huge highs and sunk to tremendous lows in his *sixty years* in show business. He blames fear for the lack of artists expressing true creative freedom in today's entertainment, saying that many are afraid of moving in a new artistic direction they will later regret.

"We're all afraid to take a step," Osmond says. "We're all afraid to say anything because we're gonna get eaten alive. Somewhere, somehow, somebody's going to make fun of you." He adds, "Don't let it bother you. Move on. Be an artist."

Michelangelo, who created some of the most famous frescoes in the history of Western art, was admired for his *terribilità*—the ability of his works to instill a sense of awe. He always aimed for the fences—without fear of rejection—when creating his art. As a quote often attributed to him notes, "The greatest risk to man is not that he aims too high and misses, but that he aims too low and hits."

As a writer and director, Kyle Newman thinks failure defines people more than success, adding, "I think failure is one of the great motivators." Perhaps having the ability to fail is one of the many benefits of achieving success. Those triumphs allow one to fail freely while being true to oneself artistically, creatively, and financially.

Ripps agrees wholeheartedly. "There are always better stories about failure than success," he says, adding that at dinner parties he does better recounting how he failed than talking about his successes. "It's much more interesting. It's much more compelling, and it's much more human."

For Young, true success only comes when you acknowledge the likely potential for failure. "You have to be willing to embrace it and really welcome it into your life with open arms. Be sure to welcome failure. Always say, 'You're okay with me, failure…come on in,' because then you have no fear."

Young almost *embraces* failure, challenging himself to not ever be negatively—or even positively—affected by what others think of his work, and thus never allowing anyone else's opinion of him to define him.

But after Lucas is gone and only his legacy and his films have survived, how will he be defined?

George Lucas was inundated with requests for everything under both suns after the success of the first *Star Wars* film. The decisions he made at that challenging time would unfairly define him, whether it was the Holiday Special or *More American Graffiti*. Some of those decisions even risk eclipsing the amazing artistic achievements of *Star Wars*.

But what Lucas did with that film will never be done again. Aside from the artistic and technical skills that helped launched *Star Wars* into the super-franchise it is now, he created an unparalleled dynamic: an entire generation of kids from the 1970s grew up loving the franchise. Then, in the 1990s, those kids exposed their own kids to the "Special Edition" versions of these films. Now, *those* children are sitting down with *their* kids and streaming the entire franchise on Disney+.

With all of Lucas's flaws and failures, there remains just one person responsible for creating all of those past, present, and future memories. He is the one to credit for all the time spent together with family and friends enjoying one of the most popular adventures ever told. While he has probably received enough plaques and trophies to fill an Elstree soundstage, unfortunately there are no awards for *that* important achievement.

Hopefully, he is aware of the bonding between families and friends his franchise has created, and he can accept his few failures as mere imperfections from a man whose amazing talent and subsequent success were great enough to afford some humility.

Our *new* hope might be that Lucas can finally let sleeping banthas lie, accept these tiny red marks in his past, and clearly know the good his works have done by bringing generations of all ages together to enjoy this simple but wondrous story about "*a boy, a girl, and a galaxy.*"

ACKNOWLEDGMENTS

WHEN COVID HIT in March 2020, I was smack-dab in the middle of a documentary I was doing about the 1978 *Star Wars Holiday Special*. Few people wanted to be interviewed in person, so, not wanting to slow down my creative process, I started writing it out—less as a potential book and more just to keep focused on moving the story forward.

But I had enough news judgment to know there might be an audience for this story, particularly a book. I reached out to a literary agent I knew named Dan Ostroff, who had since become a successful producer. Dan confirmed my suspicions and immediately emailed *his* literary agent, the amazing Joshua Bilmes of the Jabberwocky Agency in New York, about the story. Joshua told me not only that this potential book *could* be sold but that it *would* be sold (these New Yorkers with their Namath-like predictions). As this was the first book I'd ever tried to sell, Josh (and his colleague Brady McReynolds) took me through the process with kid gloves, and, as promised, he sold it. Thanks to Susan Velazquez Colmant for her efforts with the audiobook, as well as Valentina Sainato for keeping track of it all.

My publisher, Applause Books, embraced this project from its infancy—specifically my editor, Chris Chappell, whose patience and investment in this adventure has made this so satisfying—and I hope this will be the first of many collaborations. Also, thanks to the tremendously patient Tom Seabrook, another talented editor, for taking the book through to its final stages, as well as Barbara Claire for her detailed photo-editing skills, and Getty's Lyndon Umali and James McCarter for supporting the project as well.

It is my relationship with the Special's second director, Steve Binder, that brought me to tell this story. When I realized that he had directed the Holiday Special—which was legitimately stinking up his stellar résumé—he told me he was proud of the work he had done. That one surprising comment intrigued me and prompted me to want to tell that story, and he gave me his blessing to share it.

Those who produced these shows were like family to me—and some were *actually* family—and had put their hearts and souls into this wonderful schlock, resulting in me having to walk a precarious line between respecting their hard work while also being realistic enough to acknowledge that—*holy crap*—a lot if it was pretty horrific. However, a decent proportion of these shows were well done and did their job of entertaining families. I thank all of my father's friends and colleagues who allowed me to interview them, making this project a perfect match for me. (During the Special, the Empire declares a mandatory curfew to all those on "the Kazook planet," a name used for Chewbacca's planet pre-"Kashyyyk." *Kazook* is pretty darn close to my fairly unusual name of Kozak spelled backward, so I felt a second connection to the Special.)

Early on, I enlisted Jason Lenzi for help. He knew who best to interview and what to glean from them. Most importantly, his actual—yes—*love* for the Special and his almost *brave* admission that he had seen it as a child and liked it made me realize I had seen it and liked it as well, thus inspiring me to figure out *why* I liked it. He also encouraged me to treat this Special as more of a sick child—like something that needed to be understood and thoughtfully explained—than just a source for wacky memes.

In a nice twist, my dear friend, camera operator Larry Heider, unveiled several of his never-before-seen still photos, taken behind the scenes of the Special. I'm grateful that he chose this book for their commercial debut.

It was quite an honor to meet and work with the outstanding Pete Sears, whose amazing memory and great attitude helped me meander my way through the drama that was the Jefferson Starship. Also, thanks to writers Lenny Ripps and Bruce Vilanch, who embraced my writing this book and tolerated my endless emails, texts, and phone calls.

Thanks to my documentary partner Jeremy Coon, as well as Jon Heder for bringing us together. After two years of speaking with a half-dozen potential investors/partners, Jeremy was the only one who saw this as more than a *Mystery Science Theater 3000* segment. He immediately invested in the project, moving us forward in getting the stories of this Special on tape and helping me learn the film business overnight.

The doc's producers, Kyle Newman and Adam F. Goldberg, also contributed greatly to the book. Kyle, an accomplished writer/director, used his own filmmaking instincts to better understand Lucas. His quotes were strikingly profound, adding both a sympathetic heart and a deserved dose of damnation in places deemed appropriate. Thanks to Doug DeLuca for acting as my film agent early on, and for teaching me patience in waiting for the best deal possible.

Scott Kirkwood's remarkable website, www.starwarsholidayspecial.com, was a huge resource for interviews, as well as various memorabilia. His passion for this subject, and his zeal for discovering more, was inspiring. Ross Plessett was equally valuable, having interviewed some of the cast and crew years ago who had either passed away or no longer wished to talk about the subject. Thanks to Scott Dittrich Jr., for digitizing those interviews.

Legal advice was so appreciated, and many thanks go to David Blood, Cassandra Barbour, Joshua Lastine, Michael J. Wahl, Hector Del Cid, David Wardle, Randi Frisby, and the always amazing Heather Bennett.

Thanks for their background info: Antar and Omar Abderrahman, Jeffrey Berg, Bill Bracken, Mike Colasuonno, Robert Daly, John Field, Wenda Fong, Lee Gabler, Jeanne Gale, Michael Gursey, John Hamlin, Bumpy Lippincott, Gus Lopez, Jon Macks, John Moffet, Mike Ovitz, Carolyn Raskin, Daniel Saks, Frank Santopadre, Dani Tenerelli, Dave Thomas, and Pete Vilmur.

Thanks also to Nick Castle, Jay P. Morgan, Helga Pollock, Genevieve Rinzler, Michelle Erwin, Sharon Binder, Dara Gottfried, Maxine Smith, Joseph Bonjiovi, Jay Levey, Dora Whitaker, Marta Lee, Garon Lee, Melissa and George Cvjetnicanin, Romy Binder Harding, Brigham Taylor, Joe McFate, Susan Madore, Jason Morey, Brian Panella, and Tawala Sharp. Special thanks to the fantastic team of TV archivists, encyclopedias Ian Marshall and Bill DiCicco of Retro Video.

Copyediting provided by Melisa and Taylor Kozak, George Bozic, Cary Pittard, Eric Smith, Rogers Johnson, Greg Fein, Jed Woodworth, Rob Young, Andy Schrader, and Jesse Griffith. Thanks to Lucas Kozak for his massive sorting, Hunter Kozak for his help with the introduction, and Kennedy Kozak for his help throughout. Also, Theresa Coffino, Nancy Moscatiello, John Johnston, Cheri Brownlee, and Ron Vander—for opening the door.

Special kudos to my favorite previous boss, Jay Leno, who couldn't imagine himself doing an interview that would—even potentially—make fun of any project since he was responsible for the 10 p.m. *Jay Leno Show* during the ridiculous Jay/Conan dispute of 2009. His feelings on failure—as well as Jerry Seinfeld's praising of NBC for trying such a show—helped inspire the end of the book.

Special thanks go to lifetime family friend Bob Newhart, who was a huge resource and strength to me while writing this book; and dear friend Donny Osmond, whose surprise involvement in the story—*and potential responsibility for the Special*—made this all the more fun. My unique friendship with Donny has been a blessing in so many ways since he helped change my life forty years ago this summer.

Also thanks to the amazing Dominic Dare, Jim Hardy, Linda Hope, Tony Griffin, Dan Farr, Lincoln Hoppe, Leigh Savidge, Elizabeth Gibson, Tod Goldberg, Lance Stubblefield, Mark Anderson, Brent Estes, Darren and Cathleen Poulsen, Kenneth Cornaby, Jaron Poulson, Ed Johnson, Ron Valentine, Brian Barlow, Roann and Arnold Lemmon, Michael Stein, Josh Goldstein, Jodi Tripi, Greg Porter, Michael Burns, Eddie Rohwedder, Rich Brown, Richard Propper, Aaron Elswood, Dr. Chris Eddy, Dan Downs, Jim Matherly, Matt Stevens, Steven Lindberg, Sharon Deffense, Brian Ravert, Lisa Higginbotham, Joey Bennett, Brian Jay Jones, Barry Dagestino, Jeff LeSueur, Tim Arnold, Hyrum Osmond, John Skogmo, Mark Leonard, Bob Read, Sid Kassouf, Kevin Gershan, Jason Swank, and Adele Sparks.

Super thanks to my friends at *Jimmy Kimmel Live!*: Jimmy, Molly McNearney, David Craig, Matt Musgrave, Mitch Cole, Seth Weidner, Jill Leiderman, Josh Weintraub, Jimmy Dunn, Tony Barbieri, Patrick Friend, Guillermo Rodriguez, Jesse Joyce, Gary Greenberg, Craig Powell, Danny Ricker, John Wolk, Jennifer Sharron, Gary Gast, Erin Irwin, and the amazing Tom Fitzgerald, and all the rest that make it the best late-night talk show ever.

Best not to forget the wondrous Kris Hill, Drew and Susan Adams, John and Kathie Hansen, Barbara and Jeff Moffat, Renae and Shane Peck, Colette and Stan Jeppsen, Brian and Leanne Ostler, Piet and Cecile Kroon, Stefan and Christina Franck, Jared and Amber Hill, Michele and Jeff Risser, and Janeen Anderson.

I so wish that Mitzie and Ken Welch, John Carlin, Diahann Carroll, Keith Crary, Lev Mailer, Ginnie Newhart, Val Higginbotham, Naida Williamson, Peter Mayhew, David Winters, Blaine Anderson, and Carrie Fisher could have been here with me at the publishing of this book. Gilbert Gottfried, Elle Puritz, and Charley Lippincott gave phenomenal interviews; some, like Jonathan Rinzler and Mike Erwin, made their interviews with me the last ones they would ever give, and they are particularly profound.

Thanks to my family: my nephews Dustin, Jeremy, Zachary, and Liam; my nieces Chantel and Lilian; my sisters Heather and Julie; Ellen and my brother Bob, whose crazy timing for falling into my life couldn't have been better.

Thanks to my mother, Marie, who bought me my first electric typewriter and my first computer after I got my first staff-writer gigs. Special thanks to my wonderful kids and their significant others, and *their* even more wondrous kids: Taylor, Carly, Harper, Hailey, Hunter, Shelby, Porter, Susanna, Hannah, Eliza, Kennedy, Chanson . . . and yes, *Lucas*, for entertaining me with hundreds of hours of endless screaming and arguing over which is the best film of the *Star Wars* franchise. If there was a subject deemed worthwhile to debate into the wee early hours of the morning, these kids at least know their priorities.

For my godsent wife, Melisa, continuously standing by me in every leg of this adventure, encouraging and believing in me, even managing to read every revision of this manuscript several times. To this day, she is my best friend, an exemplary mother, and a beautiful woman who continues to remain in her prime.

Lastly, to my father, Elliott. Many say it must have been hard to traverse through the backstreets of his industry alone, without him. Those people are wrong. He was with me the entire trip.

STEVE KOZAK
JULY 2023

CAST OF CHARACTERS

Omar Abderrahman hologram acrobat, SWHS

Antar Abderrahman hologram acrobat, SWHS

Beverly Abderrahman hologram acrobat, SWHS

Alisa Abderrahman hologram acrobat, SWHS

David Acomba director, SWHS

Jeff Altman co-host, *Pink Lady and Jeff*

Bea Arthur "Ackmena," SWHS

Ted Ashley chairman, Warner Bros (1969–1980)

Jeff Babko keyboardist, Cleto and the Cletones, *Jimmy Kimmel Live!*

Kenny Baker operated R2-D2 internally

Marty Balin lead singer, Jefferson Starship, SWHS

Peter Barth stage manager, SWHS

Brian Bartholomew art director, SWHS

Barry Beckerman development executive, Warner Bros (1969–1972)

Newt Bellis former owner, Mobile Video Services; dated associate producer Rita Scott

Jeff Berg Lucas's former agent, International Creative Management

Steve Binder second director, SWHS

Jerry Bixman editor, SWHS

Jake Bloom Lucas's former personal attorney

Bertolt Brecht writer, *The Threepenny Opera*

Earl Brown songwriter, *Donny and Marie*, *Elvis Comeback Special*

Richard Brustein former TV variety agent, International Creative Management

Ellis Burman Thomas R. Burman's brother; showed how to make Chewbacca

Thomas R. Burman costume creator, SWHS

Bonnie Burton former editor/writer, starwars.com, *Star Wars Insider*

Ben Burtt sound designer, SWHS, *Star Wars* franchise

John Calley head of production, Warner Bros (1968–1981)

Art Carney "Saul Dann" / "Trader Dann," SWHS

Monroe E. Carol associate producer, SWHS; liaison for 20th Century Fox

Diahann Carroll "Mermeia," SWHS

James Carson conceptual designer, *The Last Jedi*

Craig Chaquico lead guitarist, Jefferson Starship, SWHS

Paul Chato performer, the Frantics, *Four on the Floor*, CBC

Howard Chaykin artist, Marvel Comics / *Star Wars* editions

Francis Ford Coppola producer, *THX 1138*, *American Graffiti*

Gene Crowe technical director, SWHS

Peter Cushing "Admiral Moff Tarkin," *A New Hope*

Anthony Daniels "C-3PO," SWHS, *Star Wars* franchise

Duwayne Dunham editor, Lucasfilm; wore Boba Fett costume

John Dykstra special photographic effects supervisor, *A New Hope*

Bryce "Kermit" Eller wore Darth Vader suit for TV, promo events

Mike Erwin stage manager, SWHS

Jon Favreau creator, *The Mandalorian*

Rudy Fehr editor, head of post-production, Warner Bros (1936–1976)

Andrew Ferguson assistant professor, University of Maryland

Todd Fisher Carrie Fisher's brother

Carrie Fisher "Princess Leia," SWHS / *Star Wars* franchise

Harrison Ford "Han Solo," SWHS / *Star Wars* franchise

Alan Dean Foster ghostwriter, *Star Wars* novelization

Ian Fraser composer, SWHS; co-writer, "Peace on Earth / Little Drummer Boy"

Stuart Freeborn "Chewbacca" costume creator, SWHS

Paul Gale "Itchy," SWHS

Sid Ganis senior VP, Lucasfilm (1977–1986)

Mick Garris R2-D2 remote operator, SWHS; receptionist

Jean Giraud a.k.a. Moebius psychedelic illustrator of the 1960s and 1970s; inspired Lucas, Nelvana

Larry Gleason former president, Mann Theaters

Andy Goldberg founder, Off the Wall Improv

Seth Green co-producer, unaired *Star Wars* project *Detours* with Lucas

Larry Grossman co-writer, "Peace on Earth / Little Drummer Boy"

Lance Guest portrayed several characters in *Special* (a play about SWHS)

Alec Guinness "Obi-Wan Kenobi," *Star Wars* Episodes IV–VI

Dorothy Hamill Olympic gold medalist ice skater

Mark Hamill "Luke Skywalker," SWHS and *Star Wars* franchise

Larry Heider cameraman, SWHS

Dwight Hemion executive producer, SWHS

Miki Herman Lucasfilm liaison, SWHS; production assistant, *A New Hope*

Marcus Herring pop-culture historian

Michael Hirsh co-founder, Nelvana; produced animation for SWHS, *Droids, Ewoks*

Vince Humphrey editor, SWHS

Willard Huyck writer, *American Graffiti*; script doctor, *A New Hope*

Henry Jaffe former head of finance, Smith–Hemion Productions

Jeff Jampol manager, Grace Slick

Roy Johns hologram juggler, SWHS

Joe Johnston conceptual designer, SWHS, *Star Wars* franchise

James Earl Jones voice of Darth Vader, SWHS and *Star Wars* franchise

Paul Kantner guitarist, Jefferson Starship, SWHS

Lawrence Kasdan co-writer, *The Empire Strikes Back, Raiders of the Lost Ark*

Jonathan Kasdan son of Lawrence Kasdan; co-writer, *Solo: A Star Wars Story*

Gloria Katz writer, *American Graffiti*; script doctor, *Star Wars*

Taran Killam writer/comedian, *Saturday Night Live*

Peter Kimmel production assistant, SWHS

Scott Kirkwood webmaster, www.starwarsholidayspecial.com

Buz Kohan co-writer, "Peace on Earth / Little Drummer Boy"

Harvey Korman "Chef Gormaanda," "Krelman," "Dromboid," SWHS

Elliott Kozak producer, *Bob Hope All Star Christmas Comedy Special*; TV variety packaging agent, International Creative Management

Marty Krofft executive producer, *Donny and Marie, The Brady Bunch Hour*

Peter Kuran animator, miniature and optical effects, *A New Hope*

Gary Kurtz uncredited consultant, SWHS; producer, *American Graffiti, A New Hope, The Empire Strikes Back*

Alan Ladd Jr. president, 20th Century Fox (1976–1979)

Verne Langdon makeup artist, SWHS; monster-mask maker, Don Post Studios

Sean Latham co-writer, "The Rise of Periodical Studies"

Joe Layton producer, SWHS; director, *Raquel*

Dick Lederer VP of worldwide advertising and publicity, Warner Bros

Stan Lee publisher, Marvel Comics

Kim LeMasters VP (1976–1984), president (1988–1990), CBS Entertainment

Jason Lenzi owner, Bif Bang Pow action figures

Bumpy Lippincott widow of Charles Lippincott

Charles Lippincott former VP of publicity, promotions, marketing and advertising for the Star Wars Corporation

Bernie Loomis president, Kenner Toys (1970–1978)

Marcia Lucas editor, *American Graffiti, A New Hope*

George Lucas wrote story for SWHS; writer/director, *Star Wars*

Rick Ludwin former executive VP of late-night and special programming, NBC

Paul Lynde former comedian, *Donny and Marie*

Bob Mackie costume designer, SWHS, *The Carol Burnett Show*, Cher

Dan Madsen founder, *Star Wars Insider*; former president, Star Wars Fan Club

Lev Mailer "Imperial Guard #1," SWHS

Patty Maloney "Lumpy," SWHS

Peter Mayhew "Chewbacca," SWHS and *Star Wars* franchise

Jimmy McInerney host, *Rebel Force Radio* podcast

Ralph McQuarrie conceptual designer, SWHS and *Star Wars* franchise

Craig Miller president, Star Wars Fan Club (1977–1981)

Bob Mills writer, *Bob Hope All Star Christmas Comedy Special*

John Moffitt director, *The Richard Pryor Show*

Mickey Morton "Malla," "Tork" (the cantina bouncer), SWHS

Walter Murch co-writer, *THX 1138*; shot Altamont concert with Lucas

Peter Myers VP of domestic distribution, 20th Century Fox (1977)

Jim Nelson associate producer, *A New Hope* (uncredited)

Kyle Newman writer/director, *Fan Boys*

Ted Nichelson author, *I Love to Love You Bradys: The Bizarre Story of the Brady Bunch Variety Hour*

Frank Nielsen layout artist, SWHS

Andrew Osborne writer, *Special* (a play about SWHS)

Brian Panella former agent to Diahann Carroll

Leslie Parsons assistant art director, SWHS

Marc Pevers former VP of licensing, 20th Century Fox

Dale Pollock author, *Skywalking: The Life and Films of George Lucas*

Don Post Jr. owner, Don Post Studios; maker of monster masks

Pat Proft writer, SWHS

David Prowse wore Darth Vader outfit in *Star Wars* franchise

Nick Prueher former David Letterman researcher; co-founder, Found Footage Festival

Elle Puritz assistant to the producer, SWHS

Jack Rader "Imperial Guard Officer," SWHS

Sue Raney renowned Jazz Singer

Fred Rappaport head of specials, CBS Television

Thurl Ravenscroft voice of Darth Vader, *Donny and Marie*

Jack Rebney foul-mouthed Winnebago salesman

Jonathan R. Rinzler former executive editor, LucasBooks

Lenny Ripps writer, SWHS

Matthew Robbins colleague of Lucas's at USC Film School

Larry Ross owner, Blast from the Past

Bernie Safronsky former head of specials, CBS

Julie Salamon author, *The Devil's Candy: The Anatomy of a Hollywood Fiasco*

Sang Jun Lee conceptual artist, *Revenge of the Sith*

Dan Schaarschmidt archival television researcher

Rick Scheckman clip researcher, *Late Night with David Letterman, The Late Show with David Letterman*

George Schlatter creator/producer, *Rowan and Martin's Laugh-in*

Steve Schuster saxophonist, Jefferson Starship, SWHS

Rita Scott associate producer, SWHS

Pete Sears bass player, Jefferson Starship, SWHS

Joel Selvin author, *Altamont: The Rolling Stones, the Hells Angels and the Inside Story of Rock's Darkest Day*

Iwan Serrurier inventor of the Moviola home-movie projector in 1917

Mark Serrurier enhanced Moviola into preeminent film editing equipment

Steven Serrurier prop house owner, Serrurier and Associates

Shields and Yarnell mime duo; co-hosts of 1978 TV series

Fred Silverman programming executive at CBS, NBC, and ABC

Grace Slick lead singer, Jefferson Starship

Clive Smith animation director, SWHS

Gary Smith executive producer, SWHS

Robert Scholes co-writer, "The Rise of Periodical Studies"

Nathan Stein hologram juggler, SWHS

Dan Stevens former TV variety agent, International Creative Management

Burt Sugarman executive producer, *The Midnight Special*, *The Richard Pryor Show*

Yuichi Sugiyama ringmaster, SWHS

Jim Swearingen senior conceptual designer, Kenner Toys

Ned Tanen VP of production, Universal Pictures (1970–1982)

Chris Taylor author, *How Star Wars Conquered the Universe: The Past, Present, and Future of a Multibillion-Dollar Franchise*

Dani Tenerelli pop-culture illustrator

Roy Thomas writer, Marvel Comics / *Star Wars* editions

Susan Trembly marketing and publicity, Lucasfilm (1977–1984)

Rocco Urbisci producer, *The Midnight Special*, *The Richard Pryor Special*

Bruce Vilanch writer, SWHS, *Donny and Marie*, *The Brady Bunch Hour*

Rick Wagner "Walrus Man," SWHS

Brian Ward pop-culture historian

Rod Warren writer, SWHS

Charles Weber CEO, Lucasfilm (1977–1980)

Kurt Weil composer, *The Threepenny Opera*

Fred Weintraub executive VP, Warner Bros (1970–1972)

Ken Welch producer, SWHS

Mitzie Welch writer/producer, SWHS

Raquel Welch actress/dancer; included in original SWHS treatment

Frank Wells West Coast VP (1969–1973), president (1973–1977), vice chairman (1977–1984), Warner Bros

Johnny Whitaker "Johnny Stuart," *Sigmund and the Sea Monsters*

Carol Wikarska Lippincott's ex-girlfriend; became Lucasfilm's publicist after Lippincott's exit

Barry Williams "Greg Brady," *The Brady Bunch Hour*

John Williams composer, *Star Wars* franchise

Stan Winston makeup artist, SWHS

David Winters choreographer, SWHS

Wolfman Jack "Wolfman Jack," *American Graffiti*; host, *The Midnight Special*

BIBLIOGRAPHY

BOOKS

Bass, Dick, and Wells, Frank. *Seven Summits* (New York: Warner Books, 1986)

Baxter, John. *George Lucas: A Biography* (London: HarperCollins, 1999)

Binder, Steve. *Elvis '68 Comeback: The Story Behind the Special* (San Diego, CA: Thunder Bay Press, 2021)

Biskind, Peter. *Easy Riders, Raging Bulls: How the Sex 'n' Drugs 'n' Rock 'n' Roll Generation Saved Hollywood* (London: Bloomsbury Publishing, 1998)

Bugliosi, Vincent. *Helter Skelter: The True Story of the Manson Murders* (New York: W. W. Norton and Company, 1974)

Burnett, Carol. *One More Time: A Memoir* (New York: Random House, 1986)

Burnett, Carol. *This Time Together: Laughter and Reflection* (New York: Three Rivers Press, 2010)

Burnett, Carol. *In Such Good Company: Eleven Years of Laughter, Mayhem, and Fun in the Sandbox* (New York: Crown Archetype, 2016)

Casey, Dan. *100 Things Star Wars Fans Should Know Before They Die* (Chicago: Triumph Books, 2015)

Cowie, Peter. *Coppola: A Biography* (New York: Charles Scribner's Sons, 1989)

Daniels, Anthony. *I Am C-3PO* (London: DK Publishing, 2019)

Eliot, Marc. *Walt Disney: Hollywood's Dark Prince* (New York: Birch Lane Press, 1993)

Fisher, Carrie. *Wishful Drinking* (New York: Simon and Schuster, 2008)

Fisher, Carrie. *The Princess Diarist* (New York: Blue Rider Press, 2016)

Frampton, Peter. *Do You Feel Like I Do? A Memoir* (New York: Phenix Books, 2020)

Friedkin, William. *The Friedkin Connection* (New York: HarperCollins, 2013)

Goldberg, Andy. *Improv Comedy* (Hollywood, CA: Samuel French Trade, 1991)

Gross, Edward, and Altman, Mark A. *Secrets of the Force: The Complete, Uncensored, Unauthorized Oral History of Star Wars* (New York: St. Martin's Press, 2021)

Hofstede, David. *What Were They Thinking? The 100 Dumbest Events in Television History* (New York: Back Stage Books, 2004)

Jacobson, Brian R. *In the Studio: Visual Creation and Its Material Environments* (Oakland, CA: University of California Press, 2020)

Jenkins, Garry. *Harrison Ford: Imperfect Hero* (New York: Birch Lane Press, 1998)

Jones, Brian Jay. *George Lucas: A Life* (New York: Back Bay Books, 2016)

Kaminski, Michael. *The Secret History of Star Wars: The Art of Storytelling and the Making of a Modern Epic* (Kingston, Ontario: Legacy Books Press, 2008)

Kenny, Glenn. *A Galaxy Not So Far Away: Writers and Artists on Twenty-Five Years of Star Wars* (New York: Henry Holt and Company, 2002)

Lucas, George. *Star Wars: From the Adventures of Luke Skywalker* (New York: Ballantine Books, 1976)

Lucas, George (foreword). *The Art of Moebius* (New York: Berkley Trade, 1989)

Luceno, James. *Inside the Worlds of Star Wars Trilogy: The Ultimate Guide to the Incredible Locations of Episodes IV, V, and VI* (New York: Lucas Books, 2004)

McCarthy, Patty J. *The Lucas Effect: George Lucas and the New Hollywood* (Youngstown, NY: Teneo Press, 2014)

McCormick, Maureen. *Here's the Story* (New York: HarperCollins, 2008)

McKeen, William. *Rock and Roll Is Here to Stay: An Anthology* (New York: W. W. Norton and Company, 2000)

McParland, Robert. *Rock Music Imagination* (New York: Rowman and Littlefield, 2019)

Miller, Craig. *Star Wars Memories: My Time in the (Death Star) Trenches* (San Bernardino, CA: Fulgens Press, 2019)

Miller, James Andrew. *Power House, CAA: The Untold Story of Hollywood's Creative Artists Agency* (New York: Custom House, 2016)

Miller, W. R. *The Star Wars Historical Sourcebook, Volume One: 1971–1976* (Pulp Hero Press, 2018)

Newhart, Bob. *I Shouldn't Even Be Doing This! and Other Things That Strike Me as Funny* (New York: Hyperion Books, 2006)

Nichelson, Ted. *Love to Love You Bradys: The Bizarre Story of the Brady Bunch Variety Hour* (Toronto: ECW Press, 2009)

The Old Farmer's 2022 Almanac (Lewiston, ME: Geiger, 2022)

Osmond, Donny. *Life Is Just What You Make It: My Story So Far* (New York: Hyperion Books, 1999)

Patell, Cyrus R. K. *Lucasfilm: Filmmaking, Philosophy, and the Star Wars Universe* (London: Bloomsbury Academic, 2021)

Phillips, Gene D. *Godfather: The Intimate Francis Ford Coppola* (Lexington, KY: University Press of Kentucky, 2004)

Pollock, Dale. *Skywalking: The Life and Films of George Lucas* (New York: Harmony Books, 1983)

Rinzler, J. W. *The Making of Star Wars* (New York: Del Rey Books, 2007)

Rowes, Barbara. *Grace Slick: The Biographer* (New York: Doubleday, 1980)

Salamon, Julie. *The Devil's Candy: Bonfire of the Vanities Goes to Hollywood* (London: Penguin, 1992)

Sansweet, Steve, and Vilmur, Pete. *Star Wars Vault: Thirty Years of Treasure from the Lucasfilm Archives* (New York: It Books, 2007)

Schlatter, George. *Still Laughing: A Life in Comedy* (Los Angeles, CA: Rare Bird, 2023)

Schumacher, Michael. *Francis Ford Coppola: A Filmmaker's Life* (New York: Crown Publishing Group, 1999)

Selvin, Joel. *Altamont: The Rolling Stones, The Hells Angels, and the Inside Story of Rock's Darkest Day* (New York: HarperCollins Publishers, 2016)

Slick, Grace. *Somebody to Love? A Rock-and-Roll Memoir* (New York: Warner Books, 1998)

Starr, Michael Seth. *Art Carney: A Biography* (New York: Fromm International Publishing Corporation, 1997)

Tamarkin, Jeff. *Got a Revolution! The Turbulent Flight of Jefferson Airplane* (New York: Atria Books, 2003)

Taylor, Chris. *How Star Wars Conquered the Universe: The Past, Present, and Future of a Multibillion Dollar Franchise* (New York: Basic Books, 2014)

Weller, Sheila. *Carrie Fisher: A Life on the Edge* (New York: Sarah Crichton Books, 2019)

Williams, Barry. *Growing Up Brady: I Was a Teenage Brady* (New York: HarperCollins, 1992)

Winters, David. *Tough Guys Do Dance* (Pensacola, FL: Indigo River Publishing, 2018)

Wynne, Patricia. *Star Wars: The Wookiee Storybook* (New York: Random House, 1979)

ARTICLES

"40 Years On: The Animated Sequence of the *Star Wars* Holiday Special," *Episode Nothing: Star Wars in the 1970s*, November 16, 2018.

Barnes, Mike. "Ken Welch, Carol Burnett's Longtime Musical Collaborator, Dies at 92," *Hollywood Reporter*, February 5, 2019.

Brown, Peter. "Starship Tries it Without Grace," *Gannett News Service*, December 6, 1978.

Brown, Tracy. "Boba Fett Had Four Lines in *Empire Strikes Back*. How Did He End Up with His Own TV Show?" *Los Angeles Times*, December 31, 2021.

Buck, Jerry. "Star Wars Special Is Bubblegum for the Brain," *Anniston Star*, November 17, 1978.

Burton, Bonnie. "In Defense of the *Star Wars* Holiday Special," *CNET*, November 17, 2018.

Burwick, Kevin. "*Solo* Writer Wanted to Include More *Star Wars Holiday Special* References," Movieweb, August 8, 2019.

Childed, Serg. "German Roots of the Moon of Alabama," *Music Tales*, August 27, 2018

Collinson, Gary. "Star Wars on the Small Screen—The Star Wars Holiday Special," flickeringmyth.com, November 8, 2019.

Consumer Product Safety Commission. "Mattel Announces Toy Replacement Program," January 11, 1979.

Cooper, Christopher. "Welcome to Lucaswood: The Studio That Struck Back," *Star Wars Insider* #197, September 2020.

Cotter, Padraig. *Screen Rant*, June 19, 2022.

Digiacomo, Frank. "The Han Solo Comedy Hour," *Vanity Fair*, December 22, 2008.

Ebert, Roger. "*Thief of Bagdad*: One of the Most Delightful Fantasies Ever Put on Film," rogerebert.com, May 6, 2009.

Fahey, Mark. "Seinfeld: 25 years of Making Beaucoup Bucks," CNBC, May 31, 2015.

Farhi, Paul. "Bing and Bowie: An Odd Story of Holiday Harmony," *Washington Post*, December 20, 2006.

Fleming, Mike Jr., "Star Wars Legacy II: An Architect of Hollywood's Greatest Deal Recalls How George Lucas Won Sequel Rights," *Deadline*, December 18, 2015.

Fong-Torres, Ben. "Jefferson Starship: Strange Times at the Launching Pad," *Rolling Stone*, May 18, 1978.

Franich, Darren. "The Best *Star Wars* Characters Disney Left Behind," *Entertainment Weekly*, May 20, 2022.

Gross, Ed. "Retrovision Exclusive: The Selling of *Star Wars*, Part 1," www.comicbookmovie.com, September 11, 2011.

Guthrie, Marisa, and Barnes, Mike. "Rick Ludwin, Former NBC Late Night Executive and Seinfeld Champion, Dies at 71," *Hollywood Reporter*, November 11, 2019.

Habeeb, Lee. "The Story Behind Bowie and Bing's Unlikely Holiday Duet Sends a Welcome Message in Divided Times," *Newsweek*, December 19, 2019.

Hibberd, James. "Anthony Daniels Says Original Star Wars Holiday Special Was 'Like Being at a Weird Funeral,'" *Entertainment Weekly*, November 29, 2020.

Leotta, Alfio. "*Apocalpyse Now* Turns 40: Rediscovering the Genesis of a Film Classic," *The Conversation*, May 6, 2019.

Lepitak, Stephen. "*Star Wars* Marketing Man Charles Lippincott on the Real Force Behind the Franchise's Success," *The Drum*, December 1, 2015.

Liebenson, Donald. "50 Years Ago, a White Woman Touching a Black Man on TV Caused a National Commotion," *Vanity Fair*, April 2, 2018.

Liebenson, Donald. "Call It a Comeback: The Inside Story of Elvis Presley's Iconic 1968 Special," *Vanity Fair*, August 18, 2018.

Liebenson, Donald. "May the Farce Be with You," *Los Angeles Times*, November 16, 2008.

Lowry, Brian. "Seinfeld Finale Ends up in Sixth Place of All Time," *Los Angeles Times*, May 16, 1998.

Malloy, Tim. "5 Mandalorian Easter Eggs That Call Back the Infamous *Star Wars Holiday Special*," Moviemaker, November 19, 2019.

Millin, Leslie. "A Beautiful Film on Mariposa," *Toronto Globe and Mail*, September 27, 1969.

Newbold, Mark. "LEGO Star Wars Holiday Special Virtual Press Conference: With Anthony Daniels," Fanthatracks.com, November 16, 2020.

Newborn, Alex. "I Have a Bad Feeling About This," *Star Wars Insider* #106, January 2009.

Pallotta, Frank. "Steven Spielberg Published This Awesome Ad Congratulating George Lucas When *Star Wars* Beat *Jaws*—And Started a Tradition," May 1, 2014.

Pasternack, Alex. "Happy Wookiee Life Day: The *Star Wars Holiday Special* was the Worst Thing on Television," *Vice*, December 23, 2012.

Plessett, Ross. "The *Star Wars Holiday Special*: After 20 Years of Silence, Its Creators Take a Critical Look Back," *Ultra Filmfax* #69–70, October 1998/January 1999.

Pollock, Dale. "A Man and his Empire: The Private Life of *Star Wars* Creator George Lucas," *Life Magazine*, June 1983.

"Producer Miki Herman on the Early Days of Lucasfilm," Lucasfilm.com, March 29, 2022.

Ross, Dalton. "What Happened to Star Wars: Detours," www.ew.com, June 30, 2021.

Rossen, Jake. "The Dark Side: An Oral History of The *Star Wars Holiday Special*," *Mental Floss*, November 19, 2018.

Rossi, Rosemary. *The Wrap*, July 30, 2020.

Sandomir, Richard. "David Winters Obituary: Energetic Dancer Turned Choreographer Dies at 80," *New York Times*, May 3, 2019.

Sharf, Zach. "Brian De Palma: 'I Was Terribly Wrong Mocking the Force After First 'Star Wars' Screening," *IndieWire*, July 7, 2021.

Silliman, Brian. "The Story of How Boba Fett's First Official Appearance Was in a 1978 California Parade," Syfy.com, November 12, 2021.

Snider, Mike. "*Robot Chicken* Digs Its Satirical Talons into *Star Wars*," *USA Today*, June 17, 2007.

Swanson, Dave. "When Grace Slick Quit Jefferson Starship After a Drunken Germany Show," *Ultimate Classic Rock*, June 20, 2013.

Taylor, Chris. "How *Star Wars* Conquered the Galaxy," *Reason*, January 2016.

Tozzi, Lisa. "Her Most Desperate Hour: Carrie Fisher Discusses *The Star Wars Holiday Special*," *New York Times*, January 12, 2010.

"Welcome to the Fillmore East Review," *New York Times*, October 11, 1970.

Wilkins, Jonathan. "The Conversation," *Star Wars Insider* #145, November/December 2013.

WEBSITES

Bea Arthur, Archive of American Television, TV Academy Foundation Interviews, March 15, 2001 (Part 2 of 5): interviews.televisionacademy.com/interviews/beatrice-arthur?clip=19999#interview-clips

Roger Ebert 1977 Star Wars Review: www.ccusd93.org/cms/lib/AZ02204140/Centricity/Domain/1089/Star%20Wars%20Review%20-%20Roger%20Ebert.pdf

"Mark Hamill: Memories of Carrie Fisher, the Holiday Special, and a Broken Promise," *Renegade Geek*, May 5, 2017: www.youtube.com/watch?v=p6dIYUoSeFQ

Harvey Korman, Archive of American Television, TV Academy Foundation Interviews, April 20, 2004 (Part 2 of 3): interviews.televisionacademy.com/interviews/harvey-korman?clip=23649

Lew Mailer (Imperial Guard) Interview: www.starwarsholidayspecial.com/swhs-old/text/lev_mailer.htm

Patty Maloney (Lumpy) Interview: www.starwarsholidayspecial.com/swhs-old/text/patty_maloney.htm

Recording Industry Association of America: www.riaa.com

Saluki Hall of Fame: www.siusalukis.com

"Star Wars Holiday Special," Fourth Draft of Script, September 15, 1978: www.starwarsholidayspecial.com

Unofficial "Star Wars Holiday Special": www.starwarsholidayspecial.com

"USC Amplified Mark Hamill," USC Annenberg School for Communication and Journalism, October 14, 2020: www.youtube.com/watch?v=JNzLho0a_uA

Charles Weber biography: novafilmhouse.com/about-us/team/charles-j-weber/

Wookieepedia: starwars.fandom.com/wiki

PODCASTS

Steve Binder interview, *Gilbert Gottfried Colossal Podcast*

Craig Chaquico interview by Scott Kirkwood, starwarsholidayspecial.com

Charles Lippincott interview by James McInerny, *Rebel Force Radio*

Bruce Vilanch interview, *Gilbert Gottfried Colossal Podcast*

TV/FILMS

The Big Bang Theory season 7, episode 22: "Star Wars Day" (CBS, 2014)

The Big Bang Theory season 11, episode 24: "Bow Tie Asymmetry" (CBS, 2018)

The Brady Bunch Variety Hour (ABC, 1976–1977)

Bright Lights: Starring Carrie Fisher and Debbie Reynolds (HBO, 2016)

Charge at Feather River (Warner Bros, 1953)

Distant Drums (Warner Bros, 1951)

Donny and Marie (ABC, 1976–1979)

The Lawrence Welk Show (syndicated, 1971–1982)

The Mandalorian (Disney+, 2019–)

The Midnight Special (NBC, 1972–1981)

Muppet Show (Season 4, Eps #17 – 1980)

The Paul Lynde Halloween Special (ABC, 1976)

The Richard Pryor Show (NBC, 1977)

Rogue One: A Star Wars Story (Lucasfilm, 2016)

South Park: Mr. Hankey's Christmas Classics (Comedy Central, 1999)

Star Wars Episode IV: A New Hope (Fox, 1977)

Star Wars Episode V: The Empire Strikes Back (Fox, 1980; Blu-ray commentary, 2020)

The Star Wars Holiday Special (CBS, 1978)

The Story of the Faithful Wookiee (Lucasfilm, 1978)

Telly ... Who Loves Ya, Baby? (ABC, 1976)

The Thief of Bagdad (MGM, 1940)

This Is Spinal Tap (MGM, 1984)

The Toys That Made Us season 1, episode 1: "Star Wars" (Netflix, 2017)

Under the Helmet: The Legacy of Boba Fett (Disney+, 2021)

Wacko (CBS, 1977)

OTHER

Duwayne Dunham: Boba Fett Costume Test (1978)

Rolland G. Smith Promo for Evening News (1978, WCBS)

"White & Nerdy," music video by "Weird Al" Yankovic, September 26, 2006

ENDNOTES

Unless otherwise noted, all quotations are from the author's interviews.

2   **"It was a bit late"**: Frank Digiacomo, "The Han Solo Comedy Hour," *Vanity Fair*, December 22, 2008

2   **"Your brain melts"**: Donald Liebenson, "May the Farce Be With You," *Los Angeles Times*, November 16, 2008

3   **the film that had recently**: Frank Pallotta, "Steven Spielberg Published This Awesome Ad Congratulating George Lucas When *Star Wars* Beat *Jaws*—And Started a Tradition," *Insider*, May 1, 2014

5   **"the worst piece of crap"**: "Emmy Guy," *All Things Considered*, NPR, September 22, 2002

5   **"the worst two hours"**: David Hofstede, *What Were They Thinking? The 100 Dumbest Events in Television History*

9   **Jeff Berg, Lucas's agent**: Mike Fleming Jr., "Star Wars Legacy II: An Architect of Hollywood's Greatest Deal Recalls How George Lucas Won Sequel Rights," *Deadline*, December 18, 2015

10 **Most importantly, the studio**: email from Marc Pevers, April 13, 2023

11 **However, Mego**: Aaron Sagers, "How Star Wars Toys Changed Everything," *Den of Geek*, December 31, 2019

12 **From a budget of**: Garin Pirnia, "13 Wild Facts About Easy Rider," *Mental Floss*, May 12, 2019

13 **"The studios were"**: Gene Youngblood, *George Lucas: Maker of Films*, 1971

13 **Despite an unusual Wednesday**: Tom Brueggemann, "The Real Story Behind the Star Wars Opening Weekend 45 Years Ago," *IndieWire*, May 4, 2022

14 **Peter Frampton had recently**: allmusic.com

16 **Among the mafioso**: Reid Goldberg, "How George Lucas Pivoted from Experimental Filmmaking to Mainstream Blockbusters," *Collider*, March 4, 20233

18 **"We chatted"**: Stephen Lepitak, "Star Wars Marketing Man Charles Lippincott on the Real Force Behind the Franchise's Success," *The Drum*, December 1, 2015

18 **To harness Lippincott's**: Mark Evanier, "Charles Lippincott, R.I.P.," *News From Me*, May 20, 2020

19 **"My thinking was"**: Ed Gross, "Retrovision Exclusive: The Selling of Star Wars, Part 1," comicbookmovie.com, September 11, 2011

20 **"To prevent this"**: Stephen Lepitak, "Star Wars Marketing Man Charles Lippincott on the Real Force Behind the Franchise's Success," *The Drum*, December 1, 2015

20 **"The real problem was"**: Jimmy McInerny, "Charles Lippincott Interview," *RebelForce Radio*, July 5, 2013

21 **Fox criticized the Marvel**: Brian Jay Jones, *George Lucas: A Life*, p.242

24 **Lucas, fresh from USC**: George Lucas, "Power of Story: Visions of Independence," *Sundance Film Festival*, January 29, 2015

25 **Ashley lent him $300,000**: Gene Phillips, *The Godfather: The Intimate Francis Ford Coppola*, p.67

27 **"They freaked out"**: Brian Jay Jones, *George Lucas: A Life*, p.118

27 **Wells—who again was**: John Baxter, *George Lucas: A Biography*, p.108

27 **Finally, the studio**: Michael Schumaker, *Francis Ford Coppola: A Filmmaker's Life*, p.84

27 **"The studio tried to recut"**: George Lucas, "Power of Story: Visions of Independence," *Sundance Film Festival*, January 29, 2015

27 **"I'm more upset"**: Gene Youngblood, *George Lucas: Maker of Films*, 1971

27 **Wells had been less**: John Baxter. *George Lucas: A Biography*, p.105

28 **"In effect"**: Gene Phillips, *Coppola: The Intimate Francis Ford Coppola*

28 **"Warner Bros not only"**: Dale Pollack, *Skywalking: The Life and Films of George Lucas*

28 **Upon his departure**: Anonymous source

28 **As soon as Coppola**: Gene Phillips, *Coppola: The Intimate Francis Ford Coppola*, p.71

28 **At the Oscars presentation**: Peter Biskind, *Easy Riders, Raging Bull*, p.181

28 **When Coppola was preparing**: Gene Phillips, *Coppola: The Intimate Francis Ford Coppola*, p.71

30 **The box-office figures**: "Weekend Domestic Chart," the-numbers.com

37 **"Prior to that"**: Kevin Smith, *A Disturbance in the Force* (2023)

38 **Just three years earlier**: Virginia Rohan, "Mel Brooks Reveals the Stories Behind Blazing Saddles," *The Record* (Bergen County, NJ), August 22, 2016

44 **"something Tarkinish"**: Anthony Daniels, *I Am C-3PO*, p.89–90

46 **"beautiful blonde-haired"**: Anthony Daniels, *I Am C-3PO*, p.89

51 **By January 1978**: "Weekend Domestic Chart," the-numbers.com

52 **According to Ian Fraser**: Paul Farhi, "Bing and Bowie: An Odd Story of Holiday Harmony," *Washington Post*, December 20, 2006

53 **pro-fascist comments**: Stereo Williams, "On Race, David Bowie Delved Deep into the Darkness and Came Back Human," *The Daily Beast*, April 13, 2017

53 **"David came in"**: Pamela Sosnowski, "Why David Bowie Didn't Want to Sing with Bing Crosby," *Rebeat*, August 2015

53 **"We decided the best"**: Lee Habeeb, "Opinion: The Story Behind Bowie and Bing's Unlikely Holiday Duet Sends a Welcome Message in Divided Times," *Newsweek*, December 19, 2019

53 **"Bing loved the challenge"**: Buz Kohan, "Bing Crosby Rediscovered," *PBS American Masters*, June 3, 2014

53 **"They sat at the piano"**: Roger Catlin, "When Bowie Met Bing: The Story of Their Bizarre Holiday Duet," *Songfacts*, December 18, 2014

54 **"I was wondering"**: Andrea Warner, "David Bowie, Bing Crosby, and the Story of the Strangest Christmas Duet Ever: 10 things you need to know about 'Peace on Earth / Little Drummer Boy,'" *CBC Music*, December 20, 2017

54 **"clean-cut kid"**: Pamela Sosnowski, "Why David Bowie Didn't Want to Sing with Bing Crosby," *Rebeat*, August 2015

55 **"We never expected"**: Thomas Curtis-Horsfall, "Why David Bowie Nearly Refused to Sing with Bing Crosby on Classic Christmas Duet," smoothradio.com, December 22, 2022

55 **RCA Records formally released it**: Since the song was never intended to be released, the original sixteen-track master was erased, so they had to use an online mix from the special, where they were able to pick up the vocals from a boom microphone. (From *Ashes to Ashes: The Songs of David Bowie 1976–2016*, by Chris O'Leary.)

55 **co-produce a few**: Soon after Disney purchased Lucasfilm in 2012, the decision was made to not air the series. Green had completed thirty-nine episodes that subsequently were never broadcast.

56 **"kind of a bastard"**: Jacob Adams, *Hanlet Episode 4 & ½: Attack of the Phantom Special*, via YouTube

64 **"fresh and innovative"**: "Welcome To The Fillmore East Review," *New York Times*, October 11, 1970

64 **"a beautiful film"**: Leslie Millin, "A Beautiful Film on Mariposa," *Toronto Globe and Mail*, September 27, 1969

64 **From the beginning**: Ross Plessett, "The Star Wars Holiday Special," *Ultra Filmfax* #69–70, p.77

64 **was never released**: Various reasons have been given for the film never being released, ranging from Harrison losing his voice to his anti-Beatles comments, his spiritual decrees, his decision to offer too much stage time to Shankar, and the shows not being very well received.

65 **"We wanted something"**: Frank Digiacomo, "The Han Solo Comedy Hour," *Vanity Fair*, December 22, 2008

66 **"It just kept getting"**: Jake Rossen, "The Dark Side: An Oral History of The Star Wars Holiday Special," *Mental Floss*, November 19, 2018

66 **"a product of rock"**: Frank Digiacomo, "The Han Solo Comedy Hour," *Vanity Fair*, December 22, 2008

68 **"I remember that Dwight"**: Ross Plessett, Rita Scott interview, 1998

69 **"what a director needs"**: Brian Jay Jones, *George Lucas: A Life*, p.275

71 **"I had an idea"**: "Charley Lippincott, "The Alan Dean Foster interviews," *From the Desk of Charley Lippincott*, November 12, 2015

75 **Proft corroborated Ripps**: Ross Plessett, "The Star Wars Holiday Special," *Ultra Filmfax* #69–70, p.76

75 **"fur-covered creature"**: George Lucas, *The Adventures of Luke Starkiller*, second draft, January 28, 1975

79 **"dress that Bob Mackie"**: Peter Brown, Gannett News Service via *Pensacola News Journal*, November 21, 1978

80 **Why is Diahann Carroll**: Ross Plessett, "The Star Wars Holiday Special," *Ultra Filmfax* #69–70, p.78

82 **After visiting some**: Ross Plessett, "The Star Wars Holiday Special," *Ultra Filmfax* #69–70, p.78

83 **"I presented him to"**: Ross Plessett, "The Star Wars Holiday Special," *Ultra Filmfax* #69–70, p.78

84 **In 1971, he had**: Robert McParland, *The Rock Music Imagination*, p.53

84 **the album still went**: Recording Industry Association of America, riaa.com

84 **Kurtz had been given**: Frank Digiacomo, "The Han Solo Comedy Hour," *Vanity Fair*, December 22, 2008

85 **"It was in my contract"**: Paul Byrne, "Harrison Ford Talks 'Cowboys and Aliens' and the Star Wars Holiday Special," *Movies Ireland / Irish Cinema Times*, August 18, 2011

85 **"I don't sing"**: Jerry Buck, "Star Wars Holiday Special: It's Bubble Gum—But Tasty," Associated Press, November 17, 1978

85 **"I'm *not* under contract"**: Mark Hamill, "Memories of Carrie Fisher, the Holiday Special, and a Broken Promise," Fan Expo Dallas, *Renegade Geek*, May 12, 2017

85 **"I remember when I"**: Mark Hamill, "Memories of Carrie Fisher, the Holiday Special, and a Broken Promise," Fan Expo Dallas, *Renegade Geek*, May 12, 2017

86 **"Just not Star Wars"**: Mark Hamill, "Interview with Dean of the University of Southern California's USC Annenberg School for Communication and Journalism," October 14, 2020

86 **Lucas reminded him**: Mark Hamill, "Memories of Carrie Fisher, The Holiday Special and a Broken Promise," Fan Expo Dallas, *Renegade Geek*, May 12, 2017

87 **"I was speeding"**: *Gossip Magazine*, 1978

87 **The impact resulted in**: Padraig Cotter, "Mark Hamill's 1977 Car Accident Explained," *Screen Rant*, June 19, 2022

88 **Lucas says that**: George Lucas interview, Blu-ray commentary, *The Empire Strikes Back* (Lucasfilm)

89 **They insisted that Fisher**: Ross Plessett, Ken and Mitzie Welch interview, 1998

90 **"great dignity and noble"**: Ryan Parker and Trilby Beresford, "Harrison Ford Remembers Star Wars Co-Star Peter Mayhew: 'I Loved Him,'" *Hollywood Reporter*, May 2, 2019

90 **"It was a wonderful"**: Ross Plessett, Peter Mayhew interview, 1998

92 **"They were doing this"**: George Lucas interview, *Under the Helmet: The Legacy of Boba Fett*, Disney+, 2021

94 **"loosely enough that they"**: "Canadian Star Wars Animation from Nelvana," *Fantastic Films Fantasy and Sci-fi Movie Magazine* #21, August 1981

95 **"She'll make point-five"**: *Star Wars Episode IV: A New Hope*

95 **"He is a master"**: George Lucas (foreword), *The Art of Moebius*

103 **"Of course I can"**: Alan Dean Foster, *Star Wars: The Adventures of Luke Skywalker* (Ballantine)

104 **"I was young"**: Charles Lippincott, "The 'Secret Weapon' Behind Star Wars," *From The Desk of Charles Lippincott*, December 19, 2015

104 **asked Lucas for $50 million**: Dale Pollack, "A Man and His Empire: The Private Life of Star Wars Creator George Lucas," *Life*, June 1983, p.94–96

105 **Lucas fired him**: Brian R. Jacobson, *In the Studio: Visual Creation and its Material Environments*, p.247

105 **Dykstra was notoriously**: John Baxter, *George Lucas: A Biography*, p.251

105 **He did the same to**: Brian Jay Jones, *George Lucas; A Life*, p.122

106 **"stupid decision"**: Dale Pollack, *Skywalking: The Life and Films of George Lucas*, p.194

106 **Pevers sued Lucas**: Chris Taylor, "How Star Wars Conquered the Galaxy," *Reason: Free Minds and Free Markets*, January 2016

106 **Star Wars profits**: Brian Jay Jones, *George Lucas: A Life*, p.256

106 **"I'm ambivalent about"**: Charles Lippincott, "The 'Secret Weapon' Behind Star Wars," *The Desk of Charles Lippincott*, December 19, 2015

107 **"Lucas's ex-wife Marcia"**: Charles Lippincott, "The 'Secret Weapon' Behind Star Wars," *The Desk of Charles Lippincott*, December 19, 2015

108 **"Charley was one of"**: Aaron Couch, "Charles Lippincott, Star Wars' Publicity Mastermind, Dies at 80," *Hollywood Reporter*, May 20, 2020

108 **"When it came to marketing"**: Mark Hamill, Twitter, May 20, 2020

110 **The first day of taping**: *The Star Wars Holiday Special*, fourth draft of script, September 15, 1978

112 **"We tried the cooking"**: Ross Plessett, Mitzie Welch interview

117 **Rita Scott and line producer**: Author's interview with Elle Puritz

119 **"What better testament"**: Taran Killam, *A Disturbance in the Force*, 2023

119 **Roger Ebert compared**: Roger Ebert, "One of the Most Delightful Fantasies Ever Put on Film," rogerebert.com, May 6, 2009

123 **"We knew we had Bea"**: Ross Plessett, Mitzie Welch interview

123 **"This is the right song"**: Ross Plessett, Ken and Mitzie Welch interview

124 **"Harvey Korman and I"**: Bea Arthur, TV Academy interview

126 **"He doesn't like you"**: *Star Wars Episode IV: A New Hope*

128 **"Some things are so contradictory"**: Taran Killam, *A Disturbance in the Force*, 2023

131 **The temperature outside**: *Farmer's Almanac*

132 **The Cowardly Lion**: Hilary Elizabeth, "The Wizard of Oz: 10 Hidden Details About the Costumes You Didn't Notice," *Screen Rant*, September 9, 2019

133 **"We were shooting"**: Ross Plessett, Ken and Mitzie Welch interview

136 **With this specific union**: Author's interview with Bill Bracken

139 **four people had died**: Joel Selvin, *Altamont: The Rolling Stones, the Hell's Angels, and the Inside Story of Rock's Darkest Day*, p.321

140 **"The spacey, otherworldly"**: Joel Selvin, *Altamont: The Rolling Stones, the Hell's Angels, and the Inside Story of Rock's Darkest Day*, p.306

140 **"The vibes were bad"**: Barbara Rowes, *Grace Slick: The Biography*

140 **Sometime in 1978**: Jefferson Airplane, 1998, via the Wayback Machine

141 **"Who won the war"**: Hamburg TV Show, VH-1's Behind the Music

141 **"Gracie has a problem"**: Ben Fong-Torres, "Jefferson Starship: Strange Times at the Launching Pad," *Rolling Stone*, May 18, 1978

141 **check into rehab**: Dave Swanson, "When Grace Slick Quit Jefferson Starship After a Drunken Germany Show," *Ultimate Classic Rock*, June 20, 2013

141 **"I'm in Germany"**: Jeff Tamarkin, *Got a Revolution! The Turbulent Flight of Jefferson Airplane*, p.296

143 **"closed on orders"**: Gannett News Service via *Pensacola News Journal*, November 21, 1978

144 **"science-fiction scene"**: Scott Kirkwood, Craig Chaquico interview

145 **"It was just a mishmash"**: Scott Kirkwood, Craig Chaquico interview

145 **"I kind of went for"**: Scott Kirkwood, Craig Chaquico interview

146 **"There was no center"**: Ross Plessett, David Acomba interview

147 **"Trader Dann does Norton"**: *The Star Wars Holiday Special*, fourth draft of script, September 15, 1978

147 **"It wasn't really"**: Ross Plessett, "The Star Wars Holiday Special," *Ultra Filmfax* #69–70, p.79

147 **Acomba's original plans**: Ross Plessett, Mitzie and Ken Welch interview

149 **"Then, when I found out"**: Ross Plessett, "The Star Wars Holiday Special," *Ultra Filmfax* #69–70, p.78

149 **"David was one of"**: Ross Plessett, Rita Scott interview

150 **"I sent a telegram"**: Ross Plessett, David Acomba interview

150 **"According to the Welches"**: Ross Plessett, Welches interview

151 **"It was traumatic"**: Ross Plessett, "The Star Wars Holiday Special," *Ultra Filmfax* #69–70, p.78

151 **"I couldn't keep calling"**: Ross Plessett, "The Star Wars Holiday Special," *Ultra Filmfax* #69–70, p.78

154 **While taping a duet**: Donald Liebenson, "50 Years Ago, a White Woman Touching a Black Man on TV Caused a National Commotion," *Vanity Fair*, April 2, 2018

154 **"For me, the '68 special"**: Donald Liebenson "Call It a Comeback: The Inside Story of Elvis Presley's Iconic 1968 Special," *Vanity Fair*, August 18, 2018

155 **"I wanted to let"**: William McKeen, *Rock and Roll Is Here to Stay: An Anthology*, p.179

157 **"I was drawing this"**: Ross Plessett, "The Star Wars Holiday Special," *Ultra Filmfax* #69–70, p.82

159 **Pevers had dangled**: Chris Taylor, "How Star Wars Conquered the Galaxy," *Reason*, January 2016

159 **"So that's why we developed"**: Ross Plessett, "The Star Wars Holiday Special," *Ultra Filmfax* #69–70, p.83

160 **"We didn't know it"**: Ross Plessett, Mitzie Welch interview

160 **"there was definitely talk"**: Ross Plessett, "The Star Wars Holiday Special," *Ultra Filmfax* #69–70, p.83

160 **"there may have been"**: T-Bone's *Star Wars Universe*, January 16, 2001

160 **"If he did the Special"**: Jake Rossen, "The Dark Side: An Oral History of The Star Wars Holiday Special," *Mental Floss*, November 19, 2018

160 **"I learned a lot"**: Peter Mayhew, Dragon-Con panel appearance, 2011

161 **"There was a redrawing"**: Ross Plessett, Leslie Parsons interview

167 **"Itchy applauds"**: *The Star Wars Holiday Special*, script revision, September 17, 1978, p.62

167 **"He takes one look"**: Carrie Fisher, *Wishful Thinking*, p.87

168 **"I have to stay with"**: Terry Gross, "Carrie Fisher Opens Up About Star Wars, the Gold Bikini, and Her On-Set Affair," *Fresh Air*, NPR, November 28, 2016

169 **"We wanted to do"**: Jerry Buck, "Star Wars Holiday Special: It's Bubble Gum—But Tasty," Associated Press, November 17, 1978

170 **"softcore porno"**: Ross Plessett, Mitzie Welch interview

172 **"a tired, off-screen"**: Frank Digiacomo, "The Han Solo Comedy Hour," *Vanity Fair*, December 22, 2008

172 **"It was cute"**: Jacob Adams, *Hanlet Episode 4 & ½: Attack of the Phantom Special*, via YouTube

173 **"The budget got"**: Ross Plessett, "The Star Wars Holiday Special," *Ultra Filmfax* #69–70, p.83

175 **"I'm not convinced the special"**: Alex Pasternack, "The Star Wars Holiday Special Was the Worst Thing on Television Ever," vice.com, December 24, 2014

176 **This gruesome crime scene**: Gary Hinman Supplemental Report, Los Angeles County Sheriff's Department (#069-02373-1076-491), July 31, 1969

178 **"I've spoken some rubbish"**: Anthony Daniels, *I Am C-3PO: The Inside Story*, p.91

178 **"Threepio has always"**: Anthony Daniels, *I Am C-3PO: The Inside Story*, p.91

178 **"I had been singing in"**: *Bright Lights: Starring Carrie Fisher and Debbie Reynolds*, HBO, 2016

179 **"the biggest thing"**: *Bright Lights: Starring Carrie Fisher and Debbie Reynolds*, HBO, 2016

180 **"But when we called"**: Sheila Weller, *Carrie Fisher: A Life on the Edge*, p.68

180 **Fisher did not seem happy**: Frank Digiacomo, "The Han Solo Comedy Hour," *Vanity Fair*, December 22, 2008

180 **"clearly intended to be"**: Anthony Daniels, *I Am C-3PO: The Inside Story*, p.91

182 **"The Best Actor in"**: Anthony Daniels, *I Am C-3PO: The Inside Story*, p.91

182 **"And there we were"**: Mark Newbold, "LEGO Star Wars Holiday Special Virtual Press Conference: With Anthony Daniels," fanthatracks.com, November 16, 2020

185 **"I saw all of those"**: Ross Plessett, Mitzie Welch interview

186 **"Actually, the show is"**: Ross Plessett, Ken Welch interview

186 **"re-editing"**: "I Have a Bad Feeling About This!," *Star Wars Insider* issue #106, January 2009, p.32

188 **"I was faced with"**: "I Have a Bad Feeling About This!," *Star Wars Insider* issue #106, January 2009, p.30

189 **ratings came in**: Simon Abrams, "The Star Wars Holiday Special Is a Brilliant Disaster. That's Why Disney Shouldn't Erase It From History," *Esquire*, Dec 17, 2019

189 **"bubble gum for the brain"**: Jerry Buck, "Star Wars cast together again on TV," Associated Press via *Corpus Christi Caller-Times*, November 17, 1978

189 **"unintentionally hilarious"**: Bill Higgins, "Hollywood Flashback: The Star Wars Holiday Special Got Past George Lucas in 1978," *Hollywood Reporter*, December 25, 2019

189 **"The plot smacks of"**: Gail Williams, "Star Wars Holiday Special—Review," *Hollywood Reporter*, November 20, 1978

193 **"I still have a soft spot"**: Kevin K, starwarsholidayspecial.com

194 **"Never got a phone call"**: Jake Rossen, "The Dark Side: An Oral History of The Star Wars Holiday Special," *Mental Floss*, November 19, 2018

194 **Herman was hired to help**: "Producer Miki Herman on the Early Days of Lucasfilm," lucasfilm.com, March 29, 2022

195 **"She started out as just"**: Ross Plessett, Mitzie Welch interview

200 **"They were doing this"**: *Under the Helmet: The Legacy of Boba Fett*, Disney+, 2021

200 **"The special from 1978"**: George Lucas, staticmultimedia.com, 2005

201 **"Pass on what"**: *Star Wars Episode VIII: The Last Jedi*

202 **As of this writing**: Hayley C. Cuccinello, "Inside Star Wars' $5 Billion Merchandise Motherlode: The 14 Weirdest Items for Jedi-Wannabees," *Forbes*, December 14, 2015

203 **Sony had launched**: A. J. W., "VHS or Beta? A Look Back at Betamax and How Sony Lost the VCR Format War to VHS Recorders," *Click Americana: Vintage & Retro Memories*

203 **Universal and Walt Disney sued Sony**: Jake Rossen, "A Brief History of the VCR," *Mental Floss*, April 1, 2021,

204 **The case ultimately went**: Sony Corp of America v Universal City Studios (#81-1687), argued January 18, 1983; reargued October 3, 1983; decided January 17, 1974

205 **It became a favorite**: The tape, as well its effect on Rebney, became the subject of the critically acclaimed documentary *Winnebago Man* (2009), directed by Ben Steinbauer. Rebney passed away on May 10, 2023, at the age of ninety-three.

205 **"It became a currency"**: Kevin Smith, *A Disturbance in the Force*, 2023

205 **"I had to get"**: Bobcat Goldthwait, *A Disturbance in the Force*, 2023

206 **"He said, 'Oh'"**: Steve Sansweet, *A Disturbance in the Force*, 2023

212 **In their article**: Sean Latham and Robert Scholes, "The Rise of Periodical Studies," vol. 121, no. 2, JSTOR, Cambridge University Press, March 2006

214 **"When you have a bunch"**: Kevin Smith, *A Disturbance in the Force*, 2023

218 **"We had done a couple"**: Mike Snider, "Robot Chicken Digs Its Satirical Talons into Star Wars," *USA Today*, June 17, 2007

219 **Disney announced its acquisition**: Press release, "Disney to Acquire Lucasfilm Ltd," *The Walt Disney Company*, October 30, 2012

220 **The Mandalorian rides a "blurrg"**: Tim Malloy, "5 Mandalorian Easter Eggs That Call Back the Infamous Star Wars Holiday Special," *Moviemaker*, November 19, 2019

220 **"definitely a point of inspiration"**: Hoai-Tran Bui, "Jon Favreau Isn't Joking About Wanting to Make a New 'Star Wars' Holiday Special, Already Has Plans," *Slash Film*, November 15, 2019

220 **"That animated piece still"**: Ash Crossan, Jon Favreau interview, *Entertainment Tonight*, September 16, 2019

221 **"I've been thinking about"**: Hoai-Tran Bui, "Jon Favreau Isn't Joking About Wanting to Make a New 'Star Wars' Holiday Special, Already Has Plans," *Slash Film*, November 15, 2019

221 **Galactic backgrounds**: "Star Wars: Galactic Battlegrounds, Episode One Campaigns," Ensemble Studios/LucasArts, 2001

221 **"That's a real thing"**: *The Big Bang Theory* season 7, episode 22, "Star Wars Day," May 1, 2014

221 **"Actually, Luke was on"**: *The Big Bang Theory* season 11, episode 24, "Bow Tie Asymmetry," May 10, 2018

223 **"I was thinking of"**: lucasfan.com

223 **Entertainment Weekly recently listed**: Darren Franich, "The best *Star Wars* Characters Disney Left Behind," *Entertainment Weekly*, May 20, 2022

223 **sneak in references**: Kevin Burwick, "Solo Writer Wanted to Include More Star Wars Holiday Special References," *Movieweb*, August 8, 2019

224 **Apparently, Itchy had almost**: Sang Jun Lee, *Art of Star Wars: Revenge of the Sith*

224 **for the uninitiated**: On the heels of that decision, Disney announced it would also begin streaming additional *Star Wars* content, including the two Ewok movies made for television, *Caravan of Courage: An Ewok Adventure* (1984) and *Ewoks: The Battle for Endor* (1985), as well as the *Ewoks* and *Droids* cartoon series that ran on Saturday mornings in 1985 and 1986, which were produced by Nelvana, the Toronto animation company that handled the Boba Fett cartoon in the Special.

226 **"I could be proven"**: Donald Liebenson, "May the Farce Be With You," *Los Angeles Times*, November 16, 2008

227 **"I'm still sorry that"**: Ross Plessett, "The Star Wars Holiday Special," *Ultra Filmfax* #69–70, p.79

228 **"That debate was the worst"**: Mark Hamill, Twitter, September 30, 2020

228 **"George once asked us"**: Dean Carol L. Folt, "Interview with Mark Hamill," *USC Annenberg School of Communication and Journalism*, October 13, 2020

228 **"I don't think I humiliated"**: Jimmy McInerney, "Mark Hamill Interview," *Rebel Force Radio*, July 20, 2008

229 **"Let's make Cheney"**: Carrie Fisher, Dragon-Con panel appearance, 2011

229 **"By that time you"**: Carrie Fisher, Dragon-Con panel appearance, 2011

230 **"I know it's a bit"**: Harvey Korman, TV Academy interview

230 **"I had no idea it was"**: Will Gardner, "The Bea Arthur Interview: A Conversation with Golden Girl Numero Uno," *Portland Mercury*, October 13, 2005

230 **"I never gave it much"**: Bea Arthur, TV Academy interview, 2001

231 **"I was privileged to"**: T-Bone's *Star Wars Universe*, January 16, 2001

232 **"I'm gonna shock you"**: Steve Binder, *Gilbert Gottfried's Amazing Colossal Podcast*

236 **Ever-so symbolically**: Mike Barnes, "Rick Ludwin, Former NBC Late Night Executive and Seinfeld Champion, Dies at 71," *Hollywood Reporter*, November 11, 2019. In addition to running NBC's specials department, Ludwin also oversaw the network's late-night programming. He is credited with managing the infamous 1992 Carson–Leno transition at *The Tonight Show*, but he has also

been rightfully faulted for 2009's not so impressive transition from Leno to Conan O'Brien—a fiasco that would soil the beloved genre for years to come.

236 **the show's finale**: Brian Lowry, "Seinfeld Finale Ends up in Sixth Place of All Time," *Los Angeles Times*, May 16, 1998

236 **$3.1 billion in syndication**: Mark Fahey, "Seinfeld: 25 years of Making Beaucoup Bucks," CNBC, May 31, 2015.

237 **"Kleig lights keep on"**: Rob Lowe and Eileen Bowman, 1989 Oscar Presentation (producer: Allan Carr)

237 **worst in Oscars history**: Seth Abramovitch, "I Was Rob Lowe's Snow White: The Untold Story of Oscar's Nightmare Opening, *Hollywood Reporter*, February 20, 2013

237 **"an embarrassment to both"**: "A second look," philly.com, April 29, 1989

237 **"The ceremony is not"**: Rob Lowe, *Stories I Only Tell My Friends*

240 **"We should consider *Cop Rock*"**: Jon O'Brien, "Cop Rock: How ABC Created the Strangest TV Musical of All Time," *Mental Floss*, October 1, 2020

240 **"If you have the guarantee"**: Will Harris, "An Oral History of Cop Rock, TV's First and Last Musical Police Drama," *AV Club*, May 26, 2016

240 **"I believe that George"**: Paul Scheer interview, *A Disturbance in the Force*, 2023

240 **"You have to trust"**: "Neil Young Brings New Concert Film to Slamdance Festival," *Billboard*, January 23, 2012

241 **"This was the right idea"**: Sheila Marikar, David Alpert, and Brian Rooney, "Jerry Seinfeld Defends NBC's Shake-up of Jay Leno, Conan O'Brien," abcnews.com, January 11, 2010

242 **"You have to be willing"**: "Neil Young Brings New Concert Film to Slamdance Festival," *Billboard*, January 23, 2012